ON BEING A
COP

Father & Son Police Tales from
the Streets of Chicago

Jim Padar
and
Jay Padar

On Being A Cop:
Father & Son Police Tales from the Streets of Chicago
by Jim & Jay Padar

Published by:
Aviva Publishing
Lake Placid, NY
518-523-1320
www.avivapubs.com

Print ISBN: 978-1-938686-86-3
Library of Congress Control Number: 2013919592

Editor: Tyler Tichelaar
Cover Design and Layout: Fusion Creative Works

Printed in the United States of America
First Edition

For additional copies visit:
www.OnBeingACop.com

Disclaimer: The views in this book are those of the authors and in no way reflect the views of The Chicago Police Department or The City of Chicago.

Dedication

This book is dedicated to our loving spouses, Durell and Barbara, with apologies for enduring countless missed holidays and family parties as well as unexpected overtime and those chilling news bulletins about officers shot.

Also to Christopher, Craig, and Timothy, sons and brothers, who grew up in the milieu of the police world, never wavering in their support or pride for their dad and brother.

And finally to Charlie and Maddie, who at their very young age are already learning that catching bad guys means Daddy sometimes misses story time at the end of the day.

All of you are more important to us than you will ever know.

In loving memory of Karla (1943–1975)

Acknowledgments

Jim: Any acknowledgments must lead off with my wife Durell, who, in addition to being my best friend, is and has been my proof-reader and editorial content advisor since I started writing these stories many years ago. Her eagle eye and suggestions have proved to be invaluable.

The now retired police chaplain, Father Thomas Nangle, is not only a priest and spiritual advisor, but over the years has become a close friend of the family. He has profoundly influenced my writing over the years and you will find him mentioned throughout the book, although not always by name. He has provided solace during difficult times and outrageous laughter during the good times. He graciously reviewed my stories as well as Jay's, and for that I am very grateful.

Theresa Choske at Chicago's Irish American Heritage Center organized and facilitated a memoir writing workshop that has continued at six-week intervals over the past several years. Led by Pat Cronin in the beginning and now by Virginia Gibbons, these sessions have helped me to improve my writing and polish the stories written in previous years. Pat, Virginia, and my "classmates" have become friends over the years—our stories have bonded us in a unique way. I am thankful to all of them.

My son Timothy and the company he owns (LP Internet Solutions) designed our web page (www.OnBeingACop.com) from the ground up as well as handling the myriad of details, including social media marketing, that arise in launching a new venture into the cyberworld.

Patrick Snow, my publishing coach, is not only a knowledgeable mentor, but has become a personal friend. Without his guidance, this book would not have become a reality. I cannot speak more highly of him.

Tyler Tichelaar, our editor, has proven to be an invaluable partner in preparing this book for final publication. His attention to detail is nothing short of mind-boggling, not to mention his ability to figure out what we really meant to say.

And finally, I have been blessed to work with perhaps the finest group of law enforcement officers anywhere in the world. Men and women who are exceptional in every way—partners, supervisors, and command staff included.

I must, however, mention a few who were beyond exceptional.

When I was a raw recruit, fresh out on the street in the 18th District, Sergeant Norm Schmit and Lieutenant Ray Skawski took me under their wings and mentored and guided me in such gentle and subtle ways that I scarcely knew it was happening. Skawski, in particular, was responsible for preventing me from resigning over an incident that over the years has paled into total insignificance. Schmit would show up on jobs when I was paired with another rookie, but always in an unobtrusive manner, allowing us to learn gradually to spread our wings in the world of police work.

And finally, I would be remiss not to mention my three long-term regular partners over my fourteen years as a patrol officer and detective.

Early on, as a recruit, I was paired with another rookie, Tony Grazioso. Tony and I were sharp, but we were brand new. The only way we survived was under the watchful eyes of the field supervisors above.

John Klodnicki and I teamed up to work as partners on the tactical unit in the 18th District. We worked the King Riots in the Cabrini Housing projects and the 1968 Democratic National Convention in Lincoln Park and Old Town. We survived without a scratch.

Mike Shull and I would become the longest continuous partners in homicide at that time. We worked together for over seven years, until I was promoted to sergeant and transferred to other duties.

Tony, John, Mike, and I literally shared moments of life and death together, and we formed a bond that can only be matched by those who have shared military combat experiences. We developed a profound trust in one another—brothers in the world of police. That relationship bled over to our off-duty hours and our wives became good friends also. I was blessed to have each of them as a partner, and, of course, you will find them all mentioned in this book.

• • • •

Jay: I begin by thanking my wife Barbara. Her constant love and support have helped make this book possible, but more importantly, she has helped create this wonderful life we share.

I thank my father/coauthor for encouraging me to write about what I was seeing as my career began. These stories not only formed a foundation for this book, but also acted as a type of therapy for a new rookie cop who wasn't used to the emotional roller coaster that this job can sometimes be.

To all of my fellow officers, many of whom have raced to my aid when I've called for help, I thank you and my family thanks you. You are true heroes and will always be considered my brothers and sisters in blue.

The Police Chaplains Unit has been such an integral part of this department. The chaplains are a constant support to the men and women who serve and protect on a daily basis. They are constantly coming to our rescue in times of spiritual and emotional need. I thank you for all you do.

To retired Superintendent Phil Cline and the Chicago Police Memorial Foundation, I thank you for reviewing my stories, providing the cover photo for this book, and allowing me to know that my family will always be taken care of should anything ever happen to me on this job.

Finally, I'd like to thank the Chicago Police command staff responsible for developing and hosting a writer's workshop encouraging and assisting all Chicago Police officers to become writers.

Contents

• • • •

Introduction

I had cheated death; a bad guy's bullet missed its mark and mine did not. But strangely, my first emotion didn't flood over me until a few hours later in the early morning hours, at home, in my children's room. My eyes welled and I swiped at my face with my black speckled hands. I could smell the gunpowder residue. Chris, age five, Craig, three and a half, and Jay, just seven weeks old, were sleeping soundly. I stroked their backs ever so gently and fought to control myself. Their mother, my wife, was being prepared for surgery at this very moment, and in a year, that monster we call breast cancer would tear her from our lives. Had that errant bullet found its target tonight, the boys would have truly become orphans.

You may ask why would anyone want to be a police officer? Particularly a man or woman with children? The truth is, law enforcement was never an objective in my planned career path. But Confucius said, "Choose a job you love, and you will never have to work a day in your life." In my case "the job," as cops are wont to call it, chose me, and it turned out to be both a major career change and a job that I loved. Sometimes, we put ourselves into a box for a variety of reasons, some of them very good reasons. But the wise person will be alert for cracks in the walls of that box and either patch them or use them to break out.

No one understands better than I do that breaking out of our personal box may be difficult. But we owe it to ourselves to be alert to the possibilities and to evaluate them with the best judgment we can apply. The fact is, throughout our lives we should strive to grow, to explore, to discover, and most importantly, to change in both small and large ways—it's called *maturing*, and it's a lifelong process.

Ride with my son Jay and me, both of us cops, as we experience the unbridled variety of police work in the City of Chicago. Jay and I only rode together for one night, but you'll be surprised at the similarity in our experiences as we laugh, cry, and cling to family, before and after moments of humor, loss, and profound tragedy—the law enforcement stew. Friends, family, fatherhood, and faith have strengthened us and helped to see us through heartbreak, both on the streets and at home. In this collection of short stories, all based upon actual incidents, it is our hope that you will grow with us in a profession that we found to be both intense and rewarding. No matter your vocation or occupation, I believe these lessons from the street can be applied to your daily living.

Most importantly, it is our hope that this book will help you to see police officers as human beings. Human beings who on occasion make mistakes, but more importantly, human beings who are spouses, parents, siblings, and neighbors. Human beings who stand between the predator and the preyed upon in our society. By that definition alone, police work is indeed a noble profession.

So escape your box for at least a brief time, double-check your equipment belt, climb into that blue and white squad, fasten your seatbelt, and experience life on the streets of Chicago as a cop. Jay and I promise you quite a ride. Then join the moderated forum at www.OnBeingACop.com and share your impressions and opinions with other readers.

–Jim and Jay

A Cop, a Baby, and the Future

By Jim

Early Christmas Day 1968, I stood at the crib of my firstborn, Christopher. In his fifth day on earth, he was dwarfed by his bed, a speck on a sea of mattress. Or so it seemed at least to me as I stared down intently. I was leaving for work now and the Magnum revolver, the nightstick, the handcuffs, the uniform in general, could seem out of place in this baby's room. Not to me, of course—this was my profession; these were my tools. Christopher slept peacefully, unaware of the contrasts in this early morning scene.

I tugged at the gun belt until the pistol rested comfortably on my hip. Welcome home, son. "Son." The word generated awe, fear, panic, and pride simultaneously. What did I know about being a father? In this quiet moment, the responsibility began to dawn with the morning sun. It became almost overwhelming. This tiny but perfect human form was so vulnerable, so dependent, and so completely powerless in the world about him.

For that matter, what did I know about being a cop? Now entering my third year on the job, by most standards, I was still a rookie. But that didn't cross my mind. Don't worry, son; I'll come home; I'll be here. Or will I? A cop in a big city, brightly marked squad, ghetto beat—so many stories yet to unfold. Am I not also vulnerable, dependent, powerless to a degree? I won't let anything happen; I can't let anything happen. I will be home tonight, son. But…where do the dangers lie? We're alike, son. The future is beyond our control.

We don't know that in five short years you'll be joined by two brothers, Craig and Jay, the coauthor of this book. We don't know that cancer will tear your mother from you and your brothers before you're seven years old. We don't know that a Daughter of Charity of fourteen years will leave the religious community and Jay will propose to her…"Do you want to be my mommy?" She'll be your second mom. We don't know that there will be still a fourth brother, Timmy, who will serve to cement firmly the new family unit.

But this morning, here in this room, I only know that I am your father. I will protect. I will control. The Lord willing, and with extra care on my beat, I will be home tonight and every night. I'm responsible for you, son. For the first time in my career as a police officer, I leave for work with a touch of fear for what the day holds in store. I can't let anything happen to me. Because at this moment, neither of us realizes how fate will rule our futures and how fate will write the stories you are about to read.

This book of cop stories marks the end of my police career and the very first part of Jay's. These tales from the streets of Chicago are of two ordinary men, father and son, doing extraordinary things. Not superhero stuff, just the fascinating daily routine of police officers that is in reality anything but routine. Each day is different and unpredictable, and yes, many times extraordinary.

Each short story stands on its own and where the subject matter dictates, similar father/son perspectives are placed together. For this reason, only a cursory attempt has been made to put them in chronological order. Ride with each of us on the street and through life as we discover that the dangers, the joys, the times to laugh, the times to cry will come when we least expect them.

Shootout at the High Rollers Pool Hall

Prelude to a Family Tragedy

By Jim

audio at www.OnBeingACop.com/soundtracks/shootout.mp3

It was 1974 on a cold February afternoon in Chicago as I headed for the 4:30 roll call at Maxwell Street, Area Four Detective Headquarters. I would be late. I had tarried too long with my wife at the nearby hospital where she had been admitted to be prepped for an operation the following day. A persistent, suspicious lump on Karla's left breast would be examined surgically. She was characteristically upbeat as always, and I found it difficult to tear myself away, but I finally made the break. I would return early tomorrow to see her off to the operating room.

The red brick building at Maxwell and Morgan had been built in 1889 and was a classic old Chicago Police Station. The single long flight of marble steps leading to the second floor detective squad room had paths worn an inch or two deep at each side rail where cops with bad guys in tow had trudged over the previous eighty-five years. It would become known to a nation of television fans as the "Hill Street Blues" precinct because it is where the opening scenes of the popular 1980s show were filmed. To those of us who worked the murders, it was just Maxwell Street Homicide.

I would be with my steady partner, Mike Shull. Mike and I worked together with comfort and confidence that had developed after spending many months together, cruising the West Side in search of the killer *du jour*. And as a bonus, he had an offbeat, intellectual sense of humor that made our hours together pass quickly.

"Padar, Shull, you've got thirteen," announced the sergeant as he read the assignment sheet. That meant our radio call for evening would be 7413. Seven designated the Detective Division, four was Area Four, and thirteen would be our homicide car for the eight-hour tour. It wouldn't be the last time that the number thirteen figured in events of the night.

As was customary, incoming cases would be rotated among all the homicide units working that night. Since my wife Karla was scheduled for surgery early the following morning, I wanted to be sure to visit with her before they took her to the OR. We asked the sergeant for the night's first assignment to lessen the chance of getting stuck with a late job. He obliged us a little over an hour later with a shooting victim at the Cook County Hospital. We interviewed the victim of a minor gunshot wound along with two witnesses, put out an all-call for the offender, and stopped by a few locations he was known to frequent. Being a chilly February night, it was highly unlikely that we would draw another assignment. Our chances of having to work overtime were now very slim.

As the tour of duty drew to a close, a forecast "light snow" started to dust the drab West Side landscape. Mike and I decided to make one last semi-circle of the area and then head into the office for the 12:30 a.m. check-off roll call. I'd be home and in bed by 1 a.m., grab a few hours' sleep, and head out to the hospital. It was shortly after midnight, the radio was dead quiet, and the streets were deserted as we coasted to a stop at the westbound traffic light at Madison and Homan. A man ran down the center of the street, and when his feet hit the ground, there was a momentary puff of the new fallen snow. He left a trail of giant footprints running straight toward our car. As a longtime ghetto resident, he could spot an unmarked squad at a hundred yards.

Mike glanced at me as Mr. Citizen approached our car. "This guy done jus' got robbed," said Mike.

I rolled down my driver's window. It was exactly thirteen minutes past midnight. In police time, 0013 hours.

"In da pool hall! Dey dere right now, stickin' up everybody!"

"How many are there?" I asked.

"Dey's like fo' of 'em. An' dey got guns!"

"Okay, okay, we got it," I replied as I picked up the mike from the dashboard. "Seventy-four-thirteen emergency."

"Go ahead, seventy-four-thirteen," was the instant response from our Citywide 2 dispatcher.

"Yeah, there's a robbery-in-progress..." I glanced across Homan to the south side of the street through the snow. No chance of getting an address. "...at Madison and Homan in the pool hall."

I killed the headlights and pulled our car slowly across Homan to the north curb of Madison directly across from the pool hall.

"Madison and Homan in the pool hall, a robbery-in-progress," barked the dispatcher.

A moment before, Mike and I could have believed we were the only police unit on the streets of Chicago's West Side, but the quiet radio jumped to life as the Task Force and Canine Units on our frequency responded in a flurry of overlapping jumbled transmissions, sirens screaming in the background. There was lots of help out there!

Citywide dispatch took the air again, "All right, quite a few units pretty close to that; they're comin' there, so units be careful now; that's a robbery-in-progress called in by seven-four-thirteen; that's a homicide car. Madison and Homan in the pool hall."

Those were the last words we heard as we got out of the car, leaving our communications firmly affixed to the control head mounted under the dashboard. In 1974, the department was in the final stages of transitioning from car-mounted radios to personal radios that would clip to your equipment belt. The Detective

Division was last on the list for the new radios. In the parlance of the day, we were "leaving the air."

As we left the squad, we looked across the street at the "High Rollers #4 Pool Hall." The plate glass windows were completely fogged with condensation. It would be best to stay on the north side of the street and use the squad for at least partial cover. Mike and I drew our two-inch barrel, five-shot, snub-nosed revolvers and rested our arms on the car roof as we peered intently through the light snow at the pool hall's doorway. A total of ten rounds of ammo against four armed robbers seemed to put us at a decided disadvantage. By now our Citywide dispatcher had notified the district dispatcher, and in the distance, we heard the distinctive wail of citywide and district units approaching. Good ol' Area Four! But for a few seconds, the scene was almost idyllic with the red neon of the pool hall reflecting on the undisturbed snow softly falling on a deserted tranquil street. It would have made a great urban streetscape painting that you might find in an upscale gallery on North Michigan Avenue.

We didn't have long to wait before all that changed. Four robbers, with dark clothing strangely punctuated with red ski masks, burst through the door onto the sidewalk, broad-shouldering each other as they competed for space in their haste to exit.

"Halt, police!" we yelled to the very much surprised group. They paused in a moment of indecision. One of them raised a weapon, and fired a shot in our direction. It went wild into the park behind Mike and me. They too heard the sirens in the distance, and while I have no way of knowing whether it figured into their decision, they turned east and as a group fled southeast through the parking lot next to the pool hall. Using the squad roof to steady our arms and with a firm two-handed grip, Mike and I squeezed off several rounds. The department's regulation high pressure ammunition was designed for four-inch barrel revolvers, and as a result, each round squeezed out of the two-inch snubnose seemed to envelop my hands in a burst of flame and unburnt powder as it spewed from the cylinder and barrel. One, two, three rounds I counted, and sixteen-year-old Tyree Brewston hit the ground as if a Bears fullback had hit him. In reality, it was only a thirty-eight Special +P Hollow Point entering his left buttock and exiting his scrotum. Tyree wasn't going any further tonight, but his older companions fled south on Homan, never looking back. I made a mental note that I had only two rounds left if they should return for their wounded companion. In retrospect, it was a ludicrous thought... attempting to imply a Marine mentality to a ragtag group of ghetto robbers. I fingered the bullet pouch on my belt for a split second, but the approaching sirens convinced me that a reload would not be necessary.

The first assist unit was now pulling up, westbound on Madison. They stopped between the parking lot and us. Fate ruled that they just happened to be a canine unit. With a light snow falling, and two dogs, pursuit shouldn't be a trick.

"Shots fired! Shots fired!" I shouted to them. "We've got one down in the parking lot." I was hoping that they would relay the information to dispatch since our radio was firmly attached inside our locked vehicle. Unfortunately, that did not happen. With a fluid situation that was still developing, the initial units arriving elected to take care of business on the street and pursue the escaping robbers. The result was several minutes of confusion for the poor dispatchers. The second assist unit was a district beat car, and the officers cautiously approached Tyree, who lay writhing in the snow. They collared a passing wagon for transport to the hospital. Mike and I headed into the pool hall. We had just shot a guy. The next order of business was to corral victims and witnesses and phone our boss!

Time swirled around us. The scene was almost surreal, but neither Mike nor I would recall any excitement or panic. Behind the scenes, our Citywide dispatcher had notified the District Zone dispatcher of the robbery-in-progress, still unaware that shots had been fired. Additional 11th District beat cars were en route from all directions. The wagon loaded up Tyree and headed to Mount Sinai Hospital. As more beat cars arrived with lights and sirens, the street was literally wall-to-wall squad cars parked askew, Mars lights still flashing. The previous scene of a lone unmarked homicide car pulling quietly to the curb had been transformed in a matter of a few moments to one worthy of the ten o'clock news. Given the hour, however, the news crews were thankfully tucked in for the night.

We started to gather vital information, victims, witnesses, and addresses. Canine and Task Force reported apprehending two additional offenders. It was becoming apparent that several of our robbery victims and witnesses had disappeared in the confusion. Our concern was very real—we had just shot a man and our cast of eyewitnesses was slipping away. We heard some talk that the canine unit had also recovered a weapon. In the pool hall, Mike grabbed a personal radio from a district officer.

"Seventy-four-thirteen on the Zone..." Mike called.

"Seventy-four-thirteen go ahead," responded the district dispatcher.

"We're here at the scene of the robbery in the pool hall, and any beat cars that are out in this area workin' on this, would they bring the patrons back to this location for interview? Any of those beat cars that have any of those patrons and victims of the robbery would they please bring them back to the scene?"

Out of a packed pool hall of multiple victims, we would wind up with only six robbery complainants/witnesses. Weeks later, only one would show up in court to testify to the robbery.

It was a full eighteen minutes before we were able to return to our radio and give a report to our Citywide 2 dispatcher.

Outside once again in our squad, I keyed the mike. "Seven-four-thirteen, do we have the canine car that recovered that weapon from that robbery-in-progress? Please return to the scene here with that weapon."

"Yeah, he is on the way to ya, and also four-thirteen, clarify: Were there shots fired by the police?"

It was now almost twenty minutes into the incident and our Citywide dispatcher and the district dispatcher had no details of the shooting. The ten-year-old "state of the art" communications center was located in the headquarters building just south of Chicago's Loop. District zone dispatchers were housed on one floor and the Citywide dispatchers were on another floor. The detective units at the scene had radios, but they were firmly anchored to the dashboards of their vehicles. Such was the state of Chicago Police communications in the mid-70s.

"Yes, there were shots fired by the police," I replied. "And there is one offender who is hit; he is on his way to Mount Sinai Hospital; his condition appears to be good at the present time."

"All right, is this by four-thirteen?"

"The shots were fired by four-thirteen; that is correct."

"All right, were there any shots fired back at the police?"

"Yes, sir, there were shots fired at us," I said.

"All right, that's what I had to find out here. Ah, four-thirteen, there's no police officers injured, though?"

"Negative. No police officers injured."

There was a flurry of questions: Who was going where? What command personnel were responding? And then there was a momentary break in radio traffic. An anonymous unit broke silence.

"Police one...offenders nothing."

Back at the Maxwell Street station, there was all the fanfare that accompanies a police shooting—commanders, deputy superintendents, internal affairs, state's attorneys, and a court reporter to take official statements from Mike and me. We would later recall that we probably experienced more stress during the next several hours than we did in those fateful few seconds on West Madison Street.

The "occasional snow" continued falling throughout the night. I glanced anxiously at my watch. It was after 5 a.m. and my wife's surgery was scheduled in less than three hours. I felt a need to go home before heading for the hospital, and the snow would be a problem. After a few consultations, the bosses agreed to let Mike complete the remaining paperwork, and I was released from my tour of duty shortly after 5:30 a.m.

The occasional snow now amounted to several inches, but I hit the expressway before the rush hour and made it home while it was still dark. In the bathroom, I scrubbed my hands vigorously and discovered tiny reddish black marks that burned under the soap and brush. I dashed cold water on my face, and then I tiptoed into the boys' room and touched each one of them. Chris, age five, Craig, three and a half, and Jay, just seven weeks old, were sleeping soundly. I stroked their backs ever so gently. For the first time, I felt some emotion as tears welled up. I brushed my eyes and was surprised at the faint smell of gunpowder residue that remained on my hands.

Karla's mother was taking care of the children. "Jim?" she called from the other bedroom. "Are you okay?"

I moved to the hallway before answering. "Yes," I whispered. "I had to work late. It's snowing pretty good. I'm heading out to the hospital."

At the hospital, it was obvious that Karla had been crying. I sat down on her bed and gave her a hug and a kiss. I told her she looked scared; she told me I looked tired. There was a roommate on the other side of the curtain between the two beds, but I had no idea who it was.

"I had to work late," I replied. "You know they can give you something to relax you." I called for the nurse, who gave Karla a shot while we held hands.

Karla loved good-natured kidding, especially if it was at my expense, but this morning, none came from her. Neither of us was up to it. When the nurses arrived to take her to surgery, I walked her to the elevator doors, holding her hand all the way. When the doors opened, she kissed my hand and suddenly brightened.

"Your hands are dirty!" she said, shaking her head in mock exasperation as the elevator doors slid shut between us.

As she headed to surgery, Karla would be alone in a very real sense. In the operating room, the doctors would discover an aggressive breast cancer with indications of metastasis. There would be no partner at her side, no sirens in the distance heralding imminent rescue. Indeed, for the next several months, it would seem as though the entire medical profession had abandoned her.

• • • •

It was just a year past that long day, and I was speaking with Karla's oncologist late one afternoon. Things were not going well, and Karla had been hospitalized for the past several days. The doctor spoke of a new experimental chemotherapy, and we agreed to start treatment that very afternoon.

Early that evening, I sat with Karla in room 1007A at Rush-Presbyterian-St. Luke's. She told me our pastor had visited, but she was noncommittal about the details.

"We prayed" was all she would say, and then suddenly, she looked at me with tears welling up in her eyes and asked, "When am I ever going to be okay?"

I encouraged her to give the new medicine a chance to take effect, and as visiting hours drew to a close, I kissed her goodnight.

Out in my car on Van Buren Street, I slid in behind the wheel. With tears streaming down my face, I gripped the wheel, closed my eyes, and prayed aloud, "Dear Lord, if you are going to take her, please...take her now."

I shed tears, but I felt none of the heart-pounding panic of the previous months...just a sense of peace and resignation. I sat quietly for several minutes and dried my eyes. Then I headed home on the Kennedy Expressway with a sense of fatigue but also, strangely, of peace.

It is said that coincidence is God's way of remaining anonymous. As I hung my coat in the front closet, the doorbell rang. It was my brother Jerry and sister Nancy. They had gone to visit at the hospital, but they had arrived too late for visiting hours. On a whim, they decided to stop by and visit me. Almost simultaneously, the phone rang. It was the hospital. Karla had taken a sudden turn for the worse. Could I please return as quickly as possible?

Jerry drove. Nancy sat in the backseat, crying quietly.

"Oh, Jim; oh, Jim," she repeated over and over.

As we headed back toward the city on the expressway, I implored my brother not to speed or take chances. Deep inside, I knew two things for certain: It was over, and I would not be alone. Jerry and Nancy were with me tonight, and Karla's family would surround the boys and me with love and support in the coming months and years. Maybe God had a plan....

Do You Want to Be My Mommy?

By Jim

video at www.OnBeingACop.com/mommy

Life had been good to me. A happy marriage to Karla, three young sons, Chris, Craig, and Jay. At work, I had been promoted to detective, and I wound up in my assignment of choice—homicide—where I was working with Mike, my partner of choice. It was a mesa point in my life, even and stable, with perhaps some mountains yet to climb. But mesas have steep edges, and as a family, we were about to crash over the edge.

In February of 1974, Karla was diagnosed with that monster we call breast cancer, and one short year later, it would rip her away from me and the boys who were then six, four-and-a-half, and one years old. I became a single father. One might think that I was left alone, but that was not true. I was blessed with a solid extended family that came to the fore. Karla's sister and brother-in-law, Kristine and Bill, were a couple who didn't preach their faith—they lived their faith. They had three children of their own, cousins to the boys, roughly the same age. As a family, they closed ranks with me, and along with help from Karla's parents for the next few years, the boys and I survived. Still, it was less than ideal. The boys knew the wheel was missing a spoke, but with a lot of help and some adept juggling, I managed to keep us together as a family unit and continue my work as a homicide detective.

Remarrying was out of the question—maybe in the distant future, the golden years, but certainly not with three young children. And where would one even start to look for someone who would be willing and able to be a wife *and* a mother?

But the Lord works in mysterious ways. Unknown to me, hundreds of miles from Chicago, a nun from the order of the Daughters of Charity was struggling with the desire to have a family of her own and most definitely become a mother. A short time later, Durell left the Daughters of Charity and arrived in Chicago, temporarily staying with her parents. She announced to friends that she was interested in meeting a widower with children. Wade and Gail were her next-door neighbors, and Wade just happened to be a homicide detective who worked out of the same office as I.

"I know a widower with children," Wade had told Durell with a broad smile.

"I told her you would call her," he later told me at the office.

And so, Durell and I began to see one another, and after a very short period of time, we knew it was meant to be. Equally important, the boys enjoyed it when Durell was with us. It was time for a formal proposal. My birthday was just two months away, and I thought it would be a novel turnabout if I were to give her a ring on my birthday. That was my plan.

But Jay was now four years old, and at that age, his world moved in his own personal timeframe. We were at a party with Karla's family, a full month before my birthday. The gathering was the normal hectic large family party—aunts, uncles, and Karla's parents. As usual, the food was good and plentiful and the boys enjoyed being with their cousins and everyone who had helped care for them since their mother had been torn from them. Jay walked the crowd, neck craned upward, gaining him a child's view of the group and bypassing everyone who had played such a giant part in his care from the time of his birth. Then he spotted Durell and grabbed her hand.

"Will you take me to the bathroom?" he asked.

"Well, of course, Jay."

Once in the washroom, he dropped his pants to his ankles, and she helped hoist him upon the toilet. His straight brown hair complemented his deep brown eyes. He put his chin on his hands and his elbows on his knees. He was swinging his feet. Durell sat on the edge of the tub, directly across from him. She cupped her chin in her hands and rested her elbows on her knees, and they looked directly at one another, barely a foot apart. They sat like that for a moment, Jay still swinging his feet before he spoke.

"Well?" he said.

"Well what, Jay?" she replied.

"Do you want to be my mommy?"

Durell felt as though she had nearly fallen backwards into the tub, and she felt tightness and a lump in the back of her throat. She recovered quickly.

"Jay, I would like nothing more in the world than to be your mommy!"

"Okay…can we go now?"

Out in the crowd again, Jay ran off with his cousins. Durell grabbed me and ushered me into the vestibule, out of earshot.

"Jay just proposed to me!"

"What?"

"In the bathroom, just now…he asked whether I wanted to be his mommy. Of course, I told him yes."

"Fantastic!" I exclaimed. "Tonight when we get home, we'll tell the other boys that Jay had this great idea…."

So, looking back on it now, I guess that was really the moment of our formal engagement, and I wasn't even there.

And my plan? Well, apparently that had been superseded by a plan made elsewhere…a plan I was totally unaware of…but a plan that was exquisitely executed.

You Can Never Go Back

By Jim

photo at www.OnBeingACop.com/gallery/goback.jpg

You can never go back. That's what they say. What is past is gone forever. Move on. Don't look back.

That's even more true for cops, I suppose. You work the street for years, and then you're promoted and catch a special assignment that keeps you inside. It's nice. You feel like you've accomplished something. It's not that you didn't like the street. You did. As a matter of fact, after several more years "inside," you begin to realize that you loved the street. It was exciting. It was fun. And you really miss it. But you can never go back. Yet another promotion and increased responsibilities...inside. You are told you are "too valuable" to the department in your present assignment. You retire and go on to other things. It is painfully obvious now. You can never go back.

Well, almost never. If you happen to have a son, who for some inexplicable reason decides to follow in your footsteps, and if that son decides to ask you to go on a ride along with him for a night, well, maybe you can go back. Just for a night. It's a rookie's ultimate expression of self-confidence to ask his dad, a retired lieutenant with twenty-nine years of service, to ride with him. It says a lot. "I am a cop too, Dad." It's a very adult version of, "Look at me, Dad!"

On a more profound level, it says, "I share your love for the job, Dad. Let me share a night with you...."

And so for eight hours, we rode together, not as father and son, not as rookie and lieutenant, but as a couple of cops in a beat car doing what cops do. It was not an exceptional night from a law enforcement perspective, but the tools had changed: handheld radios, in car data terminal, light bar with strobes and takedown lights pointing to each side. The players on the street were familiar—it was the same circus, just different clowns. But it was a profoundly exceptional night from a personal perspective because for that microcosm in time, we were partners....

Glad to Be Back
(Email)
By Jay & Jim

Subject:	**Glad to be back...**
Date:	**Thu, 09 Sep 1999 10:47:45 -0500**
From:	**Jay Padar**
To:	**Jim Padar, Chris Padar**

Dad,

I was pleasantly surprised when I returned to work last night and got into our new beat car. It's a '99 Ford Crown Vic Police Interceptor with 197 miles. I didn't realize how much I missed work until I hit the lights and siren, put the pedal to the floor, and sped to assist our sergeant. Wrong way down the one-way street, across the intersection, over the rumble strip to avoid the blue lights we just cut off, and to a screeching halt next to one of our favorite "white-shirts." He had an offender on the ground who was chasing a "half-naked woman" down the street. We were a couple of blocks away when the call came out, and we got there in about twenty seconds. To my amazement, another car beat us there. They were cuffing the offender, so it was my duty to console the "half-naked woman." (You know—We Serve and Protect.) Turned out to be a half-naked post-operative transsexual prostitute. I guess I got what I deserved. I had the last twenty-one days off, went to the Poconos, New York City, and worked a couple of side jobs. Now I'm mad that I missed the last twenty-one days at work. I missed out on twenty-one days of good stories. Nothing on vacation was as much fun as working last night, and it was just a slow Wednesday night in Chicago. Can't wait for the weekend! Make sure you keep this email and show it to me when I'm old and bitter, complaining to my kids about how much the job sucks, and lecturing them about how times have changed and how they would hate being a cop. Well, at least I have about another three-and-a-half months before they make me take furlough again!

Subject:	**Great to be back & Transvestite Prostitutes**
Date:	**Thu, 09 Sep 1999 12:03:42**
From:	**Jim Padar**
To:	**Jay Padar**

Jay,

What a great message! You'll never have more fun on the job than you're having now. If you're lucky, it will last some time. I count fourteen years of good times, patrol and homicide. And maybe the first few years in the TV Studio before I became a sergeant. When I was a new patrol officer, my partner asked me what I knew about "he-shes," and I had to admit that I had never heard the term. When he told me they were transvestite prostitutes, I couldn't believe him. Well, our goal that night became to arrest a he-she for loitering. It didn't take long—he spotted one waving down cars on Wells Street. I couldn't believe that a john would mistake this for a real woman. We got the subject spread-eagled on the squad, and my partner stepped back to the cover position while I did the frisk. (It was so nice of him.) The arrestee looked back over "his" shoulder at me and apparently liked what he saw. "Oh, search me! Search me real good!" he squealed as he spread his legs even farther. I still remember that as one of the most disgusting things that I ever had to do on the job. My partner was laughing all night long!

A Head Is Highly Portable

By Jim

Chicago: Winter—1970

The itinerant huddled at the front of the Madison Street liquor store. Any minute now, he knew he would be asked to leave, but it was bitter cold outside. It was one of those below zero Chicago nights with just enough wind to make sleeping outside a roll of the dice with the Grim Reaper. Cold enough that a handful of his less fortunate peers would not make it through the night. He was drunk, so he knew the Mission down the street wouldn't take him. That was one of its two conditions—sobriety and the patience to sit through a sermon of sorts—in exchange for some hot soup and sleeping space in the giant second floor hall. In his inebriated state, it would not be an option for him tonight. Still, he had some money for wine and a sheltered place to sleep.

The man behind the register was glancing at him now. In another minute, the bum was certain he would be asked to leave the store's warmth. He dug into every pocket and collected an assortment of lint, tobacco shreds, coins, scraps of tissue, and a key to a long forgotten door. The cashier was staring now, so the bum made his move, slowly, toward the cash register. He dumped the pocket debris onto the counter.

"A pint of Richard's," he mumbled. His blood alcohol level prevented him from counting, but it looked to him like he had more than enough for a bottle of Richard's Wild Irish Rose. The man took a bottle and a brown paper bag and placed it on the counter. Then he slid several coins through the flotsam and looked expectantly at the customer. There was money left.

"And some Camels."

One, two, three, four cigarettes were counted out.

"Matches?" asked the clerk.

The bum nodded and one of the cigarettes was replaced with a pack of matches. He retrieved the key from the counter just before the clerk swept the remaining mess to the floor with his hand. The key was precious and would be used for his next encounter with the police. (I gotta place officer! I gotta place to stay. See, here's my key!) Sometimes it worked. But tonight, he headed out the door, hoping to avoid the police altogether, clutching his purchase: a pint of fortified wine, three cigarettes, and a pack of matches.

Outside the liquor store, the 12th District wagon was making its hourly pickup of curbside drunks. If he went to jail now, he'd lose his wine. He stepped back into the doorway and waited for the wagon to pass. Then he took a long drag on the bottle inside the brown bag and stepped out into the night. He lurched down the street and took a left on Peoria. A block to the north was a lot full of abandoned semi-trailers. They were largely inaccessible with their rear doors flush against the brick wall of the next-door building. But several weeks ago, he had pried some rusted sheet metal out of the wheel well of one of the trailers and managed to climb into most spacious sleeping quarters. He stumbled around the lot, numb with cold, and after a while, he found the unit. Once inside, he took another long drink of Richard's and lit a cigarette. It was pitch black, but the light from the match provided amazing illumination, revealing a few empty boxes and pieces of a wood pallet.

He wrapped himself in the cardboard and assumed the fetal position, but the trailer's metal floor and walls seemed to suck any remaining warmth out of his body. He had never been so cold in his entire life. He struck another match and lit a piece of cardboard in an attempt to warm his hands over the flame. The heat felt good. He added some more cardboard and then some wood from the pallet. He was finally beginning to feel warm, and he moaned softly. He didn't notice the smoke gathering along the ceiling of the eighteen-foot trailer. His giant bedroom began to fill with thick acrid smoke from the ceiling downward, but by the time it reached floor level, the alcohol and carbon monoxide had done their job. He was spread-eagled on his back, totally unconscious.

The fire struggled inside the enclosure, fed oxygen sparingly from the wheel well, venting furtively from some broken seams in the metal body. Eventually, the heat melted a small hole in the fiberglass roof, and suddenly, air streamed in from the wheel well and out the opening above. In seconds, the trailer's interior became a raging inferno. It would have melted the entire roof and the aluminum walls, but as quickly as it started, it ran out of fuel. With nothing left to burn, the fire extinguished itself, save for the smoldering silhouette.

Wednesday, April 9th, 1970

Nathaniel Horton felt good. He was rich! Nate had worked every day this week, and after getting totally drunk tonight, he still had twenty-four dollars in his pocket. He was intoxicated and he had money, so he knew he was vulnerable. He couldn't spend the night at the Mission, and the Union Hotel would cost him six dollars. But no need. It was a beautiful spring evening, and if he could just find an isolated spot to sleep, he would awake with his twenty-four dollars. At Peoria and Randolph, he spotted the lot full of trailers. It was dark and the lot was poorly lit, but he found a hole above one of the wheel wells. He scrambled into the darkness and promptly passed out.

Thursday morning dawned sunny and bright. Nate awoke, staring at an almost blinding patch of bright blue sky visible through the large hole in the trailer's roof. He rolled to his left and began to focus on his surroundings. Instantly, he was awake. The grotesque, mummified body was between him and the wheel well exit. He had no choice but to climb quickly over the remains and beat a hasty retreat.

Sunday, April 12th, 1970

The rookie detective reported to Maxwell Street Homicide for the afternoon shift. He checked the assignment sheets and discovered he was working with the senior detective, Big Andy. Andy was a large, amiable old timer. His partner must have taken the day off, thought the new guy. Good. He had only been working homicide for two months, and his chances of drawing a homicide assignment would be better working with Big Andy. The new detective had seen very few actual murder scenes. Still, on a quiet Sunday afternoon, what were the chances?

The newbie stood at the open window of the Area Four Homicide office, looking north across Maxwell Street and toward the flophouses of Roosevelt Road. Andy walked over and stood next to his partner for the day.

"When the wind is right, you can smell the piss from here, kid," he rasped in his gravel voice. "Come on; let's see if we can find you a body!"

Well, even if we don't draw an assignment, it's going to be a good day, thought the rookie. Big Andy is a character with a wealth of war stories. And Area Four was nicknamed "the murder factory."

Once outside, the street proved to be extremely quiet. The radio was nearly silent. There were two follow-up interviews on some older cases, and then they found themselves cruising the West Side with Big Andy giving the young detective a richly narrated tour of previous homicide scenes.

"Seventy-one-o-three," the dispatcher broke the radio silence.

"Seventy-one-o-three, go," answered the Area One Homicide unit.

"See the beat car at 626 West Randolph, regarding a human head."

Damn! thought the rookie. That's an Area One assignment. We can't even feign an assist to satisfy our...well...my curiosity.

"Sure glad that's not our case," said the rookie weakly.

"Take it easy, kid," growled Big Andy. "That's the edge of our area, and a head is highly portable; they might try to shift it to us."

Twenty minutes later, Andy's prediction came true.

"Seventy-four-twelve," said the dispatcher, "meet the Area One homicide car at 626 Randolph regarding that human head." The rookie detective stifled a fake yawn and slouched slightly in the seat, trying to look nonchalant. For an instant, out of the corner of his eye, he thought he caught a hint of a grin on Big Andy's face.

Andy and the new homicide detective walked into the Working Man's Tavern on Randolph, now bereft of customers save one, but crowded with curious uniformed officers, detectives, and crime lab technicians. Sitting on the bar, resting on a crumpled newspaper, was a blackened mummified human head, grinning out at the nearby empty tables. In a corner, wringing his hands, was Nate Horton.

"Can't you move that thing?" whined Nate as Andy and the new detective approached the table.

"Hey, Andy!" one of the Area One detectives greeted the Area Four Team. Everyone knew Big Andy. "This guy brought that head in here, and he claims he found it in your area. He says he'll take you to the rest of the body."

Once outside, a grisly cortege proceeded west on Randolph. An unmarked homicide car was in the lead, the rookie sitting straight now, his mind racing to catalog the details of the unfolding investigation. Nate was in the backseat, and his mood also had changed. He was relieved to be removed from the gaze of the head, and he leaned forward in his seat, giving directions. Immediately behind was the crime lab sedan with a trunk full of cameras and forensic kits. Grumbling along at the end were two wagon men with a cargo of a human head…in search of a body.

On the way back to the trailer, Nate repeated his story.

"When I woke up Thursday with that thing, I ran like hell. I came over here to tell my buddies, but they just laughed at me and told me I had the DT's. We sat around drinking and they kept ragging on me. I was really getting pissed. When we ran out of money, I went back to the trailer to get some proof for them. I poked at it with a stick and the head just fell off, so I wrapped it in newspaper and brought it back to the bar. But my friends were gone."

Andy was distracted by traffic and there was a moment of silence. The new kid's mind raced. Say something…for God's sake say something; you're a homicide detective in the second largest city in the country. Contribute something!

The new detective finally asked a question: "Ya, but that was last Thursday. It's Sunday afternoon now! Where has that head been?"

"Well, when I found they were gone, I took the thing outside to the empty lot next door and set it up against the wall," said Nate. "Then this afternoon when they came into the bar, I went out and got it."

"You mean that head sat out in that lot in downtown Chicago for four days?" asked Andy.

"Well, I had it wrapped real good," said Nate. "Turn here! Turn here at Peoria!"

The macabre procession pulled slowly into the lot full of abandoned semi-trailers. The fire department peeled back the side of the abandoned truck as if it were a giant tin can. Lab technicians and detectives examined the soot-blackened scene. The charred body would yield no fingerprints. The scorched key in its front jean pocket bore no identifying information. As the fragile body was gently removed, the floor of the trailer revealed a bright silhouette where the bum once lay. In the center of the image was a pristine pack of matches from a Madison Street liquor store. The wagon crew reunited the wandering head and its lifeless body and delivered one complete corpse to the morgue.

Back at the Maxwell Street station in the Area Four office, Big Andy slipped a form into the typewriter.

"Primary Classification?" asked the first box. "Death Investigation," typed Andy.

"Secondary Classification?" "Accidental (pending autopsy)."

"Well, kid," smiled Big Andy, "it's not a homicide...but it'll be a good story to tell your kids years from now."

"Yes, it will," said the rookie detective. "Yes, it will!"

Accidental Cop

By Jim

Tribune article at www.OnBeingACop.com/gallery/tribune.pdf

I was sitting at my desk at Motorola. "Engineering Liaison Coordinator," they called me, and I was pretty good at it. It was a position that made good use of my engineering education, "to talk the talk," but didn't require me to do any hands on engineering, "to walk the walk." I was the buffer between major customers and our engineering department. When customers requested changes on a long-term project and our engineers said, "Of course, we can do it," I was the guy who reviewed the change from an engineer's perspective and said, "Yes, but it will cost you…."

I had come to Motorola from a job in New York City, where I was project manager on a major research and development project. I had discovered two things about myself in New York—I was insanely homesick for my home sweet home Chicago, and worse, I was not a good R & D design engineer. Although I had graduated in the top 10 percent of my class, I was not imaginative or innovative enough to forge new trails on the engineering landscape. When I got laid off in an 80 percent staff reduction, I heaved a sigh of relief and headed back to Chicago.

But after finishing a gigantic project for Motorola, I became bored. There was nothing on the horizon that promised to be challenging. Tom, a coworker my age who sat behind me, was equally bored. We would walk the building and scope out the offices until we found an exceptionally good-looking secretary. Then we would find out who her boss was and manufacture a reason to have some business with him. To say we had too much time on our hands would be an understatement.

Tom and I were talking one day about interesting occupations. He had a few friends who were police officers. He thought that would be interesting. Could be, I thought to myself, but I have zero interest in such a major career change.

"How much does a cop make?" Tom and I wondered aloud.

"It can't be a secret," I said. "Let me call and find out."

I called and was connected with the Chicago Police Department's Public and Internal Information Division. The man gave me the figure, obviously less than what Tom and I were presently making.

"By the way," said the officer, just before he hung up. "We're having a civil service exam for police officers this Saturday. It's a walk in—all you need is the $5 testing fee. Do you want me to send you the information?"

"Sure. Why not?" I said.

A few days later, a thick envelope arrived at my apartment. I threw it on my dresser without opening it.

Saturday morning, I was up early for no particular reason. As I dressed, I spotted the envelope. I tore it open and scanned the contents quickly. If I hurried, I would be able to make it in time for the test being held at a local high school. It would give me something to tell Tom Monday morning.

I joined several hundred other young men and was ushered into a classroom where we all filled out detailed employment applications. We were then issued multiple test booklets over the next three hours. I was supremely disappointed. I didn't quite know what I was expecting, but a generic intelligence test, reading, vocabulary, and some very basic writing was not at all what I thought it would be. There wouldn't be much to tell Tom on Monday.

I promptly forgot about the whole disappointing exercise. They could have at least had some questions on criminal law, or traffic violations, or even some deductive reasoning problems. There was certainly no challenge there, to my way of thinking.

A few months later, the phone at my Motorola desk rang.

"This is Tom Powers, *Chicago Tribune* city desk. We'd like to come out to get a headshot of you."

"Huh? Why would you want a headshot of me?"

"Is this James Padar?" he asked.

"Yes."

"Did you take the police test a few months ago?"

"Yes."

"Well, don't you know?" asked Powers.

"Don't I know what?" I asked impatiently.

"You scored number one! You're going to be in tomorrow's paper."

"Whoa! Tom, please, no. My boss doesn't even know I took the police exam. I'd just as soon you left me out of the paper," I pleaded.

"Too late," replied Powers. "You're probably already in this afternoon's *Chicago American*."

I hung up the phone and raced down to the lobby where the afternoon paper was nestled in the red newspaper vending machine. Sure enough, on page three, the bold headline read, "Oak Park man scores number one on Chicago Police exam." My name was in the very first sentence.

I tucked the paper under my arm and marched up to my boss's office and closed the door behind me.

"Milt, I've got kind of a funny story to tell you…."

Milt was ecstatic.

"Hold on," he said. "I'm calling our public relations. They'll get the *Tribune* back on the phone and tell them to come out for the picture."

"You really think that's a good idea?"

"Of course! It's great—it shows we have smart people working for Motorola." Milt was positively enthusiastic.

"If I'm so smart, why do I want to leave an engineering position with Motorola to be a cop?" I asked.

"People don't think like that," he said. "All they'll read is 'Motorola' and 'number one' in the same sentence."

The company assigned me my very own public relations representative, and after the hubbub surrounding the photographs had subsided, I found myself back in my boss's office.

"Boss, I really didn't mean—" I started.

"Jim! Jim." Listen to me for just a few minutes. You're a good engineer and I'd hate to lose you. You're good at what you do—but you'd be good at whatever you decide to do. I know you're bored here and we haven't been able to challenge you—"

"But—" I interrupted.

"No, listen…please, for just a minute. You're single, you have no family responsibilities. If there was ever a good time to break out of a mold for you, it's right now. Take a couple of weeks and think about it. If you want to give it a shot and it doesn't work out, I'll take you back here, same desk, and same job. So think about it."

Two months later, I walked into the Chicago Police Academy at 720 West O'Brien Street and never looked back.

I was dating Karla, who was Milt's secretary, so I was in occasional contact with him and the Motorola folks from time to time. Karla and I were married a little over a year after I joined the police department, and both Motorola and the Chicago Police Department were well-represented at our wedding. Milt renewed his offer of my old job, but I was having too much fun.

In another year, Karla would give birth to our firstborn son, and she would quit work. Milt never spoke to me again. It was one thing to lose a mediocre engineer, but a super secretary was hard to replace!

Cops Don't Cry

By Jim

"For those of you here today who have a police officer
as mother or father, know this:
At some time in their career,
they have come home from the street and wept for you."

Father Thomas Nangle, Police Chaplain
Family Day Mass, 2006

1978, Homicide, Second Watch...

It was a beautiful warm summer day, but the air was crisp, un-encumbered by the awful humidity that sometimes grips Chicago in mid-August. Our sports coats hung in the back, swaying gently, as Mike Shull steered the unmarked sedan around the city's West Side. Kids were everywhere. On bikes, playing baseball, and splashing in the occasional open hydrant.

Cops develop a background ear, constantly tuned to the radio's drone. We were talking about nothing in particular, but immediately picked up our call when the dispatcher paged.

"Seventy-four-eleven."

I reached for the mike. "Seventy-four-eleven," I replied.

"Seventy-four-eleven, take the death investigation now at St. Mary's."

St. Mary's was a brand new hospital in a very old neighborhood. Brand new building, that is. The hospital had been there for generations, but it had been recently rebuilt. It was a modern state-of-the-art building. All private rooms, first class emergency room. Mike slid the car into a parking place reserved for police vehicles. We left our jackets in the car. No need to cover the revolver, handcuffs, ammo pouch. The hospital personnel knew us too well.

Inside, we greeted the ER staff, which responded in subdued voices. It was a drowning. Male white, about eight years old. He was removed from the bottom of the park pool by a lifeguard who administered CPR until the arrival of the fire ambulance. The paramedics continued CPR en route to the hospital. It's tough to give up on a kid. The ER doctor pronounced the boy dead on arrival. There must have been 200 kids in that pool, so how long he was on the bottom was anyone's guess. Our job would be to eliminate foul play as a possible factor in the drowning. We gathered what little identifying information the hospital had and then headed to the examining room where he lay.

It could have been a scene from a movie. The heavy wood door with large shaded glass swung open, and on a gurney, under a sheet, was the silhouette of a small human being. The nurse closed the door behind us, and Mike and I pulled the sheet back. The boy looked to be about the reported age of eight. Light brown curly hair, still wet. His turquoise swim trunks clung to his pale white skin. My chest gave an involuntary breath—no—a single convulsive sob. My eyes welled and I turned away to compose myself. The nurse was looking at me intently. Mike never blinked. He continued with the boy's examination. Male white, approximately eight years of age, brown hair, blue eyes, no bruises, no external signs of violence. In less than a minute, I returned to the gurney, once again a stoic homicide detective. I reached across, grasped his arm, and pulled the cold, wet little boy toward me. Mike scanned the boy's backside for any marks or indications of violence. No rigor, no lividity, no bruises. We completed our notes and returned to the nurses' station, which had received some additional information, possibly the location of his mother working as a waitress at a nearby restaurant. We would need another unit to get the mother and bring her to the hospital for identification. Mike and I would go to the pool and interview the lifeguard and any witnesses.

Out in the lot, we rolled down our car windows and paused for a moment to let the blast of now superheated air out of the squad. Mike slid in behind the wheel. I waited for radio traffic to clear.

For the first time since the ER, Mike looked me in the eye. "You saw Craig, didn't you?"

"I did. I knew it wasn't him, but somehow, I saw him lying on that gurney."

Cops try to keep their family separate from their street life. Most times they succeed. It's a necessity for mental survival. When you fail and identify family with a real-life street scenario, the results can be traumatic. My curly-headed, brown-eyed, eight year old was miles from here doing his summer thing; I felt sure of that.

The radio fell silent for a moment and I keyed the mike. "Seventy-four-eleven, we're going to need an assist car to locate the mother...."

That night as Craig raced into the house for supper, I grabbed him in a bear hug.

"Dad!" he shouted as he squirmed loose, "Cut it out!"

"Wash up!" I shouted after him with just a hint of a crack in my voice.

The Encounter

By Jay

Our encounter only lasted for a matter of seconds. It happened fourteen years ago, but I think about it more often than I'd like to. I think about it intently every year at Christmastime. My stare would have, I'm sure, made him feel uncomfortable or uneasy, but I'm certain he never knew I was there. If he had seen the way I was staring at him, he would have sensed my helplessness and fear. That intent stare had an adverse effect on me. It locked his image in my memory for an eternity. It's an image, I fear, that won't ever go away. That image is the reason I hold my three-year-old boy's hand a little too tight when crossing the street. It's the reason I carry my son's twin sister across the street when she tells me that she can walk on her own. It was an event for which the police academy did not, could not prepare me. My instructors made me faster and stronger. They made me smarter and more knowledgeable. However, there are experiences on the street for which lectures and gym exercises just can't prepare you. This was one of them.

The date was December 24th, 1998. I had graduated from the police academy just ten days prior, and I was about as green as a new police officer could be. My veteran partner for the night had been on the street for about a year and a half. Thinking back, I laugh about how highly I regarded his experience. He was, and still is, a solid police officer, but at the time, he was just a kid like me. We were working the afternoon shift on Christmas Eve, just hoping to get off on time. Right before the end of our shift, the dispatcher apologetically assigned us the call.

"Sorry, Two-four-forty-four, but we have a pedestrian struck by a hit-and-run driver at Rockwell and Devon. There are no other cars available. Fire is on the way."

My partner hit the gas and proceeded to the scene. At first glance, we were relieved. No pedestrian down, no ambulance, and no commotion on the street. As we happily informed the dispatcher that we couldn't find any victim, she advised us that the victim was taken by cab to St. Francis Hospital. All right, he can't be in bad shape if he took a cab to the hospital. We'll race there, knock out a quick report, and be at check off on time. Our Christmas was just a few hours away.

We walked into the emergency room and let the receptionist know that we were there for the hit-and-run victim. Our cavalier demeanor changed dramatically when she informed us that he was in Trauma Room Three...and his parents were with the chaplain in the private waiting area. I walked hurriedly into the ER and pulled the curtain back at Trauma Room Three. That's when my eyes locked onto him. His naked and bloodied little body lay lifeless on the gurney. The doctors and nurses were working feverishly to revive him. They were pumping his chest and working on him in a manner I can only describe as controlled chaos. They were working on him the way a dying three-year-old boy deserves to be worked on. All of the medical technology available and intense effort by emergency room staff would not be enough to save this little boy. His short life would end tonight.

After what seemed like an eternity, I closed the curtain and walked slowly to the private waiting area—a waiting area where no one wants to be. The boy's father sat sobbing in a chair with his head in his hands, clothes soaked with his little boy's blood. He had held his son in the cab on the way to the hospital. His mother sat almost expressionless, in a state of shock, holding their newborn baby as the hospital chaplain spoke softly to her. I knew I could offer no comfort or be of any help to anyone. I could sense the uneasiness in my partner as he told me he had never handled a fatal accident before and that he was going to request that Major Accidents respond to the hospital. Even though, as the passenger in the patrol car, it was my job to handle the paperwork for this, my partner thankfully took the reins and completed what was necessary.

Detectives from the Major Accident Investigation Unit, who investigate all fatal traffic accidents, arrived shortly afterwards and began their investigation. They asked the hard questions like the boy's name and birthday, how did this happen, and what did the car look like that hit him.

It turns out that this young family was visiting from Indiana. They had just finished a late dinner at a restaurant when Dad went out to warm up the car. Mom waited in the restaurant for a few minutes and then carried their newborn in her arms as their three-year-old son held onto her finger while walking alongside her. When the little boy saw his dad warming up the car across the street, he let go of his mother's finger and ran into the street toward him. That's when the silver sports utility vehicle struck him. The little boy was dragged underneath the SUV for about a block before his body came to rest on the cold pavement. Not wanting to wait for an ambulance, his father picked up his little body and raced him to the hospital in a cab. I found out months later that the driver of the SUV had fled to Mexico after the accident. He later returned and was arrested.

I didn't speak of this incident the next morning while celebrating Christmas at my parents' house with my family. It would be the first of many events throughout my police career that I wouldn't speak of. Someday, God willing, years from now, my kids will be grown and read this story. And they'll understand why Daddy held their hands a little too tight at times, and why they were carried across the street when they thought they were too big to be carried. Hopefully, they'll understand how precious they are to me and how hard I've worked to protect them. And maybe, years from now, if they see me staring off into space at a Christmas Eve party, while everyone else is laughing and enjoying the celebration, they'll know that it's just that time of year when their daddy must remember December 24th, 1998 and the moments spent with that other little boy.

But It's Not Our Job!

By Jim

photo at www.OnBeingACop.com/gallery/ElMorro.jpg

Ask almost any homicide detective in Chicago and that person will probably tell you that he or she is there by choice. At least during my tenure, I never ran across any who did not want to work in a homicide unit. Murder is the ultimate crime, and working the various cases is both interesting and challenging.

Continue on and ask the detectives what is their least favorite thing about working in a homicide unit and many will tell you, paper jobs. Back in the day, the full title of the unit was Homicide, Sex, and Aggravated Assault. That meant we also investigated rapes and sexual assaults along with shootings and stabbings where the victim was not killed. These assignments were typically passed out to individual detectives at roll call in the form of case reports previously submitted by the district beat cars. They came with a deadline for resolution, so often, the pressure of murder investigations, or just plain procrastination, resulted in a backlog of paper jobs on your clipboard.

It was just such an assignment that was passed out to my partner Mike Shull one day. After roll call, we were flipping through our newly assigned paper jobs, prioritizing them as best we could, when I heard a long sigh from Mike.

"What is it?" I inquired. He answered in a sing-song voice.

"Heard a shot,

Felt a pain,

Story number nine again."

Paper jobs were enough of a distraction in and of themselves, but when victims demonstrated a total lack of cooperation, they became a colossal waste of time. Mike had long advocated that we be authorized to dispose of such cases with a large rubber stamp that merely read:

#9

Our supervisors did not agree, of course. Each case required at least a cursory investigation before it could be suspended, even if the victim continued to be uncooperative.

Mike handed me the case report, which I scanned quickly. Carlos Diaz was walking on Division Street when an unknown person ran up behind him and stabbed him in the back for no apparent reason. Carlos could not offer any description—he didn't even know whether the offender was male or female—nothing was taken from him. His story screamed #9. There was one thing, however, that would require we give the case more than passing attention. The beat officer indicated that Carlos was being admitted to the Cook County Hospital.

"We'd better stop by and check his condition, Mike. We don't want any surprise bodies showing up at the morgue."

"Yeah, I hate when that happens," said Mike.

"So does the sergeant—let's buzz by the County…but not 'til after we eat."

"I like the way you think."

After breakfast at Lou Mitchell's, we headed for the Cook County Hospital. We learned that Carlos had just come out of surgery and wouldn't be able to talk to us, but we asked to speak with anyone who could update us on his condition. Our only concern was, "Is he going to live?" For the most part, CCH was a cop friendly hospital, and the surgical resident agreed to speak with us.

"Is he goin' to die?" was our very first question.

"No," laughed the doctor. "He's going to do just fine, but he's going to have some permanent disability in his left arm because the stab wound severed a nerve…and he wants to talk to you guys to tell you what really happened."

"Did he tell you what happened?"

"Yeah," replied the doctor. "He said it happened in the half-way house where he is living, but he didn't want to get anyone in trouble. Now he's pissed because he's only going to have partial use of his left arm."

Mike and I looked over the original case report. Carlos Diaz had listed his residence in the 1800 block of North Humboldt Boulevard. If that were true, this wouldn't be our job. It would belong to Area Five to the north. On our way back to the office, we stopped by the halfway house and learned that Diaz in fact lived there. Great! We would just bounce this paper job back to the proper area.

Back in our Area Four office, the sergeant wasn't having any of it.

"It's your case. You started it; you finish it."

"But it's not our job, and we haven't done anything on it yet. Just send it over to Area Five," we pleaded.

"You heard me! It's your case…." He waved his hand, dismissing us from the office.

The desk man followed us out into the squad room.

"He's just being a jerk; it's really not our job," he said. "Give me the case and I'll take it off the log and send it over."

Mike and I pondered his offer a bit. For the most part, we were blessed with good bosses in Area Four. There were just two sergeants that gave us problems from time to time, and on a scale of 1 to 10, this was about a 1.5. No point in riling him up over a pissant paper job. We would pick our battles, and this wouldn't be one of them.

"Thanks, but we'll keep it," we told the desk man.

We kept tabs on Carlos Diaz, and on the third day post-op, he was well enough to be interviewed in his hospital bed.

Carlos was Mister Cooperation when we spoke with him. The fight had happened in the kitchen of the halfway house where he and about fifteen other men were completing their prison sentences. It was very late, and an inmate by the name of Freddie Rivera had been drinking and was arguing with the group. Carlos sensed things were going from bad to worse, so he started to leave the kitchen when Freddie grabbed a kitchen knife and stabbed him in the back. Carlos never saw it coming, but he knew for certain that it was Freddie. There were several witnesses, friends of Carlos, who would back up his story. The only problem was that his friends told him that Freddie had left the halfway house the night of the incident and hadn't been seen since.

We stopped by the halfway house and found it to be a large residential building on the west side of the street. The first floor, immediately to the left, had an expansive living room and dining room that had been combined into a sort of recreational area with couches, game tables, and a large television in the far corner. Toward the rear of the first floor was a large community kitchen. To the right of the large foyer was a desk that sat just outside what had become the director's office. The second and third floors were bedrooms for the inmates. It was a magnificent building in its prime, but now it was definitely showing its age and years of hard use.

The secretary at the desk was reluctant even to tell the director that we were there, but when we told her we were looking for Freddie Rivera, the door quickly opened and we were ushered into a large office with oversize leather chairs and a very bulky wooden desk, all of which appeared to have come from the "distressed merchandise" section of a thrift shop.

The director, John Lawson, was about fifty years old and dressed in a suit and tie; his appearance definitely commanded respect. He closed the door behind us and opened Rivera's file, which was already on his desk.

"Right now, we're getting a warrant for parole violation," he said. "But if he doesn't return within another day or two, we'll tack an escape charge on top of that. At the moment, we're carrying him 'overdue.'"

We explained that we would be seeking an aggravated battery warrant if the state's attorney approved, but first we needed background information on Rivera, and we would need to talk with the inmates who had seen the incident.

Lawson passed Rivera's file across the desk to us and told us to paper-clip any pages we wanted Xeroxed. From the file, we learned that Rivera had been working for a local butcher and his sister lived in the neighborhood. That would be helpful for whoever wound up looking for him, but we did not envision ourselves pounding the bushes for him. It was, after all, a paper job, and it didn't even belong in our area. The Special Operations Group and the 14th District Tactical Team would be happy to find Rivera and bring him in once we got the warrant.

The majority of the residents were at work, but Director Lawson would make them available for interview over the weekend. Carlos Diaz was well-liked; Freddie Rivera much less so. Cooperation would not be a problem, Director Lawson thought, especially since they were all so close to release.

The next week, we sandwiched the Diaz case in between our other cases and ultimately got the warrant and published Freddie's picture in the *Daily Bulletin*. That's the last we expected to hear of the case—someone else would find Rivera, arrest him, and lodge the warrant. In total, we probably hadn't spent more than four or five hours on the case. Four or five hours more than we should have, being that it was a paper assignment and it wasn't our job.

Mike and I rotated shifts a few times over the next several months, and the Carlos Diaz case became a distant memory of no importance. Then came the telephone call from Carlos.

"Do you know what that bastard did?" Carlos literally exploded over the phone. He didn't wait for a response. "That son-of-a-bitch applied for unemployment compensation!"

"How do you know?" we asked.

"One of the other guys works for the butcher. He heard the owner complaining—they sent the paperwork over here to the house, but the director won't tell me anything—he says it's confidential. Ain't that a crock?"

A few days later, we found ourselves back at the halfway house sitting in front of Director John Lawson's oversized desk. This time, he had to retrieve Rivera's file from a battered file cabinet along the wall.

"Yep. You're right. Freddie has filed for unemployment. That's a lot of nerve. How did you guys find out?" Lawson peered over his glasses at us.

Mike grimaced a bit and shifted in his seat. No telling exactly how Carlos got his information, but it wouldn't do anyone any good to reveal our source.

"Ah…not really at liberty to say," said Mike haltingly. "But we sure would like to know where Freddie wants his checks sent."

It was Lawson's turn to play coy, but he did so with a warm friendly tone.

"That's information I can't divulge. I'm sorry, but there's just no way I can tell you that." Rivera's file was open in front of him.

"It's really a shame because it's right here," he said, pointing at the open page.

"Will you excuse me just a minute or two?" he continued as he pushed the file across to our edge of the desk. He abruptly left the room and closed the door behind him.

Mike and I jumped from our chairs. I read and Mike wrote rapidly—claim number, current residence...Whoa! New York City! Calm down, calm down—we were like a couple of kids stealing candy before the proprietor returned. Quickly, reread, confirm... no errors permitted!

We sat back in our oversized, badly worn leather chairs. It was another minute or two before the director returned to his office. He took Rivera's file and closed it.

"It's really a shame that I can't share this information; I hope you understand my position," he spoke with sincere regret. He was dead serious.

"We understand," said Mike. "It's a shame, but we know you have to play by the rules." Sincere regret. Dead serious.

"We'll let you know if we find him," I said as we left.

"I would appreciate that," Lawson responded.

Out in the car, Mike and I tried to contain ourselves.

"Do you smell extradition?" asked Mike.

"I used to live in New York City," I replied. "We can have a good time there!"

It wasn't cut and dried. We needed to get the State's Attorney's Office to review the case and approve it for extradition, but it turned out Freddie Rivera had really riled people by being a fugitive and applying for unemployment. Approval was easier than we thought.

New York City Police was notified and its fugitive unit replied about a week later. Freddie Rivera had left its jurisdiction and the unemployment authorities would not tell the police where he had gone. Another dead end.

But who could get into those files legally? Two phone calls later, we had an answer—the FBI. Get an Unlawful Flight to Avoid Prosecution (UFAP) warrant, and if Freddie were receiving unemployment checks, the FBI would find him. Once again, our State's

Attorney's Office readily gave us approval to seek a federal warrant. We set up a meeting with a special agent in our office.

"How did you determine that he was receiving unemployment?" he asked.

"Confidential informant," we replied.

"Has this CI given you reliable information on previous cases?" asked the agent.

"No…" There was a long pause. "But we were able to examine a document that confirmed the CI's information."

"Do you have that document?" This agent wasn't giving up.

"No."

"Then how did those papers confirm the CI's reliability?"

"The document pointed to New York City and the NYPD verified Rivera was there, but now he's left their jurisdiction," we replied.

"And you're not going to reveal your source?"

"Does Coke tell Pepsi?" I replied, tiring a bit of this extended conversation.

The agent paused for what seemed like an eternity before he replied. Had I overstepped?

"I'll run it by our legal, but I think you've got your UFAP."

Ten days later, we had a federal warrant charging Freddie Rivera with Unlawful Flight to Avoid Prosecution. If the FBI mystique was anywhere near a match to the homicide mystique, all we had to do was wait for our extradition trip. Overall, it was a strange turn of events, and it was only a paper job that didn't even belong in our area.

Every day in homicide is a new day, and as the current cases come in, the old ones migrate to the bottom of the priority list. We had wrapped up the Diaz/Rivera case, tied it in a bow, and presented it to the feds. It was off our radar, and as always, Area Four Homicide, affectionately known as the murder factory, presented us with an abundance of fresh murders…and yes, the bane of all homicide detectives—paper jobs.

It was a pleasant surprise a few months later when our special agent from the fugitive squad called to tell us that Freddie Rivera was in custody.

"So ya' found him, heh?" said Mike.

"'Find' is a strong word," replied the agent. "I think our guy stumbled over him on the beach."

"Beach?" queried Mike. "Where is he?"

"Puerto Rico."

Mike and I beamed at one another—this paper job just kept getting better and better, and it wasn't even supposed to be our job. It was an Area Five case.

The FBI does not extradite on UFAP warrants. Such a warrant acts merely as a device to justify federal assistance when a bad guy flees a local jurisdiction. The Cook County State's Attorney's Office would be responsible for putting the extradition papers together, and the investigating detectives would be dispatched to return the prisoner to our jurisdiction. That, of course, would be Mike and me.

We needed to confirm that we still had contact with our victim and witnesses, but that proved to be an easy task. We garnered all the approvals, stamps, and signatures, and when the extradition package was complete, we presented it to our sergeant. As luck would have it, it was the same sergeant who had insisted we handle the case many months before.

"Hey! This is an Area Five case!" he exclaimed. We had no idea whether he remembered that months previously it was he who had personally insisted we continue the investigation, even after we had complained.

"Yeah, it's not our job; how strange is that?" replied Mike.

"It's only a paper job and you're going to Puerto Rico?" The sergeant was incredulous.

"Yeah, how strange is that? And it's not even our job," I chimed in, maybe with more than a hint of sarcasm.

The desk man stifled a laugh, but it resulted in something that sounded like a combination of a snort and a sneeze. Mike and I decided to step out of the office, if for nothing more than to contain our pleasure at the turn of events.

It was a cold winter day in Chicago when Mike and I stepped off the plane in sunny San Juan, Puerto Rico. We had arranged to take an extra day compensatory time, so we would have time to do the tourist thing. The frosting on the cake was when we stopped in the office of del Departamento de Justicia in downtown San Juan and discovered that a judicial signature was missing from one of the extradition documents. The gentleman apologized, but it would take an extra day to get the papers in order. Mike and I feigned disappointment and asked whether they would fax our office to explain the delay. A quick two-day extradition had turned into four.

Mike and I filled the days with a few of the normal touristy things, but we concentrated mostly on historical sites, the highlight being Fort San Felipe del Morro, or Morro Castle. Evenings, we explored restaurants in downtown San Juan; daytime would find us at a beachfront cabaña enjoying our favorite rum drink.

The fourth day we "returned to work" when we picked up Freddie Rivera and headed for the airport. On most of our extraditions, we had little trouble with our prisoners and Rivera was no exception. He was too frightened to be any trouble. Once on board our flight, he bowed his head as if in prayer. After takeoff, beads of sweat appeared on his brow as moderate turbulence buffeted the Delta plane.

"Freddie, surely you have made this trip before?" I asked as we bounced about the sky.

"Si, señor," he replied. "But never before sober!"

The turbulence gradually increased to the point where it became the roughest flight Mike and I had ever experienced. Loose objects bounced about the cabin. An overhead popped open several rows ahead of us, spilling the contents on the passengers below. We could feel our bodies straining against the seatbelts as the plane plummeted, only to be immediately followed by a feeling of soaring in a rapid ascent. The pilot warned us periodically to keep our seatbelts snug and not to leave our seats. Even the flight attendants had themselves strapped in.

"Is this our punishment for manipulating the system?" I thought. "Plunging to our deaths in the Atlantic Ocean?" It seemed a bit harsh to me. But as we approached the coastline, the flight became silky smooth. Thoughts of divine retribution evaporated. "Hey, we were only doing our job, and a very fine job at that!"

Epilogue: Freddie Rivera never went to trial. He elected to plead guilty to the plethora of charges awaiting him—parole violations, escape, and aggravated battery among them. He was forty-three years old—he would be an old man before he would walk the streets again.

Bennigan's

By Jay

Cops are different. We are taught things that most times never cross people's minds. We see things that most people never dream of. Some of it is horror beyond belief. While off duty with family and non-police friends, something will strike us in the context of the moment...appropriate for a police mind, but totally outside the realm of "civilian" experience. Often, it generates a moment of silence—there's no way we can springboard the thought into general conversation; nor would it be appropriate. We do an etch-a-sketch shake of our brain cells and we're back in "civilian" mode. Make no mistake, our minds are taking us to real scenes, real experiences. In the mind of a cop, deadly tragedies are a vivid memory of yesterday and just around the corner tomorrow....

I went to Bennigan's the other night for dinner with my soon-to-be wife. We were seated, we ordered, and shortly thereafter, we were served. As the waitress set down my girlfriend's chicken fajita, I could notice her eyes focusing on the waitress's hand.

It seemed as though I could read her thoughts by looking into her eyes: "Where did she get her nails done? I know my engagement ring will look better than hers. I don't know how she keeps all the orders straight."

As my club sandwich was laid down in front of me, I couldn't help but make observations myself. Observations that I prayed my girlfriend could never decipher: "We have to bag those hands in case there is any DNA evidence underneath those fingernails. God, I'm so glad I didn't tear the skin off that dead woman's finger when the family asked me to remove her wedding band. Will I get the blood stains out of my uniform shirt, or will I have to spring for a new one?"

This isn't the way I used to think. I never had these images running through my head before. I used to think about hitting the game-winning home run during Little League. I'd sink the tie-breaking shot in the last seconds of my grade-school basketball games. I would make that diving catch, just crossing the plane of the goal line to score the winning touchdown.

When did my thoughts change? Am I just more realistic now? Or was I more realistic then? A line drive shot should never hurt an infielder. Children can't experience heart failure during a basketball game. Spinal cord injuries never happen to kids playing football.

Am I thinking about these things because of what I see during my shift, or is it just because I'm getting older and wiser, and accepting that these things happen? Gunshot victims are for real. Infants burned in scalding water are for real. The bodies struck by hit-and-run drivers are for real. They are more real than that home run, tie-breaking basket, or game-winning touchdown.

Maybe at the end of my shift on Saturday morning, I'll stop by Warren Park and watch a kid score that touchdown. Now that would be the perfect end to a very real night.

"Waitress, how about dessert?"

A Police Family

By Jay

photo at www.OnBeingACop.com/gallery/limo.jpg

I guess I never really thought long and hard about how my career choice would affect my family. When I became a cop, I was twenty-four years old, single, and living on my own. I knew my parents would worry, but I never knew how much until I had kids of my own. Oh, how their hearts must have stopped for a moment that time when I was working midnights and their doorbell rang in the wee hours of the morning. They rushed downstairs, groggy and in a daze, to find a blue and white squad parked on the driveway and a lone uniformed police sergeant at their door. This scene has played out countless times in the history of the police department. Bad news, news that could change the rest of your life, might be right around the corner. Nobody rings your bell at this hour to chat. My mom struggled to get the door open as my dad stood by wanting—maybe not wanting—to hear why the sergeant was at their home. Both their hearts were pounding and their hands trembling, waiting to hear....

"What happened?"

"Why are you here?"

"Which hospital?"

"Just tell us he's okay."

It's all racing through their minds in an instant. The shaking hands finally got the door open.

"Sorry to wake you. I was on patrol and saw your garage door open. I just wanted to make sure you weren't burglarized."

Ahhhh, sighs of relief, deep breaths, and a quick "Thank you." How do you go back to sleep after that?

My dear wife has been by my side at wakes and funerals for officers who are no longer with us, looking at picture boards of families that will never be the same. She's attended fundraisers for the families of the officers killed in the line of duty. I know that tucked in the back of her mind is the realization that our family could be turned upside down in an instant by this job. I've come to understand how difficult it can be for her when I try my best to keep my work and home life separate.

"Work was fine. Nothing eventful happened."

That's what I tell her. You can't sit around the dinner table and talk about how the decomposed body you just removed was so stuck to the carpeting that you had to get a shovel out of the garage to scrape it free. Or how you watched a man burn to death in a car crash because the flames were so intense you couldn't get near it. That's just not appropriate dinner conversation.

I still get the occasional call from my oldest brother, Chris, wanting to make sure I'm okay. He's just heard breaking news on the radio:

"A Chicago Police officer is listed in critical condition after being shot on the South Side. His name is being withheld at this time, pending notification of his family."

God forbid I inadvertently let his call go to voicemail.

My brother Craig is a man of few words, but his actions are loud and clear. He is a scientist, very methodical in his thinking, an information gatherer. He is a great person to talk to because he just listens without interrupting. He takes it all in and carefully crafts his response. I know that he realizes how important my job is to me. When he was the best man at my wedding, one of his duties was to decorate the limo while my wife and I were having our pictures taken in the church. When we exited the church, we saw before us a white Lincoln Navigator stretch limousine all decked out like a Chicago Police vehicle. He had spent countless hours in the prior weeks handcrafting magnetic decals with the same markings in the proper color, font, and size that you would find on a squad car. Pictures of that limo still make me smile.

Tim, my youngest brother, has always been my confidant. I can talk to him about things that I know would only upset my wife and parents. Having been raised in a cop family and surrounded by many close friends who are cops, he truly understands the culture. He is another good listener.

My four-year-old twins certainly know that I'm the police, but they're not exactly sure what I do during my tour of duty. Each morning before I go to work, they ask me not to work late. My son tells me how many criminals to arrest each day.

"Get four bad guys today, Daddy."

They'll learn soon enough that my job will sometimes keep me from their ball games, dance recitals, and family parties. I just hope they'll understand why.

Being a cop is not just a job or career. It is a lifestyle. Whether you like it or not, it affects your family, friends, and so many other aspects of your life. You now pick the table in the back of the restaurant so you can see everyone who comes in and out of the door. You pick your wardrobe based on what conceals your gun best. People at parties introduce you by your profession.

"This is Jay. He's a cop."

Neighbors bring you their complaints about other neighbors. People use you to scare their misbehaved children.

"He's a policeman. If you don't start behaving, he'll put you in jail."

In the end, the tradeoffs are worth it. No single officer is going to change the world. But the lives of countless individuals have been positively impacted by police officers all across this city. Kids have been carried out of burning buildings by police. Babies have been delivered by police in the backs of squad cars. That gunman's assault has been cut short due to the bravery and dedication of the responding officers. These are all heroic actions taken by mothers, fathers, brothers, sisters, sons, daughters, friends, and neighbors, all who share the same title: Chicago Police.

The Police Test Emails

By Jim, Jay, and Tim

(used with permission)

My son, Timmy, paid his twenty bucks and was scheduled to take the police exam last Saturday afternoon. It was kind of a rough week for him. He spent a lot of time with some close friends who are now the police. And, of course, he spent a lot of time with his brother Jay talking about it. At the last minute, after much soul searching, he decided not to take the test. He called me Sunday. I think he was expecting me to be upset. Nothing could be further from the truth. I've always maintained that I would never encourage or discourage any of my boys from being the police. Nevertheless, I recognize that my sons could possibly feel some unspoken, subtle feelings that they might disappoint if they chose other careers. Many times, the truth is in the perception of an individual. That is a shame. Each of my sons is his own person and must find his own way down the path of life.

Timmy got the message below today from his big brother Jay. It speaks of love for "the job" but even more of brotherly love. It brought a tear to my eye. I am proud of them both.

-----Original Message-----

From:	Jay
Sent:	Tuesday, February 21, 2006 4:15 a.m.
To:	Timmy
Subject:	Police Test

I know you asked me the other day whether I was disappointed that you didn't take the police test. My answer is absolutely not. I guess I'm just sorry that you won't experience some of the things that I've been able to.

I remember the day I responded to a traffic accident at Peterson and Western. A fifty-year-old lady was trapped in her Jeep Cherokee upside-down. I lay in the street, held her hand, and talked to her until the jaws of life arrived. She was cut out of the car and taken to the hospital. When she was released, she brought a bouquet of flowers to me at the station. That gesture really meant something to me. I knew I had made a difference. I've never told that story to anyone before.

On another occasion, I responded to assist an officer who called for help. He was working alone and yelled out the address for the vestibule into which he was chasing an offender right before his radio went silent. When I got there, he was being thrown around like a rag doll. His body had been thrown through the drywall twice during the fight. Needless to say, that officer put up quite a fight waiting for his back-up. He was hospitalized, as was the offender. Our bad guy had just beat an old lady waiting for the bus in order to get her purse. He was sent to jail for a long time.

And nothing's better than being on an entry team for a search warrant. It's got to be the ultimate adrenaline rush when you kick in a door and run in, yelling "Police!" with your gun drawn. These are the good times I'd love for you to experience.

But the other day, I sat down with three guys I graduated with from the academy. We talked about the thirty-five of us who all became police together. Three of the officers have left the job for other employment opportunities. One officer resigned because of the toll the job was taking on her family life. Four of the officers are now on permanent disability due to injuries sustained on the job. And one officer shot herself in the head, leaving behind two young twin boys. That's 25 percent gone in just seven years. I won't even mention the countless lawsuits that many of the officers have endured. I've missed countless holidays and birthday parties because of this job. I'll miss many more picnics and barbecues.

I thought quite a bit about you taking the police test the Thursday before it was given. I was on the South Side at about twelve noon. It was another day that I'd be up for twenty-four hours straight. I stood in the pouring rain, listening to "Amazing Grace" being played on the bagpipes and saluting the casket of another young police officer as it was slid into the hearse. He was killed in the line of duty. He was my age. I looked at his mother and felt a tremendous amount of guilt. I felt that we had failed her. We didn't get her son back to check off safely. Once again, I was witness to the grief and devastation that this job can have on a family. It was then that I thought maybe you shouldn't take the test. I know that you'd be an excellent officer, but I also know that you'll be excellent at whatever you do. Know that I am proud of your decision to explore other employment opportunities, and know that I'll always be proud of you. This job must be a passion of yours if you choose to take it. And if it is not, you must look at other professions. I know that if you offered me the greatest sales job in the world, I wouldn't take it. It's just not me.

I respect your decision and know that you'll be successful in any profession you feel passionate about. When you get there, and I know you will soon, remember to lift a drink with me and say cheers. For it is a wonderful thing to find a rewarding career that you love. Always remember that I love you and will support any endeavor you choose to embark upon.

Jay

-----Reply-----

From:	**Timmy**
Sent:	**Tuesday, February 21, 2006 11:15 a.m.**
To:	**Jay**
Subject:	**Re: Police Test**

It really means a lot to hear that from you.... Part of me did feel like I was disappointing you.... There wasn't one particular reason I chose not to take the test.... In fact, it was multi-faceted.... Keep in mind that you and Dad have left some pretty large shoes to fill.... All of the men in my life (Chris, Craig, you, Dad) have played a major role in the decisions I've made.... It's a scary thing to think about filling the shoes you have both worn within the department.... And I agree with you, Jay; I think I would make a great cop.... I just feel like I would be doing it for all the wrong reasons.... There is no doubt in my mind there is a place for me in this world.... I've just yet to find it.... And I don't think the police department is it.... Consider yourself lucky you've found your place at such a young age.... I can't tell you how difficult it is to wake up every day and not know what you're doing with your career.... But know this: I couldn't do it without you.... You have been such an important aspect of my life.... I love you so much.... I thank God every day I have someone like you to confide in...someone who *has* to love me back...someone who will be there no matter what.... It's truly priceless.... Thanks for just being my brother.... For always being supportive, even when you may disagree with me.... I respect you so much, not only as a brother, but as a human being as well.... And thanks again for the email. I needed to hear that from you....

Timmy

Faith, Hope, and Charity

By Jim

We knew something was going on when we arrived for the "Police Mass" on my sixty-sixth birthday. Although we were five minutes early, the seats were filled with more than the usual uniformed cops. Outfitted with safety vests and radios, it was obvious that some of them were on duty. We broke out three rows of folding chairs for ourselves and the others. Father Tom Nangle greeted Durell and me and wished me a happy birthday.

"Are you guys staying for coffee after? There's going to be a raffle, and since it's your birthday, we'd like you to draw the tickets."

Mass proceeded with Tom's unique blend of holiness, reverence, and laughter.

After the service, down at coffee, I was visiting with the big good-looking cop who was running the raffle.

"It's for my partner's son," he said. "He has autism and we'll cover a good part of this year's expenses for treatment and therapy. The city doesn't cover any of it. Last year, we did a benefit at the FOP Hall." He glanced over at his partner at a nearby table. "That's him over there. I love that guy. Next year, we'll maybe do a golf outing. Ya know, something different each year. We've already seen some improvement. We've got to keep going with this thing."

There it was, buried in a series of staccato sentences. *"I love that guy."* It was almost a throwaway line.

Cops don't say that often. They act it out daily—but they don't say it. A by-product, no doubt, of our macho, homophobic society. But there it was, all around us at a Sunday Mass. The street cop's uniforms out in the seats, the occasional crackle of the police radio. There it *all* was, the three great virtues—faith, hope, and love—all wrapped up in one package on a Sunday morning, inspired by a little boy whose world prevents him from reveling in the moment.

The Lord works in mysterious ways!

We Have an Officer Shot...

By Jim

The nightstand phone rings and the police chaplain knows it is probably not good news. Incoming calls are restricted on this line—it is either one of his fellow chaplains or the Chicago Police Operations Command. It's 1:30 a.m. as he lifts the receiver.

"Good morning, Father. Sorry to wake you, but we have a police officer shot on the North Side. He's en route to the hospital now—no word on his condition, but he's headed for a Level I Trauma Center. It should be on your Blackberry now."

The chaplain rubs his eyes, swings his feet to the floor, and picks up his dormant Blackberry. With the press of a button, it comes to life. The screen fills with notifications from the past several hours—a water main break, an extra alarm fire, a power failure, and at the very top, a police officer, age twenty-six, shot while serving a warrant.

"Okay, I've got it. I'm on my way."

The unmarked Ford sedan speeds north on the Kennedy Expressway. There is no traffic. At the Kennedy/Edens junction, the chaplain heads the car north on the Edens, but suddenly, his brain begins to clear. "Where am I going?" he asks himself. "I'm heading north…to a Level I Trauma Center…Saint Francis Hospital maybe…Evanston Hospital?"

He pulls his car to the shoulder, calls up the notification on his Blackberry, and smiles—it's Saint Francis—his cerebral autopilot was correct.

The emergency room is a beehive of police activity with supervisors and command members of the department. In the examining room, it is only slightly less hectic—two detectives at the officer's head, a portable x-ray machine just departing, and a cluster of medical people. The young officer is clad only in a T-shirt and boxer shorts. His right foot rests in a stainless steel basin of Betadine solution, and as a nurse gently lifts his foot to a fresh basin, the chaplain sees a badly mangled foot with a middle toe mostly detached. The officer is arguing with a police supervisor.

"I'm t-t-tellin' ya, I g-g-gotta call my wife! If you send a car out, she'll f-f-freak. I g-g-gotta tell her I'm okay. It's gotta c-c-come from me!" The officer's teeth are chattering and the supervisor is shaking his head.

"He's in shock; he's in no condition to talk to her," says the impatient sergeant as he turns to the chaplain.

"What happened?" asks the chaplain as he moves to the head of the gurney, between the officer and his sergeant, with an eye, at least momentarily, to diffusing the argument.

"I sh-sh-shot myself in the f-f-fuckin' foot, Father, with a sh-sh-shotgun! Goin' through a door…."

"He was on a team serving a warrant," added the sergeant. "The arrestee was behind the door as they went in, and he tried to slam it on them. The door hit the shotgun."

"Are you cold?" asked the chaplain.

"N-n-no…I just sh-sh-shake like this whenever I g-g-get shot."

The officer had lightened the moment.

"Nurse! Can we get this man some blankets?" called the chaplain.

Moments later, the officer was covered in heated blankets, and within fifteen minutes, he was talking calmly with his wife and explaining why a squad would be coming by to pick her up.

As police shootings go, this probably was an unexpectedly good outcome, but the chaplain knew that all too often the call might have morphed into a full honors funeral where the challenge would be to prevent the pomp and circumstance from overshadowing a meaningful service for the family. Line of duty deaths, suicides, and catastrophic injuries inflicting permanent disabilities—those are the worst of times.

A retired officer recalls an ancient Egyptian blessing:

"God be between you and harm in all the empty places where you must walk."

"That's what the chaplains mean to me," he said. "So many times, they stand between us and the dark side of our work."

There are good times to be sure. Officers frequently ask department chaplains to officiate at weddings, baptisms, and other family functions. Lasting bonds are formed and cherished family memories are created.

Another highlight for the chaplains is their regular interaction with the officers on the street. They will tell you, without hesitation, that here is where they get a sense of what their flock is about, especially when officers discover that the unmarked car entering the opposite end of the dark alley is occupied by members of the Chaplains Unit. Chaplains cruise the streets regularly and monitor the radio, and yes, respond to calls where they sometimes become a most welcome assist. There are more than a few "chaplain assist" stories out there.

The police department is a group of men and women of all faiths, and the members of the Chaplains Unit are representative of that diversity. Within their unit, they work closely together for the common good of their mission and the people they serve. Their service to individual officers in times of crisis generates another whole collection of chaplain stories, most of which will be forever untold. But sit with a group of cops on most any occasion, prod them gently, and they will tell you poignant, heartfelt chaplain stories, at least the ones that can be told aloud without opening old wounds.

The chaplains sum up work in law enforcement by telling their officers that they are the ones who stand between the weak and the forces of evil. Police are truly in a noble profession, doing God's work on a daily basis.

The chaplain was on the street when he monitored radio traffic, indicating unusual police activity at the emergency room of a West Side hospital. Moments later, he was standing with two officers, surveying a scene of organized chaos. There were shooting victims, stabbing victims, and at least one DOA. The scene was repugnant testimony to man's inhumanity to his fellow man. Doctors and nurses, sprinkled with women in religious habits, worked with urgency and efficiency, tending to those most seriously injured and offering comfort and assurance to those who would wait for their turn in the triage world of trauma care. Lives would be saved here tonight.

"How can you look at this and believe in God?" questioned the one cop.

"How can you look at this and not believe in God?" replied the second cop.

Touché, thought the priest silently.

Christmas Mass with the Police

By Jim

Christmas morning in Chicago never really dawned. The dark orangey skies reflecting the sodium vapor lights remained a dark gray when the timers finally killed the street lamps. The thick clouds allowed the temperature to sneak above freezing for the first time in two weeks, and the heavy snow cover actually started steaming a bit, adding to the day's overall dullness. By 10 a.m., the dawn finally gave up and the sky settled into the dreariness of a dark, cloudy winter day.

The marked 12th District squad and the unmarked detective car pulled to the curb in front of the Mercy Home for Boys and Girls on West Jackson Boulevard. The century old building appeared to loom ominously in the background. There was no call that brought them here this morning; rather, Christmas Mass was to be held in the small second floor chapel, officiated by the police chaplain.

The four men gingerly exited their vehicles and cursed silently as they attempted to navigate the high piles of soot black snow that lined the streets. The homicide detectives and uniformed patrolmen nodded to one another in a silent, grim greeting of sorts. The detective in the black trench coat cursed aloud when he slipped and fell against the salt-laden squad, leaving a white swath of salt on the side of his coat. The detective in the rumpled Colombo trench coat laughed and in a distinctive, slow, hoarse voice said, "See, you gotta have a tan coat for da' winter."

"Yeah, aren't you the Beau Brummel of the police world," his partner replied.

They climbed the stairs to the room where the ambiance was a bit warmer. The place of worship seated forty without breaking out folding chairs. It was a simple chapel, with small stained glass windows at the front and rear. There were no Christmas decorations, but the edge of the altar bore a blue and white checkered band matching that of the police hats. The ceiling held a battery of black box Fresnel stage lights, barn doors, and scrims, belying the fact that one of the chapel's primary uses was for videotaping the Mass for shut-ins. However, on the second and fourth Sunday of each month and each Christmas and Easter, the Chicago Police chaplain held the "Police Mass."

The priest, in street clothes, moved easily among the gathering group, exchanging greetings and an occasional emotional hug. Retirees, spouses, and off-duty police with pistols at their waists mingled and exchanged Christmas greetings. This morning, there were a few more on-duty officers than normal; the district officers in full street uniform, tactical officers in jeans with their black safety vests festooned with star, nametag, radio, and extra magazines of ammunition, and, of course, the two detectives who sat at the chapel's very rear. For many of the on-duty officers, it would be their only chance to attend a religious service for Christmas.

The priest disappeared into a makeshift sanctuary at the front of the chapel and emerged moments later in his robes. He stood in front of the altar.

"Good morning," he said quietly.

The congregation members were busy chattering among one another.

"Good morning," said the priest a bit louder than before. No reaction.

"Roll call!" shouted the priest in his best watch commander voice. The group laughed and they all took their seats. As they did so, the chaplain beamed. These were his people—this was his flock. He had married them, baptized their children, ridden the streets with them, and prayed with them in emergency rooms across the city as one of them lay wounded or dying. His chest almost visibly puffed with pride as he surveyed the room.

"Let's take a moment to quiet our souls before we proceed."

The two uniformed officers keyed their radio briefly.

"Twelve-twelve, hold us down for lunch at the Mercy Home."

"Ten four, twelve-twelve; you're down for lunch." That would give them some thirty minutes without a radio assignment. The tactical officers and detectives were on a bit looser leash, generally not subject to assignments from the dispatcher, but they kept their radios on and on low volume.

"Before we dare go on, let us call to mind our sins and ask forgiveness," said the priest.

The chapel was totally quiet until the radios broke the silence.

"Twelve-sixteen, cars in twelve and cars on citywide, we have a man with a gun at 2323 West Lexington. No further information." That was about a mile and a half from the tiny chapel.

From the very back of the chapel came the unmistakably growly drawl of the detective.

"Guess what he got for Christmas?"

The Mass continued, and almost as if on cue, at the next momentary silence, the radios in the room burst to life again.

"Attention cars in twelve and on citywide, we now have shots fired on Lexington."

"They must be opening the rest of the presents." Same voice... from the chapel's rear.

The tactical officers got up quietly and exited the side door, the rapid pace of their boots echoing on the stairway.

"Attention cars in twelve and on citywide, one more time, we now have a man shot at that Lexington address; that's 2323 West Lexington."

The uniformed officers exited the south chapel door. The detectives exited the opposite side door.

"Twelve-twelve, cancel that lunch; we'll take in Lexington."

From the opposite hallway, "Yeah dispatch, this is homicide seventy-four-o-three; tell our office we're heading for that Lexington scene."

The priest paused for a long moment. Less than five minutes into the service, the radios, along with their officers, had left the building, the sirens now fading into the distance.

The chaplain resumed, "Let's take a moment and pray for our people on the street this Christmas morning...."

Little Blue Canaries

By Jay

Tanker explodes on Kennedy
Northbound lanes reopened

June 9, 2005—A tanker truck containing 6,000 gallons of ether crashed into the cement side of Kennedy Expressway and burst into flames. The explosion sent a ball of fire into the sky above the Kennedy Expressway at Kimball early Thursday morning. The northbound lanes were closed to traffic for about an hour and a half after the accident, which occurred around 3:50 a.m. They have since been reopened. No one was seriously injured in the incident....

As I stepped out of the squad car and into a stream of ether, I heard the beat car in front of me ask the dispatcher why EMS (Emergency Medical Services) hadn't arrived yet to tend to the driver of the tanker that had just rolled and burst into flames on the Kennedy Expressway. She told us to stand by while she checked with fire dispatch. Moments later, she got us on the radio and told us we were in the middle of a hazmat (hazardous material) scene. EMS would not respond until the fire department said it was safe to enter the area.

It was at that moment that I thought back to my hazmat training at the police academy and laughed to myself. The instructor had been part of a fire department hazmat incident team, and he had told all of us in the class how much the firemen appreciate the police for showing up at these dangerous scenes to help out. He said we help them determine just how dangerous a scene is...in fact they even had a little nickname for us: their "little blue canaries." You see, long ago, coal miners would bring canaries with them into the mines. If the canary died, the miners knew that the tunnels were full of dangerous gas and it was time to get out. The instructor explained that when the hazmat team shows up and sees police lying all over the ground, it knows not to approach.

Needless to say, I got back into my squad and reversed down the Kennedy until I saw where the ambulances were set up.

I Hate Fires

By Jim

Being a cop brings you to the scene of fires from time to time, mostly for traffic control, which can be supremely boring at best, or cold and wet at worst. Worse even than that, however, are those rare instances when you arrive at the scene of a fire before the fire department. If it is an occupied residential building, it is incumbent upon you to initiate some sort of rescue attempt until the pros arrive.

Now, I've never pretended to understand the science of firefighting any more than firefighters understand the mechanics of running into a building where gunshots have been fired. Fires are probably more complicated than men with guns. Police officers and firefighters are different animals with different training and comfort levels in the scenarios where they have chosen to make their livelihood. Many police officers, to be sure, have received accolades and official lifesaving awards for rescuing people from burning buildings. Me? While I have succeeded in rescuing perhaps as many as two dozen people from burning buildings during my career, I have received nothing but reprimands—both written and oral—as well as causing myself great discomfort and scaring myself half to death. I hate fires.

It was March 29th, 1968, a brisk early spring day. My partner, Tony Grazioso, and I were working days in the 18th District. When we climbed into our beat car at 8:30 a.m., it was sunny with a temperature just easing out of the forties. The sun warmed the car rapidly so we hung our jackets on the hooks in the rear seat. Because we anticipated wearing our jackets whenever we left the car, we turned the cuffs on our fresh long sleeve shirts under one time. If the day were not too messy, the cuffs would remain clean and we could get one more day of wear before laundering the shirt.

We took a few radio assignments, dutifully donning and buttoning our jackets each time we left the vehicle.

At about noon, the chatter on our radio picked up as the 1st District began to mobilize traffic control beat cars and foot posts for a department store fire on State Street. Wieboldt's and Montgomery Ward reported fires, very quickly followed by Carson's. Three simultaneous fires within a two block area quickly became a major incident as fire equipment sped into the Loop from all directions. But outside of seeing fire equipment stream south through our district en route to the Loop, units from our district were not affected. That is, until the dispatcher paged our car.

"Eighteen-twenty-two, take the fire at 636 North State—Fire is not on the scene." That was a bothersome choice of words. Normally, the phraseology would have been "Fire is en route."

Tony caught the subtle alteration in semantics and looked at me, "Of course, they're not en route—they're all downtown!" We knew our fire department was among the finest in the country, but common sense told us that, at this moment in time, we would be on our own at whatever we found on State Street.

We were only a few blocks away, and in moments, we were at the fire. A street-level restaurant was burning, but the waiters, cooks, and customers were standing on the sidewalk. An adjacent stairway led to apartments on the second and third floors, immediately above the storefront. We parked the squad several doors away to avoid obstructing the fire equipment, and then we dashed from the car. As we approached the stairs, panicked people coming down called to us.

"There's still people up there!"

Tony and I ran up the stairs and began pounding on doors. There was smoke in the stairwell, but things were tolerable. We led several people down to the safety of the sidewalk.

"Mr. Lee! Mr. Lee! He's still up there. Third floor rear. He works nights; he must be sleeping."

Tony and I headed up the stairs for the second time, and on the third floor, we pounded on the rear apartment door and screamed the best we could in the ever-increasing smoke. Still sleepy-eyed, Mr. Lee, a small Asian man, finally opened the door. In seconds, we had him safely out on the sidewalk in front of the burning building.

And then we did something incredibly stupid.

A hysterical woman approached us.

"My puppies, my puppies!" she screamed. "They're on the third floor front, in a box in the living room."

"What kind of box? Exactly where is it?"

"It's just a cardboard box on the floor in the living room." Tony and I headed to the stairwell for our third trip.

"And my parakeet!" she yelled as we disappeared into the smoke.

As we passed the second-floor landing, we could hear snapping and popping from the front apartment. The smoke was rapidly becoming extremely uncomfortable. No fire units were yet on the scene. In the third floor apartment, we quickly located the tiny puppies and the parakeet. We headed downstairs, Tony carrying the box of puppies and me following with the bird. Somehow, even then, I realized the image of a cop fleeing a burning building with a birdcage was not exactly heroic. I should have grabbed the puppies and given Tony the bird.

When we reached the second-floor landing, things were not good. Smoke and heat were streaming up toward us, and the crackling sound was even louder than before. The only comfort was the sound of the first fire unit finally arriving out on the street. As we headed down the last flight of stairs, a portion of the stairwell wall broke away, tumbling into the restaurant, which was now a raging inferno. We had no choice but to make a dash for it. Two seconds later, we were on the street, turning the parakeet and puppies over to a woman, who was now sobbing uncontrollably with relief.

The only good thing about our third trip out of the building was that no media were present to snap a picture of the dramatic bird cage rescue. The news types were all downtown, covering the trio of department store arsons that ultimately caused over twenty million dollars in damage.

As we coughed and blew the black soot out of our noses, I glanced across the street and saw our district commander standing quietly in civilian clothes. I gave a quick report to the battalion chief, telling him I thought we had everyone out of the building. A hose was in position, but not yet charged, a ladder company was moving its unit into position in front of the building, and firefighters were preparing to climb up to the roof. We could feel the intense heat from the middle of the street. Tony and I walked to the far curb to catch our breaths, calm down, and watch from a safe distance. Our commander had left the scene.

Several minutes later, our field sergeant approached us.

"Hey, guys, go into the station and report to the watch commander." He would want a written report, no doubt, to give him background to initiate a department lifesaving award.

Once in the watch commander's office, we immediately noticed the pink form-sets on his desk: SPAR forms—Summary Punishment Action Reports.

"The commander wants you two disciplined."

"For what?" we asked incredulously.

"Your sleeves were rolled up."

"Oh, for Christ's sake," I said. "Let us talk to him. We just rescued a whole shitload of people from a burning building."

"Were your sleeves rolled up?"

"Well, turned under once," I said, looking down at my sleeves, now smudged with soot.

"Then you better not talk to him. He saw you and he is really pissed. Just sign the SPAR for a written reprimand and it's over with. Don't make it any worse by challenging him."

"Probably saw me with the goddamn parakeet," I muttered.

"What?"

"Never mind."

It was our first formal department discipline. Did I mention how much I hate fires?

• • • •

Several years later, a promotion to detective found me working out of Maxwell Street Homicide. Homicide detectives don't get assigned to traffic control at fires, but on occasion, we found it necessary to visit fire buildings after the fact to investigate deaths by arson. I found that far preferable to being inside burning buildings.

It was a cold February night, around 2 a.m., as Mike and I headed back to the Maxwell Street Headquarters to catch up on some typing. As we were northbound on Morgan, approaching our office from the south, we saw flames in the first-floor apartment just three doors south of our building.

"Seventy-four-o-seven emergency," we paged the Citywide 2 dispatcher.

"All units stand by. Seventy-four-o-seven, go ahead with your emergency."

"Yeah, squad, we have a residential three-story building fire at 1341 South Morgan; looks to be occupied. Fire's not on the scene—we're going in."

We jumped from our unmarked squad without waiting for a response.

As Yogi Berra would say, "It was déjà vu all over again."

We dashed up the five or six steps to the vestibule door, which was locked. We each carried an expired credit card in our front pocket, but Mike was first with his. He jimmied the latch in about ten seconds—ten precious seconds. Once inside the hallway, we felt the door to the first floor front apartment. Hot! We hesitated just long enough to hear a distant siren, probably from the fire station at 1123 West Roosevelt. Leave this door for the pros, we thought as we started pounding on the other doors, gradually working our way up the stairs to the third floor.

Sleepy people started appearing. The smoke this time was worse, and it only intensified as we reached the top floor. As soon as we satisfied ourselves of a response from each apartment, we turned to head back down the stairs into the ominous heat and black billowing smoke roiling up from the first floor. Things had deteriorated rapidly, and now Mike and I had serious doubts about our ability to get ourselves safely out of the building. What to do? Well, if you're paying attention, the Lord sends angels in many forms.

"Office!" screamed a heavyset black lady. "Ya' all come through here," she said as she motioned to her third-floor apartment. "We be goin' out the back way!"

Well, that's probably covered at the fire academy in Basic Firefighting 101; you do not have to exit the same way you came in, but I never had that course at the police academy.

As we went through her apartment, the air became cooler and less smoky, and when we got to the back porch, the crisp, cold air was positively refreshing. We made our way, coughing heavily, downstairs and to the front of the building as the fire department was charging its first line.

"Are you guys the coppers who went in?" yelled a fireman.

We nodded, still coughing, unable to speak.

"Lieu, the cops are accounted for!" he called over his shoulder.

The fire lieutenant was heading into the building as we walked over to the battalion chief, who was being briefed by another fireman.

"Hey!" my voice was surprisingly raspy and I spoke between coughs. "We didn't get into the first floor front."

"We're in there now," said the chief. "Damned space heaters!"

Our car was blocked by fire equipment, so Mike and I walked around the corner and up the long flight of stairs to our office on the second floor. At the top of the stairs was the men's room. We stopped and splashed our sooty faces with cold water and blew an unbelievable amount of black out of our noses before we headed back to the homicide office.

"You guys are in deep shit now," announced our cantankerous and paranoid midnight sergeant.

"How's that?" we asked with genuine surprise.

"I don't know what you're up to, but the First Deputy's Office just called and asked for the name and star numbers of the detectives on seventy-four-o-seven. I'm tellin' ya, whatever ya done, you're both in shit now. I gave them your name and star numbers... and I'm not covering for you!"

"Sarge, we just got a dozen people out of a burning building down the block. Downtown will probably be expecting a report from you nominating us for a lifesaving award."

"That's all bullshit. I'm not covering for you no matter what you did!" he sputtered. He was turning beet red, and we thought he might stroke out, so we found typewriters as far from his office as we could and started typing up some old cases.

The incident would rate a line or two on the twenty-four-hour report for the department brass, but without any further input from our supervisors, it would die there. Our sergeant would spend the rest of the early morning hours locked in his world of paranoia, muttering about the trouble we were facing.

Did I mention to you that I hate fires?

Two Kids Playing Fireman

By Jay

It was the type of address you would have difficulty finding unless you lived there. The small block of apartments sat tucked off the main street, only accessible by an obscure alley. The fire department had problems finding it as well. As my partner and I climbed the exterior stairs to the burning apartment, we could see the fire engines' red lights flashing through the trees from the next block, trucks trying to turn around to find this hidden spot. It would be a few minutes before they were on the scene. As we reached the second-floor landing, I noticed the deep black soot covering the windows from the inside. The glass was hot, as was the locked door. From the small crowd of tenants who gathered below us, I heard someone yell that an elderly man was still inside.

My partner looked at me with eyes wide open.

"Should we kick it?" he asked.

"You ever see *Backdraft*?" I replied.

Together, we shrugged our shoulders, turned, and began kicking the door with all our might. The damned thing wouldn't budge. Over and over, we kicked until we were out of breath. We looked at each other in disbelief and then down at the crowd below.

A young man stepped forward, holding up a small plastic key ring.

"You guys want the key?"

I didn't know whether to hug him or shoot him. I ran down the stairs, grabbed the key, and returned back to the door. With a quick turn of the key and twist of the knob, the door swung inward. A billowing cloud of hot black smoke rushed out, forcing us to our knees. We crawled through the kitchen to the living room threshold. Here we were, two relatively new officers in our early twenties, crawling into an inferno. I look back now and realize that we were just two kids playing fireman.

I only know two things about fire. Number one, if you're in a burning building, get out! Number two, if you're on fire, stop, drop, and roll. Up to this point, I wasn't doing very well with rule number one. The flames and intense heat forced us to turn around and head back to the second-floor landing. As we crawled out, we saw the "real" firemen come charging up the stairs, right at us. They crowded the landing, knelt down, and began donning their oxygen tanks. My partner and I were trapped between the fire and a stairwell blocked with firemen. We lay on the landing, coughing from the smoke still pouring out. Silently and in unison, the firemen rose to their feet and stormed past us into the flames. They didn't even have a water line charged yet. This was nothing like the movies. They sprang into action without saying a word. There were no instructions being yelled out or directions being given. Everyone knew exactly what had to be done. It was just them, their flashlights, and the fire. As the last one passed us, we scurried down the stairs to the lawn, gasping for fresh air.

After a few seconds of retching and coughing, we looked back at the building and saw another door on the side swing open. Apparently, it was the front door to the apartment. A fireman came racing out with the old man over his shoulder. The others followed him out and down the stairs as he laid the victim down. He began performing CPR as the crowd of tenants left us and gathered around the firemen. We heard a cough and the crowd began cheering. Here I was kneeling next to my partner in the grass, staring at the crowd of tenants who were clapping for the firemen and patting them on their backs.

Our heads hung low as we got up and walked back to the squad car to begin the paperwork.

"We're cops, not firemen," my partner stated.

"We were pretty close today," I replied.

"Nah... not really," he said.

Lunchbox, Nerf Football, and My Spelling Book...

By Jay

"Lunchbox, Nerf football, and my spelling book...Lunchbox, Nerf football, and my spelling book."

If I forget any of these today, I'm in trouble. Mom will kill me if I let another lunch spoil on the kitchen table when I should be eating it at school. Danny will kill me if we don't have the football to toss around at lunch. Today is my turn to bring it; besides, his is stuck on the gym roof. My teacher has been reminding us all week to bring our spelling books. If I forget mine again, today I'll be in trouble.

"Boots, badge, and gun. Boots, badge, and gun."

That's the simple phrase I repeat to myself now as I walk out the door for work every day. I know everything else is in my locker at work. When I open the locker, I grab my shoe polish kit. If I don't polish away the scuff on my boot from hopping the fence last night, I'll be in trouble with the watch commander. I make sure my uniform is looking neat and pressed. My badge goes on my vest cover, which is fastened securely around my torso. The heavy gun belt gets wrapped around my waist and is attached to my trouser belt to insure that it doesn't slide around in the event of a foot chase. My gun slides into my holster and both security snaps are pressed tightly together. I have to make sure that if my gun comes out of my holster tonight, it is my hand that pulls it. If it isn't, I'm in trouble. The unused can of pepper spray is taken from the pouch on my duty belt and shaken vigorously. This gives me the false sense that it'll work properly if I need it. If it doesn't, I'm in trouble.

I start walking to the roll call room and pause briefly in front of the mirror. I look myself over as I read the sign above: "Does Your Appearance Command Respect?" I line up in formation and make that final adjustment. The Field Contact cards and Miscellaneous Incident cards are pushed down deeper into my vest pocket so they don't block my nametag.

Roll call is over and I proceed to get my radio. It is slid tightly into the holder on my side, and the cord is tucked into my vest cover. I'm not gonna get it caught on a fence tonight. The car is full of gas, and no weapons or drugs are in the backseat. The blue lights on the light bar work. Left alley, right alley, and takedown. They all work. The air horn and sirens sound louder than ever. I'll need these if we get a hot call.

Friday is coming up, and that means time to clean my gun again. Gotta make sure it shoots every time I pull the trigger. I'll have to practice clearing a Level II Malfunction again. Lock, strip, cycle, tap, rack, assess. I can't let a stovepipe jam slow me down.

I make it safely through another night and park the squad car in the lot. I have once again fulfilled that promise we all make to our sergeant each night:

"See you at check off, Sarge...."

So much has changed. My responsibilities are different now. Years ago, I was keeping myself out of trouble. I was remembering the little things that would help keep me out of trouble. If you think about it, I guess things haven't changed all that much. That list of things to remember has grown. The items on it have changed. I still go through the same ritual, though.

"Yeah, Danny. I gotta work in an hour, but I was hoping I could stop by and toss the Nerf ball around a little.... Great! I'll be right over.... Yeah, I'll bring the ball."

"Boots, badge, gun, Nerf football.... Boots, badge, gun, Nerf football...."

The Giant

By Jay

He was a giant of a man, barrel-chested, with fists like sledge-hammers. His mere presence could cause you to turn and walk away from fear he might decide to fold you in half and tuck you away in his pocket. As our squad cars pulled up on him, he was holding a lantern in his left hand and directing us west down the tracks with his right. Our spotlights went on and scoured the ditch that ran along the stopped coal cars. About a hundred feet down, we found the man's body. Bruised and bloodied, it lay motionless on the rocks. He was dead.

I walked back to the giant who was afraid to get too close. He was the engineer. His voice trembled and his massive arms were wrapped across his chest as if he were holding himself. He just kept muttering, "I couldn't stop the train in time." I told him to wait for us where he was.

The fire department arrived and confirmed what we had suspected. We searched the body's pockets for I.D. and found some papers. All folded up were his Social Security card, a commercial driver's license certificate, and a handwritten note. There was a woman's name at the top with a phone number under it and the words, "Tell her I can't live without her and the baby. I love them both."

Then another woman's name with "Mom" written next to it, a phone number, and the words, "I love you."

Finally, a man's name with Dad written next to it, a phone number, and the words, "I love you."

I walked back to the engineer. In his trembling voice, he explained that the thirty-three-year-old man had come out of nowhere. He stepped onto the tracks, stuck out his chest, and stared at the engineer. His body tumbled about thirty feet before it came to a rest. I assured the engineer that there was nothing he could have done. A man had been determined to die today.

As I waited for the evidence technician to arrive, I couldn't help but think about the countless lives that this suicide victim would affect today. Commuter trains filled with people late for work waiting for us to process the scene and remove the body. An engineer who would look forward to sleepless nights, bad dreams, and an undeserved sense of guilt. The anger of a fatherless child. The pain of parents who must attend their child's funeral. The spouse or significant other who might have been considering taking him back just one more time.

I was just a witness to another life taken too soon. A senseless act this time, one that would cause so much pain and anger for so many people. An act that made a giant curl up and tremble with guilt. God bless them all.

The Lakefront

By Jay

To my left, the waters of Lake Michigan encroached upon the sands of North Avenue Beach and then slowly receded. On my right was an endless line of headlights, which traveled north up Lakeshore Drive. My right arm was planted firmly upon the blue metal railing as my left arm wrapped around my brother's shoulders. We swayed back and forth as we listened and sang along with the band in front of us. I needed this. I needed to return to this beautiful lakefront under better circumstances. I don't believe my brother was aware that just twenty-four hours ago, I had stood on this lakefront just a mile north. I wasn't smiling or singing then, just staring.

Eight minutes out of roll call the night before, I had heard the dispatcher send a job to a beat car. She assigned me to that same job without even asking whether I was available. I tapped the screen on my computer to retrieve the call just as she began reading it over the air. The caller had just found a suicide note left by a family member. He was nowhere to be found. He was a Chicago Police officer.

All available units responded. Some went to the caller's house. Others went to the park where the note said the family member was headed. We scoured the park on foot and in cars, looking under every bush and up into every tree. We were searching for something we didn't want to find. When our initial search was completed without success, we called in the K-9 units just to double check. The marine unit was summoned to check the river and its banks, which bordered the east side of the park. Patrolmen from other districts in the city responded to assist with the search. A unit was stationed in front of the police officer's home just in case his family heard any good news.

When our initial search yielded nothing, the family informed us that this officer also spent a lot of time at the beach. We notified all of the districts along the lakefront. This officer had left his house on foot and shouldn't be too far. It was still like looking for a needle in a haystack. We searched every late night bar and stopped every person on the street. We woke up every homeless person, asking whether he or she had seen anything. We sent a formal flash to all units citywide, asking for their eyes and ears. We had nothing.

6:03 a.m. A beat car searching the lakefront pulled up on a man sitting against a tree with a gun in his hand. He wasn't moving. A towel was over his head. The officers called out but got no response. They approached slowly and pulled the towel from his head. They immediately called for an ambulance. I was notified and responded with my lights flashing and sirens wailing. I didn't want it to be him.

To my left, the waters of Lake Michigan slowly rolled up onto the beach. To my right was an endless stream of morning commuters traveling north up Lakeshore Drive. In front of me was the lifeless body of the missing Chicago Police officer, a bullet in his head. My right arm was planted firmly upon my squad car as my left hand covered my mouth. I stood motionless and watched as officers strung crime scene tape from tree to tree. A steady flow of squad cars with flashing lights pulled up onto the lakefront.

I gave my brother a little hug, smiled, and fought back a tear. We swayed back and forth, still singing with the band. He was unaware of where my thoughts were, but he hugged back and smiled at me. I was trying to reclaim the lakefront. I was trying to erase the tragic scene I had just witnessed. I was trying to see the lakefront as it should be seen. This was not just another image of a dead body to be filed away in my mind. This was a Chicago Police officer. He was a protector of the weak, a crime fighter, and a friend to many. He could have been my backup had I ever needed help. He was a fellow officer I couldn't reach in time when he needed help the most.

The Chill

By Jim

Author's Note: I wrote this piece in June 2009, the morning after the shooting of Chicago Police Officer Alejandro "Alex" Valadez. I include the story here in memory of Officer Valadez and as a tribute to his family and a solemn salute to all police families in Chicago and across our great country.

June 2009, Chicago

I woke to the news that a 007th District police officer had been shot in the head…extremely critical condition. No name, pending family notification.

My own son, who on occasion takes his squad into 007, had his day off last night. In fact, we had dinner with him, his wife, and their twins.

But Danny…Danny works in 007. "The Chill" went up my spine, "Please, God, don't let it be Danny!"

Danny was my son's grammar school and high school buddy. They both grew up wanting to be policemen. But Danny had several issues, any one of which would preclude him from joining the force. We would talk about those issues. "One thing at a time,"

I would tell him. He would overcome one hurdle and then we would talk some more. One by one, he tackled every obstacle, and through self-perseverance and determination over the course of several years, he beat them all. On the night before his graduation from the police academy, I cut short weeklong meetings on the East Coast and flew home to be there. He gave me a bear hug that I swear broke several ribs and brought a tear to my eye. They assigned him to 007, certainly one of the most dangerous districts in the city. I got The Chill then too…. "You're responsible for him," I told myself in an absurd moment of self-importance, "Please, God, keep him safe."

We had seen Danny and his wife Terri a couple of weeks ago when we babysat for our son and his wife. Danny and Terri had picked them up for a night out, a class reunion as I recall.

"Please, God, don't let it be Danny!"

I could feel my pulse pick up as I rapidly scanned the news on the computer screen for clues.

Unmarked car—last I heard Danny was working a marked car.

Plain clothes—last I heard Danny was working uniform.

Three years on the job—I was sure that Danny had five or six.

Age twenty-seven—Danny was our son's age, thirty-five.

"Thank you, God!"

I sat there, staring dumbly at the screen, cradling my coffee cup. I took an occasional sip to quiet the not too irrational fears that had momentarily inhabited this retired cop's body. How many times did some variation of this scene play out across Chicago this morning as the "Police Family" woke to the news? For all but one family, The Chill faded and the adrenaline washed slowly out of their systems.

For all but one family….

Rest in peace, Alejandro "Alex" Valadez. May God be with your family in the coming days…and with police families everywhere who will have to endure The Chill all too many times in the coming years.

In Memory of...

By Jim

During National Police Week in May each year, several days are set aside to honor those law enforcement officers who have paid the ultimate sacrifice as a result of adversarial action on our nation's streets. They are truly the modern day heroes of our society. Another group of officers, equally as large, have lost their lives to an unseen adversary—suicide. This story serves to remember them also, but unfortunately, it offers no profound insight because, in the words of an unknown poet, "'tis hard to understand."

It was a drab waiting room on the second floor of Saint Elizabeth Hospital. The light was poor, furniture nondescript, and the walls were painted a dull unidentifiable color. My mom, twenty-one-year-old sister Nancy, and I waited nervously. It was the day of my father's surgery. At twelve years of age, I was not supposed to be there. The plan called for me to take the nearby subway to my aunt's apartment and spend the day with her. The actual surgery would take several hours, so I prevailed upon my mother to spend just another hour with them before I left. We sat and bantered like nervous people do when greater, unknown things loom ahead.

My sister reviewed my instructions. The subway station was just two blocks away at North and Clybourn. I was to take the outbound train, not the downtown train, and get off at Addison. My aunt would be waiting for me and walk me to her place on Sheffield Avenue, a stone's throw from Wrigley Field. As I was preparing to leave, the surgeon walked into the room, unannounced, in full operating room scrubs. My mother and sister looked at me nervously; I really was not supposed to be there.

The doctor didn't notice me and began without hesitation. It was cancer, a tumor attached to the posterior wall of the heart. They would proceed with the surgery, hoping to make him more comfortable in the coming weeks. But at best, he gave my dad six months to live. I staggered against the wall. My mother and sister most likely reacted in a similar manner, but I did not notice.

A bit too late, I was dispatched to my aunt's.

The subway station at North and Clybourn was well below street level and was damp and putrid smelling as I proceeded down the long stairs. I stood on the platform alone. The distant lights of the oncoming train turned to a roar as it sped into the station. My mind was spinning, my heart racing. The news was incomprehensible. I felt physically ill. As I stared down at the shiny tracks, now reflecting the lights of the oncoming train, for the first and only time in my life I considered suicide.

I was alone on that subway platform, and it was a moment of total despair. I was losing my father, my world was crashing to bits, and I could not begin to absorb the news.

Why?

Why me?

Why now?

There is a poem that I heard very recently:

Up in a quaint old attic
As the raindrops patter down
I sat paging through an old schoolbook
Dusty, tattered, and brown.
I came to a page that was folded down.
And across it was written in childish hand:
"The teacher says to leave this for now,
'tis hard to understand."

A lifetime later on a sunny June day, I stand with my police officer son at the Chicago Police Memorial Park for the Family Day Mass. He's been unusually quiet this morning, and for a moment, he breaks away from me, and I watch as he has some words with the superintendent of police.

"Walk with me," he says as he returns. The words are forced and he is visibly upset. We walk a distance from the crowd.

"My former teammate committed suicide last night." He is literally choking on the words. "It was a rumor last night; I couldn't believe it, but I just confirmed it with the superintendent."

The conversation is strained and disjointed; his throat constricts with each word: "A great guy…married…children…"

When it comes to a death like this
About all we can do is fold down the page and write
"The teacher says to leave this for now,
'tis hard to understand."

Elsewhere in this book, I've written about working with my partner Mike. He lost a long bout with the ravages of alcoholism and took his own life on another sunny day in May. I was out of town when I received the news, and I sat for some time in my darkened hotel room.

There are lots of pages in the book of life
that are hard to understand.
All we can do is fold them down and write:
"The teacher says to leave this for now,
'tis hard to understand."

Danny is the subject of still other stories in this book. A family friend since he was eight years old, he was a close friend of my son Jay. They grew up together and became police officers a couple of years apart. The call came on a Monday afternoon:

"Dad...Danny...he..." then garbled words. Maybe wind noise? Damned cell phones!

"What? You cut out. What are you saying?" I stood up as if that would provide a clearer connection.

"Danny committed suicide." The words choked in the back of Jay's throat.

It hit me in the gut like a baseball bat, and I recoiled back into the couch as though I had actually been physically struck. Marital problems, divorce...we knew. But Danny had fought and conquered so many other obstacles....

Someday—maybe only in heaven
We will unfold the pages again, read them and say,
"The Teacher was right; now I understand."

Author's note: The poem, paraphrased above, is "The Folded Page" and the author is unknown. My personal thanks to Father Greg Sakowicz for sharing his copy with me for this story.

Mike

By Jim

photo at www.OnBeingACop.com/gallery/mike.jpg

Ask any urban cop working a two-person unit what factor is most important on a day-to-day basis and he/she will tell you, "My partner." There is no place where that is truer than in Chicago. Now there are partners, and then there are *regular* partners. A partner can be for a day, a week, or even a month as sickness, days off, and vacations dictate.

A regular partner, however, is an altogether different thing. It's mostly a matter of choice and lasts for months or even years. In my nearly thirty-year career, I count only three regular partners.

As a rookie, my partner was Tony Grazioso—another rookie. Between us, we didn't have a year on the job. What was the department thinking? Nevertheless, we made it through a year and a half without making any major mistakes, under the watchful eyes of a more than attentive supervising sergeant and field lieutenant.

When I was selected for a plain-clothed tactical team, I paired up with John Klodnicki and somehow we survived the King Riots in Cabrini and the 1968 Democratic National Convention in Lincoln and Grant Parks without a scratch. We were truly kindred spirits. We were both engaged to be married and eventually started families while working together. Our wives became good friends.

After a couple of years, I was promoted to detective and assigned to a homicide unit. The first two years as a new guy, I bounced around from partner to partner in sort of a haphazard training program.

The third year, I began working with Mike Shull. We were both detail-oriented, good writers, and enjoyed working complex cases requiring lengthy investigations and reports. We would remain a team for over seven years until my promotion to sergeant forced me to move to another unit.

Mike was a college grad and a history buff with a somewhat offbeat sense of humor that on occasion would sink to the depths of irreverence and obscene outrageousness. While that is common to cops in general, and homicide detectives in particular, Mike carried it to a whole new level. In short, working with him was fun.

One of his specialties was parody lyrics invented on the fly…

"Attention cars on citywide…that shooting in the 11th District now has multiple victims. Fire is calling for an EMS Plan 1" (multiple ambulances).

In response, Mike's rich baritone would sing, to the World War II tune of "Bless 'em All:"

Shoot 'em all, shoot 'em all
Shoot the long the short and the tall
We'll handle the case with ease and grace
Including the ones who are shot in the face
Shoot 'em all, shoot 'em all…

The dispatcher interrupted. "Homicide Seventy-four-o-three, your office wants you to handle the morgue on that shooting in 11. There should be two victims en route there now."

"Seventy-four-o-three, ten-four, we're on the way." We headed to the old morgue, a drab building behind the Cook County Hospital where the bodies were housed in the basement in large refrigerated walk-in crypts. We would do a preliminary examination to determine the number and location of wounds and relay that information to the primary detectives on the case.

Mike sang to *The Wizard of Oz* tune "We're Off to See the Wizard":

We're off to see the bodies
At the beautiful Cook County Morgue
They go where bodies go
Below, below…

Songs were sung on more mundane occasions also.

"Jim, take me to the Henrotin." The Henrotin was a near North Side hospital that was cop-friendly and offered a "Police Room" with an ever-present pot of hot coffee and clean staff washrooms.

"And why, may I ask, are we going to the Henrotin?"

Sung to the tune of "I Feel a Song Coming On":

I feel a shit coming on
My asshole it rumbles and grumbles its song
[Finale, rising crescendo]
I feel a shit coming onnnn!

"Do you need lights and siren?"

"No, just don't take any detours."

In the course of our regular workday, we had jargon to describe three classifications of murders.

First was the "smoking gun," the easiest of all. For instance, after years of domestic abuse, Mom uses a butcher knife to stab Dad to death. Upon completing the dastardly deed, she calls 911, reports the crime, and awaits the arrival of the police. That's a "smoking gun." The weapon doesn't matter; these types of cases are all "smoking guns." Mike and I once suggested to our fellow homicide detectives that we add the classification of "dripping knife," but the group wouldn't buy it. Then we'd have to have the "broken bat" and the "rusty tire iron." Where would it all end? Nope, they're all "smoking guns," regardless of the weapon. Mike and I could knock out a "smoking gun" in most instances without incurring any significant overtime. Invariably, as we pulled the last page out of the typewriter, Mike would push back from the desk and announce:

"I don't like it Jim; it's too simple."

Second, a "known but flown" was similar. Jack shot Fred at a family party in front of a dozen witnesses and then fled the scene. It became a high stakes game of hide and seek, but most of our clients would cross paths with law enforcement sooner or later and the game would be over.

Finally, a "mystery" was just that…a body would be discovered. We'd have to piece every element of the case together from the start. Most times after identifying the remains, we would begin with a complete background investigation of the victim. Odds were that the killer was family, friend, or acquaintance. On some occasions, we would discover that the deceased had been living a double life that contributed to his or her death. It was homicide investigation at its best.

Homicide also investigated all suicide cases, which could get messy, especially if the family could not accept the incident as a suicide, opting instead for outlandish foul play conspiracies. The other common scenario was the incomplete suicide. Many of these were meant to be incomplete, of course—a dramatic call for help on the part of a distressed individual. Attempts with firearms, however, were generally accepted as being a genuine suicide attempt. Too many tried it the Hollywood way—the classic gun to the temple. What they didn't realize was the frontal lobes of the brain are least critical for life functions, and the forehead area also houses the sinus cavities. Depending on the caliber and exact angle of the gun, one ran the risk of inflicting a critical but non-fatal wound. Many would die a slow death days later, but we were certain that was not their original intent.

Mike and I facetiously discussed writing a public service pamphlet, "Suicide: Get It Right the First Time." We would discuss proper gun placement and also other less obvious factors such as how not to leave a mess in your home and how to insure your remains would be discovered relatively promptly. The very idea of such a bizarre publication was perhaps a new low in irreverent, gruesome, macabre police humor, but such was the inclination of homicide detectives with too much time to think outlandish thoughts.

In addition to pounding the streets of the city on a daily basis, sometimes a murder case would generate an extradition. The killer would be arrested in another state, and Mike and I would fly out and transport the prisoner back to Chicago for trial. Over our many years together, we traveled the country, bringing back bad guys and soaking up local history wherever we had the opportunity. We walked the Independence Mall area of Philadelphia and climbed the walls of the El Murro Fortress in Puerto Rico. We loved every minute away from the ghetto.

Mike and Mary Rita had no children, but Mike enjoyed interaction with my sons, and since we carpooled, he had an opportunity to see them several times a week. On Christmas, he would come by early to play with their gifts. He was fascinated by some of their toys, and of course, the boys loved the attention from him.

Every day when we left, Christopher, my oldest boy would be at the door for inspection. He would lift our suit jackets on each side.

"Gun, bullets, handcuffs. Okay, Mike."

And again, "Gun, bullets, handcuffs. Okay, Dad."

Only then would he allow us to leave for work.

After over seven years together, I accepted a "temporary" assignment outside of Homicide, and shortly thereafter, I was promoted to sergeant. Department policy mandated that I be reassigned to another unit. Mike and I would never again work together.

Over the next several years, I found it difficult to stay in touch with Mike. He would break dates for lunch, and he missed my surprise sixtieth birthday party. Since he no longer carpooled with anyone, Mike was in no hurry to get home after work. My homicide buddies told me he was stopping with the guys every day and drinking heavily. They implored me to do something, so I redoubled my efforts to reestablish contact, but Mike would have none of it.

Mary Rita left him, promising to return if he could remain sober for two years. She remained in regular contact with him, offering support from afar to avoid enabling his addiction. During crisis times, Mike would call her and she would respond to arrange hospitalization or whatever was necessary for his immediate welfare. At one point, she told me he was in the rehabilitation unit of a local hospital. Visiting was encouraged. I visited, and we had a candid and congenial conversation, most of it centering on his battle with alcoholism. His "demon," he called it. He promised to meet for lunch after his release from the hospital. It never happened.

On a brisk spring day in early May 2003, during the mid-morning hours, Mike left his modest bungalow on Chicago's far northwest side. He sat in the driver's seat of his compact pickup truck, placed the barrel of his snub-nosed revolver in his mouth, pointed it at the roof of his mouth, and pulled the trigger. It was just the way we would have written the pamphlet.

I was in Kansas City, attending a weekend meeting for a professional law enforcement organization when my wife called. Mary Rita had immediately reached out for me, but I wasn't there for her.

"Be sure to call our boys—they need to know," I said. My wife promised she would. Then I closed the drapes and sat on the edge of my bed in the hotel room over 500 miles from Chicago. I was shocked, numb, and alone. The group I was with was in a hospitality suite two floors above, but that hardly seemed to be an appropriate place for me to be at this point in time. The police chaplain back in Chicago was a personal friend. I sat in the darkened hotel room and slowly dialed his number, but I had no idea what to say or even how to start the conversation. He answered on the second ring.

"Tom? This is Jim…" I started hesitantly.

"I've been expecting your call," he said. So he knew. Of course he knew. It was one of his all-too-routine callouts.

"I'm in Kansas City. Tom…I should be there…. I should have…." I started into a spontaneous litany of shoulda, woulda, coulda, but he cut me short.

"Don't!" The sharpness of his voice startled me. "Don't try to take ownership of this. I'm sorry you're out of town, but only because you need to be with other coppers now."

I explained I was with other coppers. They were having cocktails just two flights up.

"Then get yourself up there now! Tell the person you know best what has happened, get a drink, and go sit in the corner. If they're the real police, they'll know what to do."

I walked into the noisy room hesitantly, trying to retain my composure. I wasn't quite sure how this was going to work. Chuck, a local Illinois chief of police and my traveling companion for this trip, spotted me from across the room. He made his way to me.

"My partner…" I started to speak, but my eyes welled and the words stuck in the back of my throat. No sound could come out. Chuck grabbed my elbow and pushed me out to the hallway.

"What the hell is wrong?" he asked as he half-pushed me against the wall.

"My partner committed suicide." I managed to get the words out. The enormity of saying it aloud hit my whole body, and I allowed myself to sag against the wall behind me.

"Oh, shit! Are you okay? Shit! That's a dumb question!" He grabbed my arm and ushered me back into the room to an empty table. "What are you drinking?"

The table didn't remain empty for long. Marital problems, alcoholism, and suicide are the trifecta of police hazards—far more common than the public's perception of a tough cop facing an armed assailant. (More than twice as many law enforcement officers succumb to suicide as they do to violence on the street.) Mike was unfortunate enough to have run the gamut of each of them. Most of the cops in the room had been touched in some way by all three. I heard no gallows humor, no outrageous comments, not one irreverent moment. For those few hours in Kansas City, at that corner table, we were family, police family, and together we mourned a Chicago cop whom only one of us knew. Tom was right—they knew what to do.

Each year, the anniversary of Mike's death coincides with Chicago's Annual St. Jude Police Memorial Parade to honor all officers who have passed away. Thousands of off-duty officers march in full dress uniform, and a brief service follows at the Chicago Police Memorial on the lakefront just east of Soldier Field, a spectacular venue. Mary Rita, my wife Durell, and I will attend, and Jay will march with his fellow officers. After the service, we'll find Mike's memorial brick among the hundreds that pave the area in front of the water wall. I'll brush my fingers across his brick and sing the real words to myself…

Bless 'em all, bless 'em all.

Bless the long and the short and the tall….

Postscript from Mary Rita

"A wonderful fact to reflect upon, that every human creature is constituted to be that profound secret and mystery to every other."
— *Charles Dickens*

Jim was very concerned about even allowing me to read this piece and doubly concerned about sharing the story in his book. I have a very strong feeling that Mike's story should be shared because it may help to bring the horrific thought of suicide "out of the darkness." Mike's story is not an easy read as, unfortunately, his life was not an easy one. I had to read it over a few times because a flood of memories washed over me, causing some few tears.

Jim captured the essence of Mike's life. The JOB was Mike's life. The years that Jim and Mike were partners were his happiest times. Mike was an only child, and it seemed to me that their relationship was very much like brothers. In fact, many times, Mike enjoyed telling me that either a bad guy or a witness would ask, "Are you guys brothers?" Once, after Jim gave a speech at the St. Jude's Hall, a lieutenant came up to Mike and complimented him, "Great speech!"

Mike suffered for many years with depression and alcoholism. These two diseases made it extremely difficult for him to function well on a daily basis, and it's a testament to his great intelligence and strong will that he worked for over twenty-five years. The combination, of course, made it very difficult for me to live with him. Jim tried many times to help Mike, as did others, including me. Mike was in tremendous psychic pain for such a long time; tragically, the depression won out. He could only see one way to stop the pain of mental illness.

Unfortunately, Mike's death by suicide allowed me to become a member of a club no one wants to join. Fortunately, Father Charles Rubey of Catholic Charities of Chicago formed an organization, Loving Outreach to Survivors of Suicide (LOSS) Program. The LOSS Program started in the late 1970s and has become a model around the world to help those who have lost a loved one to suicide. I am so filled with gratitude that I was able to speak without embarrassment to Father Rubey and the other mental health professionals at first, when I was scarcely capable of speaking clearly to anyone else. The beauty of this program is that there are monthly and weekly meetings, along with counselors who are available to help.

After being a LOSS member and attending meetings, going through training, I was able to become a facilitator, and that allows me to give back a portion of the gift I've received. And so, I feel that sharing Mike's story will shed light on the terrible problem that affects so many of us. I don't want Mike to be remembered for how he died, but rather for his life. And just as we can call 911 for help from the police, you can call 312-655-7283 for help from LOSS or for referral to a similar organization close to you.

On the Fence

By Jay

As I hung there upside down from the six-foot chain-link fence, I knew I was in trouble. It was dark and secluded. We were the only two people in sight. He saw my vulnerability and knew that this was his chance to exploit it. The smirk on his face let me know that I needed to act immediately. Calling for backup was not an option. As he walked slowly toward me, I saw his hand start to reach. I put my hand on my gun, unsnapped it, and slid it out of my holster. With a string of expletives, I advised him in no uncertain terms that I would not be his victim tonight. The tone in my voice and the fire in my eyes let him know that if he followed through with his plan, it would come at a price; a price he might not be willing to pay.

My partner and I were a couple of hours into our midnight shift when we got the call. He wasn't my regular partner, but we worked well together and trusted each other. It was a routine burglar alarm at a commercial business.

"Generic burglar alarm, key holder notified and will be on scene in about thirty minutes," said our dispatcher.

We crept down the block slowly, with our lights off, and parked a couple of doors down. We exited the squad car and quietly pushed the doors shut so as not to alarm any potential intruders of our arrival. With our radios turned down and flashlights in hand, we approached the front of the building and scanned the front and side windows and door. All appeared to be secure. As we walked to the back, we came to a six-foot chain-link fence separating us from the rear door and windows. Our view of the building was now obstructed by the crates and dumpsters.

My partner was the first to go over the fence as I covered him. I followed after his safe landing. With our hands on our guns, we checked the rear door and windows. All secure. I notified our dispatcher to give any other responding units a disregard. As I turned back to the fence, I noticed that my partner had already made it over and was heading back toward our car. I scaled the fence, put one foot on top, and attempted to push myself over. As I did, my shoelaces on my right boot got tangled on the fence. I came crashing down, head just inches from the pavement, swinging upside down. Try as I might, I couldn't reach the laces with my knife. I hung there, upside down, and took a deep breath, contemplating my next move.

That's when he approached. I heard his footsteps, and then I saw him slowly emerge from the shadows. The grin on his face was ear-to-ear. His laugh was devious. As he began to reach, I started my tirade and drew my weapon. He paused for a moment but called my bluff. With a hearty laugh, he grabbed the mike and called out.

"Squad, does anyone on the zone have a camera?"

Yes, prior to the days of camera phones, my partner was trying to capture this priceless moment on film before I could get myself down. My language and threats of retaliation got stronger. Before the dispatcher could respond, my partner keyed the mike again and gave a disregard.

I breathed a sigh of relief and muttered, "Cut me down, asshole."

With a smile and a laugh, he cut my laces as I did a handstand to keep myself from landing on my head. Back on my feet, I walked with him back to our squad parked in front.

"That could have been so bad," I said.

"It could have been so good," he answered.

What Scares Cops?

By Jim

"Courage is resistance to fear, mastery of fear—not absence of fear."
— Mark Twain

What scares cops? I mean what *really* scares cops?

I guess a good general answer is: Not much.

If we want to be more specific, the answer becomes murky, more complicated. In reviewing this story in my mind before setting this account to the printed page, I think a good answer, which most police officers would agree with, is "the unknown." Tactics can be taught in the academy and honed on the street with years of experience, but no matter the breadth of training and experience, there come the incidents that have no safe, tactically defined approach. You master your fear, tough it out, and do what you have to do.

It was a late summer evening, cool enough for a light jacket, especially after the sun had set. Mike Shull and I were working homicide, driving west on Madison Street in the 3800 block. About twenty-five yards ahead of us, a young man came darting out of a gangway, looking over his shoulder, running from right to left into traffic. He had reached the traffic lane directly in front of us when a very loud shot rang out from the gangway. He went face down, rolled onto his back, staring at the gangway as he tried to use his legs to push himself further away to no avail. He lost consciousness almost immediately.

Mike picked up the microphone and shouted.

"Seventy-four-o-seven. Emergency! We have an on view shots fired, man shot on the street at 3830 West Madison."

I eased our car closer to the victim but remained about ten yards back from the gangway. I put the car in park, positioning it to shield the victim from traffic. We paused for a moment to hear whether our dispatcher had read our message. He did.

"Attention, cars on citywide, we have a homicide unit with shots fired on the street and a man shot at 3830 West Madison."

This was the 11th District, and we knew that in a matter of seconds, citywide units would be on the scene with district units close behind, delayed only by the time it took their dispatcher to relay the call. We approached the victim slowly with our revolvers drawn, all the while glancing warily at the dark gangway to our right. The victim appeared to be unarmed and unconscious. A Task Force unit arrived with siren wailing from the opposite direction and positioned its car to shelter the victim from the west.

"Call an ambulance!" we shouted as we headed to the gangway.

"You guys got a description?" they called to us.

"Negative—the shot came from the gangway."

We got to the mouth of a narrow gangway, not more than four feet wide, lined with solid brick walls on both sides for the entire length. No cover, no concealment. The smell of gunpowder hung in the air as we peered down the dim length of the now empty passageway. Mike and I slowly crept toward the rear, revolvers drawn, sitting ducks for anyone who might suddenly reappear at the far end. It seemed a hundred yards long when, in reality, it was probably no more than a hundred feet. These are the moments when cops hear their own heartbeats. After an eternity, the rear opened onto a narrow lot occupied by a small construction office trailer. The lights were on and the door was ajar. We approached, again very slowly, remaining on the ground level as we gently pushed the door at the top of two stairs. An older black gentleman had his back to us as he carefully hung a shotgun on the far wall. We waited until he turned toward us, empty-handed.

"Police! Keep your hands where we can see them."

"I'm okay; I ain't did nothin'." He looked harmless...even kindly...as he responded. Maybe he was threatened by the gunman also.

Mike spoke first.

"Did you shoot that boy?"

"Yassuh, I capped that niggah's ass. He kept messing with me. I tole him not to mess with me no mo."

Moments later, we exited the gangway onto the sidewalk. Mike had his hand on the handcuff chain as he walked the prisoner out. I carried the shotgun.

"That was fast!" commented the Task Force unit.

"Ya, we don't fuck around," I answered with a smartass air of confidence and just a bit of swagger.

The scene out front had changed dramatically since we had entered the gangway. Marked squads were curb to curb. Paramedics had cut away the teenager's pant leg and were applying a dressing to the worst area of a buckshot wound. The boy was awake and alert now, lying in a puddle of urine. Perhaps he had just fainted from fright.

The distinctive wail of a lone Chicago Police siren heralded the arrival of still another unit. A homicide car pulled into the center of the milieu.

"Didn't you get the disregard?" I asked as our cohorts from Area Four rolled down their windows.

"Yeah, we were on the South Side, but we kept coming because you sounded scared."

I looked them straight in the eye, searching for a hint of insult or sarcasm, but found none. I saw instead an expression of genuine concern to which cops will seldom admit. I diverted my eyes to the pavement before I replied.

"Yeah...well...maybe that's 'cause we were scared."

Have No Fear, the Police Are Here...

By Jay

It was a simple call, very routine.

"Twenty-four-twelve."

"Two-four-one-two."

"Twenty-four-twelve, see Mr. Mohammed regarding someone knocking at his rear window. He stated someone broke that same window last week and he's afraid they're back."

"Twenty-four-twelve—ten-four—on our way, squad."

My partner and I proceeded to the address and decided to drive through the alley first. We were rolling down the alley with the lights off, but we weren't sure which building it was. We headed to the front, found the address, and parked the car. Our complainant could probably give us a little more background into the problems he was having, so we went into the three-flat and rang his buzzer.

Sure enough, Mr. Mohammed appeared, all ninety-eight pounds of him. He was a skinny little East Indian, dressed in pajamas. There wasn't much of a story behind this call, so we decided to check the yard and see what we could find. Mr. Mohammed decided he would follow us and wait at the mouth of the gangway. Assuring him that we would check things out, my partner and I proceeded to the rear of the building with one hand shining our flashlights and one hand on our guns. Mr. Mohammed watched, wide-eyed.

The gangway was narrow and completely dark, not even enough room for us to walk side-by-side. Just as we were about to reach the backyard, our good sergeant pulled into the alley behind the building. He would cover the rear and also write us down on his log. Just one problem with this plan—his squad car scared a skunk that was out for a midnight stroll. The skunk shot right up the gangway, right at us. Retreat was our only option.

With a quick yell, my partner and I were running at full speed, right toward our complainant. Our keys were slapping together, nightsticks clanking against our radios, and the beams from our flashlights were going from ground to sky with every stride. Mr. Mohammed could also run fast. It must have been half a block before we caught up to him and assured him we were only running from a skunk. He never blinked his eyes or said a word to us as we explained that there was no one in his yard. I still laugh, thinking about what he saw. Two of Chicago's finest, twice his size, running right for him with fear in their eyes. It probably took him a while to calm down and get back to sleep.

He hasn't called us back since that night.

Morgue, a Verb
By Jim

Darkness came early to Chicago's West Side ghetto. The mid-July sunset was totally obscured by stationary clouds that hung like black curtains along the western horizon. Silent lightning blinked in the distance: heat lightning we called it. The air was hot and still, and the suffocating humidity magnified the city's natural odors, the most easily identified being outdoor cooking, automobile exhaust, and stagnant garbage.

Bill Foster and I were working a homicide car out of Maxwell Street, and we were parked just off Taylor Street, around the corner from Mario's Italian Ice stand, enjoying one of its large frozen lemonades. I didn't have quite six months in yet in homicide, so that definitely qualified me as a new guy. The dispatcher chattered at an almost constant pace about street disturbances, stabbings, shootings, and a homicide on the street in the far southwestern corner of our area. Another homicide unit was told to "call the office." No doubt, it was getting the assignment. We waited, slowly spooning the icy mixture so as to avoid the inevitable brain freeze. On a night like tonight, our turn would come.

"Seventy-four-o-three, call your office." That was us—perfect timing—we had just finished our lemonade.

"Two bits says they want us to morgue that case," said Bill.

"Morguing" was a basic step in all new murder cases. Detectives needed to make a detailed examination of the body, noting the type and location of wounds. If circumstance permitted, many times a body could be morgued at the scene or at the hospital, but if things moved too fast and the victim was whisked away, a trip to the Cook County Morgue was required. A quick phone call confirmed Bill's prediction, so we headed to the morgue just as a fetid breeze began to stir.

We arrived in the parking lot just behind the Cook County Hospital as huge, widely spaced raindrops hit our windshield. The lightning now had an ominous rumble. Inside the morgue, we checked in with Freddy, the attendant. Ours was Case #137, July 1970, Crypt 12, John Doe, male/white, about sixteen years of age. Pronounced at Saint Anthony's Hospital at 2105 hours by a Doctor Whitney. Since he was as yet unidentified, we would need to get a very detailed overall physical description, in addition to noting the wounds.

Bill and I took the elevator to the basement level. As we stepped out, the building PA blasted the silence:

"Detective Foster, your office on line fourteen."

"Get started; I'll grab that call," said Bill as he quickly reentered the elevator. The door was closing before I could protest. Was this a test? I had been to the morgue many times in the past several months, but not quite under these circumstances.

I checked my notes for confirmation: The toe tag would read July #137 and he would be in Crypt 12. Crypt 12 was at the end of a short hallway lined with oversized white refrigerator doors. The walls were painted institutional dung beige, which might not have been a bad color except for being bathed in the garish green tint of the overhead fluorescent lights that lent a surreal ambiance to the scene. The floor was terrazzo with a tan/brown pebble pattern. I walked gingerly past the doors—Crypt 9, 10, 11, and there was 12.

It was at the end of the hallway, next to a window well to the outside world. As I arrived at my destination, the storm that had been hanging to the west all evening broke loose with a fury. I reached for the large chrome handle, and the instant I touched it, a bolt of lightning filled the window well with an almost immediate crash of thunder. I stepped back quickly from the handle, eyeing it warily. Try again, I told myself; you've got to do this. As I slowly opened the crypt door, rain pounded angrily at the window, punctuated by repeated thunder and lightning. If I hadn't been alone, it could have been an over the top scene from some cheap horror movie.

But I was alone. I swung the door wide and reached into the pitch black room where I thought the light switch would be. I stretched around the edge of the doorjamb and felt for the switch without actually entering the room. I couldn't find the damned switch! I backed away from the darkened room and there was the switch on the hallway wall. I knew that! Click. The crypt filled with a very dim incandescent light. Each crypt held twenty-five to thirty bodies, mostly on shelving on three walls. Recent arrivals would still be on gurneys, and if I were in luck, my case would be closest to the door.

There he was, just inside the door, #137 tied to his big toe. Another stretch, this time across the threshold, and again without entering the crypt, I pulled the gurney out into the hallway and began taking notes. Male/white, slender build, brown hair. I now had to touch him to raise an eyelid. Blinding flash! Deafening crash! Blue eyes.

His body was warm, warm enough still to detect his body odor. The boy looked to be perhaps the reported sixteen years of age. I glanced nervously into the crypt and saw that most of the bodies had been processed and wrapped. There were two or three others, naked on gurneys…late arrivals like mine. What was taking Bill so long?

Wind was now whipping, rattling hail against the window, well-punctuated with almost constant lightning and thunder. I glanced at the window, fully expecting to see someone trying to get in—or out. Where was Bill?

Concentrate! Wounds. Measure and note the wounds. GSW (gunshot wound), chest, four inches to the right of the right nipple. GSW, chest, one inch right of the left nipple, probably the cause of death. Small caliber contact rings, no powder burns. Probably shirtless at the time of the shooting. I lifted each of his hands and carefully examined them for defense wounds. Each time I touched the body, there were simultaneous cracks of thunder and lightning.

"John! Take it easy—I didn't do this to you." Another blinding crack-flash—concussion thunder shook the building. I found myself talking to the body now.

"I know, I know, your name's probably not John."

There were no defense wounds.

Number 137—he apparently didn't like being called John—was a little over a foot shy of filling the length of the 82" stainless steel morgue tray, so I marked 5' 8" for his height.

The elevator doors opened and Bill Foster stepped out into the hallway.

"How ya' doin'?" he asked nonchalantly.

"Good," I answered, trying to sound equally nonchalant. "We just have to roll him to check for exit wounds."

Bill grabbed an arm and pulled the boy toward him as I braced for the flash and the crash...but there was none. I examined his back, brushing some gravel and stones from his skin. There were no exit wounds. We were done. The storm stopped as suddenly as it had begun.

Outside, the air was cool and there was a pleasant summer breeze. The ozone from the lightning had deodorized the city, so everything smelled clean and fresh.

Our next bit of detective work was to find the homicide team handling this case and give it our morgue notes. There was no answer on the air. They were probably out of the car, canvassing the neighborhood, so we headed over to the crime scene to find them—it was best to get this done now since the night was young and we were probably next up on the assignment sheet. I could work with Bill, I told myself. He was easy to be with, and even if he had been messing with me at the morgue tonight, I proved to both of us I could handle it. Besides, sometime soon I wouldn't be the new kid. The tour of duty drew to a close without any further excitement.

While Bill and I would never work as regular partners, over the next ten years, we would "float" into one another on occasion, working together for short periods with ease.

Fast forward another thirty years: Bill and I, along with Jesse Acosta, another homicide old-timer, are sitting at the Red Apple Polish Buffet on North Milwaukee Avenue just this past week. Having finished our third plate-load of home-cooked delicacies, we pause, if for nothing more than to breathe. I tell Bill this story and he listens with a smile.

"So tell me true, Bill. Did this just kinda happen, or were you messing with me? Ya know, the new kid?"

Bill mops the last of the mushroom gravy from his plate with the remnants of a potato pancake.

"The real truth?" says Bill. "The real truth is: I don't remember that night, but if it happened like you're tellin' it," he pauses to wipe some of the gravy from the corner of his mouth, "I was most definitely not screwin' with you. If I were screwin' with you, I would have locked you in the crypt and shut the lights off before I went back upstairs."

Jesse shudders visibly at the thought....

Roller Coasters, Skydiving, and Bee Stings...

By Jay

I am afraid of roller coasters, skydiving, and bee stings.

The last time I was on a roller coaster had to be about ten years ago. I haven't been on one since. My brother convinced me to take the exciting ride. It was the "Demon" at Great America. After the first two loops, the ride came to an unexpected stop. The power at the park came to an end. Apparently, a truck on the highway had an accident and ended up striking a transformer. The next thing I knew, I was six stories above the ground with no hope of returning to the unloading platform. The long torturous climb down an emergency catwalk convinced me that this was not the excitement I was searching for.

A couple of my best friends went skydiving in Urbana, Illinois. Just another activity that I was deathly afraid of. There's no way I'm jumping out of a perfectly good airplane. Their stories were great, and I admired them for taking that risk. But not my cup of tea.

I haven't been stung by a bee since I was about six years old. Back then, I knew he was buzzing right by my ear. I followed the advice I had always been given: "Just stand still and it won't bother you." So much for that advice. At six years old, it was probably the worst pain I had ever felt.

"Forty-three, Sam, twenty-four, traffic stop at Division and Larrabee. We got four on the hood. One more car, please; no emergency."

I think I know what I'm getting into before I turn on the blue lights.

"Units in twenty-four, units on citywide, we have two calls of shots fired at Juneway and Ashland. Anonymous citizen heard four to five shots and people screaming...no further information."

"Twenty-four-twelve, we're goin'," I answer.

I almost have to fight to be the first one on the radio responding to this call. The lights and sirens go on and we're racing into an area which all the citizens are running to exit. That should be the first sign. It doesn't bother me. I get excited. It's a natural high, a high you could never find in any pill or bottle.

I can't explain why I'm not afraid. I should be. Maybe I am. My thoughts are racing a mile a minute. There's no time to replay my training. I just have to react. I have to draw my gun and run through the many innocent citizens who are just trying to get away from the gunfire. I don't know who the bad guy is. Neither do they. I do building searches, hoping that behind every corner I turn there is no one there. I find a bad guy hiding around one of those corners.

"Stop. Let me see your hands. Stand up. On the ground. Hands against the wall. Don't move...."

There is no single command I can give that will make the bad guy do what I want without some compromise of my safety. I have yet to come across the suspect who is already on his knees, facing away from me, legs crossed, with his fingers interlaced behind his head, and his head pressed against the wall. It never happens that way.

Why do I love it? Maybe, for a moment, I think I'll make a difference. Maybe I try to believe that I can do the same job my father successfully did for so many years. Maybe I believe that, no matter what I do or how safe I am, the good Lord already knows when He will pass His judgment on me.

Why am I afraid of roller coasters, skydiving, and bee stings? Maybe I'm just afraid of the slow trek up the wooden giant, the anticipation of the acceleration into the two loops. Maybe I'm afraid of sitting in the plane waiting to jump. Maybe I'm afraid of the constant buzzing around my ear, hoping not to get stung.

I don't want time to think about it. I just want to do it. Maybe anticipation is my greatest fear. Maybe I'm just afraid of waiting for what I think is going to happen next.

Accidental Murder

By Jim

Levi Wilson sat back on the living room couch of his brother-in-law's second-floor apartment on South Lawndale Avenue. A beer in hand, snacks on the coffee table, the smell of a ham cooking in the kitchen—it was turning out to be a fine Saturday afternoon. Levi and his wife Lativia thought they were just going to Lattie's sister's apartment for an early evening dinner, but when they arrived, it was a full-blown anniversary party for Levi and his wife. Thirty years of marriage, three successful daughters, and the family had gathered to help them celebrate.

"Lattie!" shouted Levi. "Bring me a beer."

The women were all in the kitchen, alternately hovering over the side dishes and basting the ham. The men and older boys were in the living room, watching the Bulls game. The younger children were playing board games on the dining room table.

"You kids are going to have to clear that table soon; we're fixin' to set out dinner."

Levi was annoyed as he pushed himself up from the couch. He strode purposefully through the house to the kitchen.

"Bitch!" he shouted at Lattie. "I tol' you to get me a beer!"

He took a wide swing at his wife. He connected, but the previous beers and Lattie's evasive action caused the blow harmlessly to graze the back of her head. The family had seen this side of Levi all too often.

"Daddy!" shouted Delilah, their adult daughter. "Not here! Not today!"

Delilah stepped between her mother and father as Levi prepared to swing again, but instead, he shoved his daughter aside, and she momentarily lost her balance and fell to the kitchen floor. Even Levi realized that he may have just crossed some unspoken line. In their entire marriage, he had never laid a hand upon his daughters.

"Bitch!" he repeated as he grabbed himself a beer and retreated to the living room. Moments later, the women heard the men laughing.

Lattie helped her daughter up, unhurt, from the floor, but both were crying. The other women tried to direct the group's attention to the final preparations of the afternoon meal, but Lattie scanned the kitchen counter and picked up a six-inch narrow-bladed boning knife. If any of the women saw her, they said nothing as she marched toward the front of the house.

Lativia stood in front of Levi. He waved her to get out of his view as he strained forward to see the television. He never saw the knife as his wife took a half-step forward and struck him once on his left shoulder. She turned and went back to the kitchen, still holding the knife.

"Goddam crazy woman!" exclaimed Levi as he brushed his shoulder as if to straighten his shirt.

"Levi, you be cut, man!" shouted his brother-in-law.

Levi looked at his fingertips and saw just a trace of blood.

"It ain't shee-it, man," he said as he tried to look at the top of his shoulder. He couldn't quite see the wound.

His brother-in-law pulled his shirt aside and observed a small 3/8-inch laceration with just a trace of blood at the edges.

"You'll be all right, man, but stay in here. Let her cool off and we'll all have supper."

Levi nodded silently as his fingers traced his left collarbone area.

There was silence in both the kitchen and the living room, with the only sounds coming from the television. The entire apartment was still, save for the sound of the Bulls announcer. Levi dropped his hand to his upper left chest area now, just below the collarbone. He rubbed it slowly.

"Hurts," he said, just before he lost consciousness.

• • • •

"Seventy-four-o-seven, call your office," the dispatcher paged. We found a phone nearby.

"Listen, ya guys; sorry to give you a late job, but the next shift is short tonight. Take a DOA stabbing victim at Mount Sinai—one in custody now at the 10th District."

It had been a quiet Saturday afternoon up to that point, but with less than ninety minutes to go, my partner and I were now stuck for the evening.

At Mount Sinai Hospital, the ER personnel directed us to a private examining room where Levi Wilson awaited transportation to the Cook County Morgue. His shirt had been cut away, but treatment had not proceeded much beyond that. He was pronounced dead on arrival. There was a single 2" x 2" gauze patch on his left shoulder on the hollow just above the collarbone. When we removed it, we saw a very small laceration with clean edges and a trace of blood. An ER nurse came into the room to retrieve some supplies.

"Is this what killed him?" we asked in a dubious tone of voice.

"We're guessing, yes, unless they find some surprises at the morgue tomorrow."

"Maybe heart attack?" asked my partner. If it were a heart attack, we might get to go home relatively on time.

The nurse shrugged and left the room.

We looked over the ER report. The only injury noted was a "laceration of the left supraclavicular hollow." Chalk up another mini-lesson in anatomy—that cavity on top of your shoulder is really a "supraclavicular hollow."

The 10th District was a madhouse with not only our case, but all the other flotsam that makes up a normal Saturday afternoon in a busy district. The watch commander was only too happy to give us permission to move all parties to the Area Four Homicide office on Maxwell Street, and we wound up transporting Lativia Wilson.

Mrs. Wilson was a somewhat heavyset woman, fifty-three years of age, well dressed with salt and pepper hair, obviously extremely distraught.

"Please, sweet Jesus! Tell me Levi's not dead," she pleaded. "I just hit him on the shoulder."

"Hit him on the shoulder with a knife," countered the uniformed patrolman as he removed his handcuffs from her wrists. He looked expectantly at us, but we shook our heads. Lativia would ride with us without handcuffs, but I would ride in the backseat with her.

At the area office, we separated the witnesses as best we could and succeeded in reconstructing the incident with very little disparity in the accounts:

Levi hit Lativia and then pushed Delilah, who fell to the floor. Neither were injured. Lativia took a kitchen knife, followed Levi to the living room, and struck him on the left shoulder with a knife. Levi most likely died within five to ten minutes of the incident. Levi had a documented history of domestic abuse over the last twenty-five years.

We called the Cook County Felony Review Unit for a recommendation on charges. The assistant state's attorney was working a double homicide on the far South Side. Could we review the case with him over the phone? He listened patiently as my partner ran down the particulars.

"Listen," replied the ASA. "Normally, I would call out someone else from home, but this seems pretty cut and dried. Charge her with murder. Put my name down as approving."

"Uh…well…" my partner was at a momentary loss for words. "Uh…I don't think we were exactly looking for a murder charge here."

"What!" shouted the ASA. "All the times I fight with you guys when you don't have a complete case, and now I'm giving you a murder and that's not what you want?"

"Well, we're just sayin', she's fifty-three years old, never had so much as a parking ticket, and he's been beatin' on her for years…."

"Yeah, but this time she's not hurt, she picked up the knife in the kitchen, followed him all the way to the living room, and stabbed him. That's murder. Let her defense attorney bring up that other crap and maybe we'll plead it out when it comes to court."

"Well…" (my partner wasn't quitting) "we're not even sure she caused his death. He's got a tiny laceration on the top of his shoulder. Maybe he died of a heart attack, or a stroke, or something."

"Yeah, right after she stabbed him. Charge her with murder."

My partner and I looked at one another and shrugged. So be it.

In total violation of our normal practice, Delilah was in the interrogation room with her mother when we entered to explain what was going to happen. Lativia would be charged with murder and removed to the women's lockup to await a bond hearing the following morning. We knew it would not be a pleasant experience for her. The women embraced and cried.

"Don't they have something like 'accidental murder'?" cried Delilah.

• • • •

Sunday morning roll call came too soon. The sergeant tossed us the Wilson case file.

"We've got no morgue man today. One of you will have to take the autopsy and the other the bond hearing. Work it out between you."

"I'll take court," replied my partner.

Since I was the junior man on the team, that left me with morgue. It might be interesting, I told myself. I still wasn't convinced that that tiny cut had killed Levi Wilson. We'd find out soon. I decided to skip breakfast for the time being.

I had only been in homicide a few months, but I had at least a half-dozen autopsies under my belt. The initial shock of watching a pathologist's assistant cut into a human body had worn off after the first two or three. Revulsion had been replaced by inquisitiveness.

At the morgue, I learned that the Wilson case was number three in the morning lineup—the double homicide from the night before would be first. While I waited, the morgue office paged me. It was my partner from court.

"Have you got a cause of death yet?" he asked.

"No, we're number three. What's up?"

"Well, the judge is a friend of mine. I'm thinkin' maybe we can get Lativia a personal recognizance bond."

"On a murder?" I asked skeptically.

"Well, we're not even sure it's a murder. Call the court bailiff on this number as soon as you get something."

About twenty minutes later, Doug, the diener (pathologist's assistant), rolled Levi Wilson into the room. He was naked now. We both looked at the small cut on his left shoulder and then scanned the rest of his body. Doug turned Levi to each side, but we found no other wounds.

"What do you think? I asked.

He shrugged and called the pathologist over. The pathologist shrugged also.

"Get started," he told Doug.

At the Cook County Morgue, the diener did most of the initial work opening the body, and Doug was one of the best.

The shoulder laceration was relatively close to where Doug would start his "Y" incision to open the chest, so he called for some photos before he started.

He cut a long incision from each shoulder to the center of the chest where the incisions joined. He then extended the incision downward to the pubic area. Next came the saw. Doug cut a triangular section of the ribcage out and then lifted it free.

"Oh yeah!" he exclaimed.

Looking into a normal chest cavity, one could readily discern the major organs of the chest; most prominent were the heart and lungs. But Levi Wilson's chest was filled with free blood.

"Doc!" called the diener.

The pathologist nodded for Doug to proceed. He carefully used an oversized soup ladle to remove and measure the blood volume. The three of us were peering at the chest cavity intently now. The doctor placed the handle of a scalpel lightly into the wound and then inserted his gloved hand into Levi's upper left chest and found the wound from the inside. He nodded to Doug, who used a hose to rinse gently the injured tissues. The trajectory of the knife blade was clearly visible now, from the left shoulder supraclavicular hollow directly down to the ascending aorta and left ventricle of the heart. Levi Johnson had quite simply died of a stab wound to the heart.

I called my partner at court to give him a report.

"You're too late," he told me. "The judge already gave Lativia a personal recognizance bond on my recommendation."

"Is that on the record?" I asked.

"No, I talked to him in chambers before the court call. The ASA is having a fit. I'll wait until the next recess and tell Kenny—I mean the judge—maybe we goofed."

"I don't think we goofed. She'll show up in court. Tell 'Kenny' I said 'Hello.'" I laughed.

• • • •

Weeks turned into months, seasons changed, and the Bulls didn't make the playoffs.

"Padar, you've got a court notification, the Civic Center downtown. That's the Wilson Homicide; how come it's downtown?"

"The defendant's out on recognizance bond, Sarge. Maybe that's why they sent it to the Civic Center."

"Recognizance bond on a murder charge? How did that happen?"

"Hey, she's a nice lady. We pulled strings."

"Yeah, I'll bet," replied the sergeant sarcastically.

It was my first time in court at the relatively new Chicago Civic Center, later to be renamed the Richard J. Daley Center. The ambiance was more genteel than the gritty antiquity of the Criminal Courts Building at 26th and California. The courtrooms were small, new, and lacked the "prison smell" of 26th Street. I could get used to this real quick, I thought.

Lativia Wilson had arrived before me and was accompanied by two of her three daughters. When Delilah saw me, she slid into the bench and sat next to me.

"Thank you for getting Mama out on bail," she said.

"Who told you that?"

"Our lawyer. He said someone put a word in to the judge."

"Well, it wasn't exactly me," I replied.

"Well, thanks anyway, Detective. Our family really appreciated it," she smiled.

Lativia's case was the first called.

"Your honor, may I approach?" asked her attorney.

"In camera," replied the judge. "Court reporter please come to chambers."

"In camera" can be loosely translated as "in chambers" and merely denotes a private portion of the proceeding that is conducted away from the open courtroom.

The judge, the assistant state's attorney, the defense attorney, and the court reporter disappeared into chambers. Hey, this was Cook County; nothing surprised me—well not too much. But I was surprised when the bailiff appeared and asked me to step into chambers.

Lativia's attorney introduced himself to me.

"Delilah works for us," he said with a smile. "We're very fond of her."

So…Lativia's getting pro bono representation from a downtown law firm, I thought to myself. Not too shabby.

The judge spoke…

"Detective, we have been reviewing the circumstances of this case. The State and the Defense have agreed to a plea bargain to Voluntary Manslaughter, if I concur. What do you think of that?"

"I think that's appropriate in this case," I responded.

"And regarding sentencing…if I pronounce sentence today, this case will be off my docket. I'm thinking of a prison term of two years with five years felony probation…."

Whoa, I thought, just let her go. I didn't know what to say, but he wasn't quite finished.

"And I'm going to suspend the prison sentence, pending completion of her probation—if she can keep her nose clean," he smiled at himself. "What do you think of that?"

"I think that's appropriate in this case," I repeated and returned the judge's smile.

"Then it's done. Let's return to court."

It was the first and only time in my police career that I ever attended a criminal trial at the Civic Center. It was also the first and only time in my career that a criminal court judge ever asked my opinion on anything.

Once back in open court, the plea and sentencing were repeated. Lativia Wilson would walk out of court, essentially a free woman. Her daughters hugged her and they cried together.

Accidental murder. Sometimes, the system works in mysterious ways....

The Green

By Jay

October, 1999

In 1942, the Chicago Housing Authority built a low-rise apartment complex on Chicago's near West Side. It was called the Frances Cabrini Homes. In 1962, it added high-rise buildings called the William Green Homes. The complex then came to be known as Cabrini-Green, or to many Chicagoans, simply as "The Green."

We've been working in Cabrini-Green this week, and let me tell you, public housing is new to me. The crime is so concentrated and every building has its own drug market. It's near impossible to sneak up on anyone.

Last night, we tried a makeshift Trojan Horse. We hid in the back of the paddy wagon and had the wagon guys stop in the rear of 660 West Division. They walked through the parking lot, and when all eyes were on them, my partner and I snuck out of the wagon and into the building. After the wagon drove off, we waited about fifteen minutes. Then we sprinted to the rear of 714 West Division as two squad cars pulled in front.

As we were running, all of the young kids, adults, and even seniors began yelling out "Five-O!"—a phrase lifted from the popular police series *Hawaii Five-O*. They were not even inconspicuous about it. It was nice, though, to see that our youth and elderly have such a strong bond together.

Well, we were able to grab a kid with five rocks and a bag of weed. He had nowhere to run. We brought him into the station and cuffed him to the wall in an interview room. The 18th District only has two interview rooms, so we had to double up with another unit that had brought in this kid's uncle on a DUI. How nice.

Today, we tried something similar at the same building. We chased a guy up to the ninth floor and found him in some lady's apartment. Once we reminded her about the policy regarding allowing a person with narcotics to enter Chicago Housing Authority property and the eviction ramifications, she immediately explained how he ran into her apartment without permission and she demanded that he leave. Said she never saw him before in her life, and she signed complaints for criminal trespass to residence.

He made us run up nine flights of stairs, and he was able to get rid of the dope before we grabbed him. And guess what? Remember the kid from yesterday? This was his father. Small world, isn't it? He starts rattling off the hiding spots for dope in the projects, where the dealers run when we pull up, the major players, and how they do their thing. He told us that he always wanted to be a confidential informant, but he didn't know who to talk to about it. We'll see how his information pans out.

Thank God, these guys aren't smart or we'd have a big problem.

The King Riots— the First Day

By Jim

photo at www.OnBeingACop.com/gallery/mlkriot.jpg

Thursday, April 4, 1968, I was working the Tactical Unit out of the 18th District. My "baby furlough," eleven days of combined regular days off and accumulated compensatory time, would begin the next day. My wife Karla and I grabbed a quick bite to eat at a local restaurant and took in *No Way to Treat a Lady*, starring Rod Steiger. On the way home, we stopped by my folks' house. My mom was standing outside as we pulled up.

"Martin Luther King has been killed," she said with shock and disbelief in her voice.

I stared dumbly at her, across the passenger seat and out the open car window.

"Wow!" was the brainiest comment I could mutter. Both the immediate and the historical implications were beyond my comprehension. I had been a cop less than two years, and the first several months of that time had been spent at the police academy. To say I was green would be an understatement. It would be a major news story for sure, but any personal implications were totally beyond me at that moment.

Twenty minutes later, Karla and I entered our West Side apartment on a quiet street directly across from Merrick Park. The phone was ringing as we entered. My wife answered.

"It's for you," she said. "Your sergeant."

"Padar!" he said without any preliminaries. "Report for roll call at 10 a.m. tomorrow in the tact office…leather jacket and helmet… figure on a twelve-hour shift."

"But I start baby furlough tomorrow," I protested.

"Not anymore!" he snapped. "All days off are canceled."

"Leather jacket?" I questioned. The spring days were getting warmer and leather jackets were optional.

"Yes," he said impatiently. "They tend to do better with bottles and rocks—see you at ten hundred tomorrow."

"Bottles and rocks?" I responded.

"Padar! King was a hero in the community. There may be widespread rioting—in fact we're expecting it. Just be here!" His tone left no doubt he was perplexed at my total naiveté.

For the first time, my pulse quickened just a bit. Riots? Bottles and rocks?

"What was that all about?" asked my wife.

"Ah…they're canceling days off tomorrow because of this King thing. I have to be at work at ten." I didn't mention anything about riots, bottles, and rocks.

I called my partner, John Klodnicki, to make sure he realized we would be carpooling tomorrow. He and I had been working together for several months, having started together in a beat car and then being invited to join the tactical unit as partners. We had hit it off from the first time we worked together, and of course, we jumped at the chance to work tactical together. We had complementary styles for working the street and that made us a better team than most.

I was newly married and John was engaged to Elaine, to be married the following month. The girls knew one another, and more importantly, they liked each other. That made it more than nice for the four of us. We would remain "police family" forever.

The next morning, the mood in the tactical office was somber. The phones were ringing madly as the brass wrestled with how to allocate manpower. With more than double the number of personnel on hand, there were not enough cars available to provide us transportation. That problem was momentarily solved when we learned that the public schools were being released at 11 a.m. A group of us were loaded into police wagons and transported to Waller High School (now the Lincoln Park High School) at Orchard and Armitage.

As the mostly black students left the school, they were greeted by helmeted police standing in the street. We had no idea why we were here, and we eyed each other warily, each side not knowing what to expect from the other. We attached ourselves to a cluster that began to walk south on Orchard Street. As we proceeded, individuals dropped off, apparently heading for home. By the time we reached North Avenue, they had dispersed without incident.

John grabbed me, and in a moment of spontaneous genius, we flagged down a passing squad and got a lift back to the station. It was genius because when we got back to the tactical office, we were given a squad and told to report to the vicinity of the Cooley High School, at Division and Sedgwick, on the edge of the Cabrini-Green Housing projects. We had a car and a radio—we were ready for action.

As we neared Cooley High School, we monitored a call of police officers calling for help at 1159 North Cleveland, a Cabrini high-rise. We pulled into the lot west of the building and immediately found ourselves in the company of several other officers, all pinned down by sniper fire from the building. John and I scrambled out of the squad and took cover on the far side of the car. We crouched and peered up at the myriad of windows, but aside from frightened people looking back at us, there was nothing to see. The gunfire from the building had ceased momentarily.

I squatted at the driver's door of the squad and peered intently at the windows. I felt an arm resting on my left shoulder as another officer steadied himself, and out of the corner of my eye, I caught the familiar blue of a police shirt. Where's his leather jacket? I wondered to myself.

A moment later, the world exploded into the left side of my head. I thought that somehow I had been shot, and I reeled to my right, went down to the pavement, and put my hand to my left ear, fully expecting it to have been shot off. There was no blood and the side of my head felt intact, but the inside of my ear hurt badly, and it was ringing loudly. The officer leaning on me had a shotgun, and as he braced himself on my shoulder, he discharged the weapon just inches from my ear. He quickly moved to the hood of the car and readied himself for another shot. I felt as though I had lost my hearing in that ear, except for the ringing. Years later, I would be diagnosed with classic noise-induced hearing loss in my left ear, but for the moment, I just wanted to get away from that building and that officer. There seemed to be a momentary pause in gunfire from the building. John and I scrambled into the car and sped north through the lot and out onto Division Street, just in time to hear that we were being paged on the radio.

I was encouraged that I had been able to hear the radio and tried to put the ringing out of my mind. We were being asked to report to the field lieutenant at our district desk.

At the desk, our lieutenant introduced us to two young men dressed in dark suits. They were the owners of the currency exchange just a few doors west of the Cooley High School. Our assignment was to escort them to their place of business and stand by with them until they emptied cash from the safe on the premises.

None of us were particularly enthused with the task, and the businessmen appeared to be petrified.

"Do you really want to do this?" we asked.

"Do you think you can help us?" they replied.

That was the wrong question to ask two young cops. Of course we could help them!

On our way to the currency exchange, our squad was hit with some rocks and bottles, and I swerved to avoid them as best I could. We passed an occasional burning building with no fire department in sight. It was then we noticed that our businessmen had disappeared. We turned to find them lying atop one another on the car's rear floor. At their place of business, I nosed the squad up on the sidewalk, close to the building door. Strangely, it was still intact. John and I peered into the backseat.

"Do you still want to do this?" we asked.

They peeked up from the floor and saw the door just a few feet from the car.

"Yeah…ya think…?" they asked hesitantly.

"Get your keys ready and move when I tell you," said John as he exited the side of the vehicle closest to the building. John went to the rear of the car with his revolver drawn and fired two shots in the air.

"Go! Go! Go!" he shouted.

I scrambled out with them and they fumbled only momentarily with the keys in the relative shelter to the recessed doorway. It was going well, but my pulse was racing and my left ear was still ringing loudly. Once inside, they unlocked more gates, and when they reached the safe, they opened it and emptied bundles of cash into a duffel bag in record time. We ran, crouched down, back to the squad. They jumped into the backseat and promptly took refuge atop one another on the floor. John and I jumped into the front and exchanged an anxious glance. Almost done…and then, we were on our way. Back at the station, we had to invite them several times to crawl out of the car.

In the station lot, John and I looked worriedly to the west where black clouds of smoke rose high into the sky. Inside the station, we scanned teletype messages and noted reports of widespread rioting and fires in the districts. I called Karla and learned she was at our apartment, having been released early from work. John called Elaine. She was in their West Side apartment at the city's edge, but just off Madison Street.

John and I weighed the options for the girls. My apartment on the quiet little side street across from a small park seemed preferable to John's place so close to Madison Street. The girls agreed. Elaine would go to our apartment, and they would stay together until John and I were released from duty.

The shortage of cars was solved by assigning four men to a car. We picked up a third man, Bennie. His partner was out of town. We would spend the balance of our tour as a three-man unit. Bennie had checked out a carbine rifle so we had additional firepower on board.

From the station, we took Chicago Avenue west toward the projects, turning north on Larrabee Street. John was driving, I was front passenger, and Bennie was in the back with the carbine. The street was littered with rocks and bottles, and as we approached the 1015-1017 Larrabee building, I saw a man with a shotgun in the building breezeway. He stepped forward, raised the gun, and aimed toward our car. I slid to the left, pushing hard into John just as he fired at us. John swerved the squad away as if he could somehow avoid the gunfire. The man fired directly at us, but he was probably over fifty yards away, and the buckshot load rattled harmlessly against the side of our car as we sped north on Larrabee. We exclaimed simultaneously. Bennie wanted to go back, but the man had retreated back into the building.

We paused at the fire station at Division Street to catch our breath and allow our hearts to retreat back into our chest cavities. Inside the fire station, we took a short break and called the girls to confirm that they were now together at my apartment, nestled away from main streets. Back on the road, we headed north to North Avenue. We needed to be away from Cabrini for a while, at least until our pulses recovered to a somewhat normal level. We spent the next couple of hours in the Old Town area, responding to sporadic incidents of looting. It turned out to be a fruitless task. Looters would flee upon our arrival, but once we left, they would return. We just didn't have the manpower to remain in any one place for long.

Dispatch put out a call for all available units to report to Oak and Larrabee, with instructions to approach from the north per orders of a deputy superintendent on the scene. When we arrived and looked to the south—where hours before we had been fired on—it was obvious the climate had changed considerably. One lone gunman had been replaced by several hundred people milling about and looting the supermarket on the west side of Larrabee.

The deputy called us to assemble around him, and he explained that we were going to form a skirmish line and take back the street. I could not believe that he was going to commit us to such a foolhardy scheme. We were outnumbered at least ten to one. It would be absolute suicide for us. Most of us had completed riot formation training in preparation for the Democratic National Convention several months ahead, but I don't think anyone ever believed that we would use it, much less that it would work.

Nevertheless, we formed a single skirmish line of widely spaced men that stretched from sidewalk to sidewalk. Behind us were three wagons and about a half-dozen more men. The crowd eyed us warily. In theory, we would march at half-step with batons at the ready. The crowd would disperse, and those who didn't would be allowed to penetrate the line only to be arrested and put into the wagons at the rear. Yes, we had practiced this at the local armory. Yes, we understood the theory behind the formation. But no one expected it to work—except for the deputy; he positioned himself with us at the center of the line and gave the order to advance. Now I was a young man, in peak physical condition, but I didn't think my system could take another round of hyperventilating and tachycardia. I felt I was running low on adrenaline and my left ear was still ringing loudly.

The deputy gave the command, and en masse, we began to advance toward the crowd that vastly outnumbered us. The crowd just stared at us in total disbelief, and then the most amazing thing happened. They scattered in all directions. Not a single one broke our line. Maybe a half-dozen bottles and bricks were thrown, but from a distance that rendered them harmless. It was classic. Just like we had practiced it in training. We took back the street and stationed a car at the supermarket. We owned the street. They always told us that the police were a quasi-military organization. Well, for those few minutes on Larrabee Street, we were far more military than we were quasi.

The hours wore on and we rushed from clash to clash. The ominous black clouds of smoke in the western sky were accentuated by the setting sun. We had no further phone contact with the girls, and all we could do was assume that they were still together and safe.

Some thirteen hours after we had started our tour of duty, we found ourselves parked at the closed gas station at Clybourn and Ogden. A gradual relief was being effectuated, and we waited for our turn to go into the station and end our tour. Things were quiet at the moment, so we allowed ourselves a moment of reflection.

"John, on Larrabee, when we did that skirmish line thing… how many people were on the street?"

"Realistically? I'd say at least three or four hundred."

"And how many live in Cabrini?"

"They say 15,000," John answered.

I did some quick math in my head.

"So that's about three percent, right?"

"I guess."

A car pulled slowly into the gas station. An older black gentleman was driving, his wife in the passenger seat, three children in the back.

"Office', can we go home now?" he nodded toward Cabrini.

We listened to the occasional gunfire. Spirals of smoke from small fires curled upwards.

"I don't think so...especially not for them," I said, nodding toward the children.

He and his wife had some conversation and somehow settled on an alternate destination for the night.

"Thank you office'. You be safe out here, ya hear?"

We nodded as he pulled slowly out of the lot and headed north out of Cabrini.

"There's the other 97 percent," I said.

Moments later, we were told to report to the station for our relief—it was about 11:30 p.m. We had worked a thirteen-and-a-half-hour tour on the first day of my baby furlough.

At the desk, we called communications to inquire about the safety of the Eisenhower Expressway for our trek home. They told us it would be safe as long as we did not exit until we got to Central Avenue. Perfect. That was our exit. We called the girls and told them we were on our way home.

The drive west on the expressway was beyond anything we had ever seen. South of the highway in particular, we saw blocks and blocks of buildings burning with no evidence of the fire department. It too had been overwhelmed and forced to tailor its responses where they could do the most good. It was literally a war zone, and it was a somber drive home. Neither John nor I had ever witnessed such devastation. We hardly spoke. We were emotionally and physically spent from the day.

The girls welcomed us with hugs and kisses and tears. The ambiance of the apartment was surprisingly comforting. The relief of being home safe was almost overwhelming. Our mood shifted. The soft, warm incandescent lighting, the table set, sandwiches at the ready, and of course, our sweethearts. All was well. We had survived the day. We were safe and we were loved.

"You guys need to wash up," announced the girls as they grimaced and handed us fresh towels and washcloths.

In the small washroom, John and I looked at ourselves and were surprised at the dirt and soot on our faces. We elbowed one another for access to the wash basin as we relived portions of the day.

"Those two guys in the backseat—man, I thought we'd have to shovel them off the floor!"

"Not to mention cleaning the crap off the seats after they left."

We laughed.

"And when you climbed into my lap—I thought you went queer on me."

"Yeah, sure; you didn't see the guy with the shotgun."

More laughter.

"You know, you're the only person I ever saw get knocked over by a sound."

"Well, believe it or not, my ear is still ringing. You should try it sometime."

"No thanks. You can just tell me about it...."

More laughter. Playful shoving.

We finished cleaning up and returned to the table, but the warmth had turned to ice.

My wife was not happy.

"What's the matter, honey?" I asked, genuinely mystified.

"We spent the whole day here, worried sick about you two, not knowing what was going on," she was nearly in tears. "And now you come home, and we find out you were...you were...*having fun!*"

Well, not really....

Epilogue

Later that night, the midnight shift pulled the security car off the supermarket on Larrabee, the one we had retaken with our classic skirmish line. I don't know what played into that decision, but when we returned to work the following day, the store had been burned to the ground along with other small businesses in the vicinity.

John and I would work twelve-hour shifts the next several days and survived without further injury. I never reported the injury to my ear, although it continued to ring for several days afterwards. We were involved in very real urban warfare, so I couldn't picture myself in an ER complaining to the doc that my ear was ringing. Specialists would later confirm that my classic "notch" hearing loss in my left ear was most definitely caused by a fellow officer with a shotgun that April day in 1968.

Some years later, my wife would observe that "baby" furloughs were aptly named. In late December of 1968, Christopher, our first son, was born. Apparently, she hadn't stayed upset with me for long....

Do You Hear What I Hear?

By Jay

My partner and I were rolling on Hudson Avenue, just north of Chicago Avenue and east of the Cabrini Row Houses. I saw two officers assigned to the housing unit walking alongside of the projects at 929 N. Hudson. They hadn't called anything in over the air, so we weren't looking for anyone in particular. My partner and I were just looking for a car full of gangbangers to stop, or maybe a dope peddler walking down the street.

Bang, bang, bang, bang, bang. Five or six shots rang out, and they were close. The two coppers from the housing unit called it in instantly.

"Forty-five-fifty-seven, loud reports at 929 N. Hudson."

We were next.

"Forty-three, Sam, twenty-four. We heard five or six shots and are with forty-five-fifty-seven. We are going to the rear of the building."

I can still see their faces. They were two black officers, one male and one female. As the shots rang out, they looked directly at us. Their eyes opened wide and their mouths dropped open. They knew instantly that we had heard exactly what they had heard.

They crouched down and drew their weapons. In a mad dash, they ran alongside the building and made it safely inside. I hit the gas and circled around the back. The squad was thrown into park, and my partner and I ran into the building, just following where our guns were leading us. Neither of us knew what we were looking for other than some cover. Maybe the housing officers saw something, but we sure didn't. The four of us grouped together in the lobby. No one saw where the shots were coming from or where they ended up. We walked back outside and inspected our squad cars for bullet holes. Nothing. We all got back into our cars and drove off to continue our patrol.

I think back on it now and realize that I will never know if those five or six shots sailed right over the roof of our car. Maybe they were shot straight up into the air. Maybe they came from a block away, or maybe they were intended to hit the blue and white passing down their street.

My partner and I made it home safely that night. So did the two officers from the housing unit. None of us will ever know if we were potential murder victims that night, or just four cops listening to the gunfire that the residents of that area listen to each and every night.

Rocco

By Jim

Coincidence: God's way of remaining anonymous.
—Albert Einstein

Synchronicity: A term coined by Carl Jung to explain what he believed to be the underlying order of the universe that manifests itself through meaningful coincidences that cannot be explained by cause and effect.

One morning in January 1975, Jack Regan, my homicide sergeant, threw an arrest report on my desk and said, half-jokingly, "Hey, maybe this is your uncle."

I looked at the mug shot and arrest sheet of a Rocco Padovoni that he had retrieved from the Robbery office next door. Could be, I thought, but who could say for sure?

Literally over a hundred years ago in Baragiano, Italy, our name had been Padovoni. The guys in the unit knew that my family name had been mangled, first at Ellis Island in the 1890s, then again when my dad and his older brother became wards of the state at Maryville Orphanage, and then one last time around 1924 when my father—perhaps not so inexplicably—dropped the last three syllables from his thoroughly corrupted surname.

Rocco had been arrested for the armed robbery of a Fannie May Candy store while using a blank pistol. His record indicated that at age fifty-eight, he had spent the vast majority of his adult life in Illinois state prisons. He was soon to be headed back.

I brought Rocco's mug shot and arrest record home, and he became sort of a scurrilous inside family joke, a real live authentic armed robber who might be my uncle. He became a living family legend, an armed desperado, no less. Our very own family felon. Truth was, he favored sticking up Fannie May candy stores with plastic guns. He was a poor soul who had fallen through the cracks of meager social services and had become institutionalized to the point where he found comfort and security in a prison setting. But I didn't know that at the time.

Then in the early '80s, I was doing some genealogy research that confirmed Rocco Padovoni was in fact my uncle, a product of a second marriage of my grandfather. Our family's sly references to Rocco only increased. Oh, we were so smug and clever.

To add fuel to the fire, at the age of seventy-four, Uncle Rocco was arrested during the 1990 Christmas season, sticking up another Fannie May Candy Store. The newspapers reported he walked with a cane, was blind in one eye, and once again used a plastic gun. The responding officers were directed to a bus stop outside the candy store where he was waiting for his getaway vehicle, a CTA bus. Uncle Rocco pleaded guilty—he always pleaded guilty—and the judge sentenced him to "intensive" probation, whatever that is. Somehow, our image of an armed felon faded a bit, but we clipped the newspaper article and filed it away.

Then, in the summer of 1992, everything changed. My wife Durell called me at home from the local hospital where she worked as a nurse.

"What is Rocco's date of birth?" she asked. I looked it up and gave it to her.

"Well, your uncle Rocco is in the hospital. He was brought in last night by ambulance. He's had a serious heart attack."

"My uncle Rocco." That simple phrase had a sobering effect upon me. Now the butt of insensitive family jokes had a face, and a physical presence in the intensive care unit a few miles from our home. A man I had never met needed help. "My uncle Rocco." He was an indigent patient, and his hospital stay would be as brief as the doctors could justify. He'd be moved to a nursing home facility as soon as possible.

Suddenly, Rocco was indeed family. Durell visited a friend in the social services department of the hospital.

"Is there any nearby nursing home that could provide our uncle Rocco with a public aid bed?" she asked.

As a matter of fact, there was, and within a week, Uncle Rocco was resting most comfortably in an upscale nursing home on Chicago's northwest side. It provided not only for his physical care but also the institutional structure that gave him comfort and security. Uncle Rocco was in heaven.

Perhaps not so strangely, he appeared at ease with the fact that I was a cop. But whenever anyone from our family visited him, he would find a way to express his opinion of our fractured family name.

"Padar, PADAR," shaking his head with displeasure. Then he would hold his thumb against his fingers, palm up, and shake his raised hand. "Padovoni! PADOVONI!" he would exclaim with a broad smile. He made no effort to conceal that he thought what had happened to our family name was a travesty. He was right.

Uncle Rocco passed away in December of 1994 at the age of seventy-eight.

Rest in peace, Rocco Padovoni!

A Run for the Border
By Jim & Jay

During the early morning hours of my midnight shift as Operations Manager of the 911 Center, I would punch up my son's radio zone on my office monitor. I would try to listen for his voice or call sign. Many times, I missed it, but this night, at 1:30 a.m., I caught his beat number immediately.

"Twenty-four twelve, emergency."

I turned my full attention to the monitor and my pulse quickened a few beats. It's probably not a good idea to have a father monitoring his son so closely and in real time.

"Four-twelve, go with your emergency."

"Ya squad, we've got an on view auto accident at Howard and Clark, and I think this lady is having a heart attack. Send us an ambulance." It was Jay's partner's voice and the tone was the typical, almost bored, matter-of-fact inflection that says, "Nobody get their shorts in a knot; we've got this handled." Relax, Dad; this is routine, I told myself.

"Ten-four, they're on the way."

Less than a minute passed and then my son's unmistakable voice broke the silence.

"Twenty-four twelve, emergency." There was an edge to his voice that was definitely not routine. The dispatcher acknowledged and Jay continued. "Squad, I've got a second victim here, about a hundred yards north of the intersection.... He's pretty bad."

I could tell from the timbre of his voice that the scene before him was a bad one. "There'll be a story from this one." I told myself....

• • • •

Judge Webster called out his name in traffic court this morning and my eyes scanned the large group of defendants with disbelief. Up rose Mr. Hancock. He slowly limped up to the bench; his hands were swollen and a discolored scar covered his skull. A quick plea of guilty to a red light violation and he limped painfully out of the courtroom to pay his seventy-five dollar fine. Last time I had seen him, his twitching body looked like that of a carnival contortionist, limbs all twisted and tangled, lifeless eyes staring at the dark blue sky. Traces of his own blood and skin spotted the pavement for 150 feet, from the point where he landed to the point where his concave skull came to a rest.

It started with a "routine" traffic stop. The dark figure curbed his 1992 Suzuki 900 sport bike shortly after seeing the blue lights flashing from our squad car. A simple ticket for running the stop sign and he would be on his way. As I exited and approached the motorcycle, I could hear the bike go into first gear. A quick glance back at me and Hancock took off like a rocket, making a run for the Evanston border. Before my partner and I even made it back to our car, I heard the motorcycle redline through three gears. I turned off the blue lights and refused to look at the citizens who were on the street, waiting to see how Chicago's Finest would react to such a blatant disregard for the law. My partner and I both knew that we were not allowed to chase a vehicle for a minor traffic violation so we proceeded to the Evanston-Chicago border in hopes of finding the abandoned bike.

At the corner of Howard and Clark stood a woman, waving frantically for us to stop. Her car was missing its right rear wheel and had extensive damage to the rear quarter panel. There was no other damaged car in sight so it looked like a typical hit-and-run accident. As I asked for a description of the person who hit her, she pointed north into Evanston and yelled, "He's right over there!"

"The cabbie?" I asked, looking at the two taxicabs parked a block down.

"No, the guy on the motorcycle!"

My eyes grew wide as I started to run down the block. I saw his body between the two cabs, whose drivers had stopped to help. The Suzuki 900 had broken through a cinder block wall 100 feet past the point of initial impact. Later the Major Accident Investigation Unit would estimate that Hancock was traveling at between 100 and 130 mph when he struck the car, turning left in front of him. His body was launched, landing 100 feet from the accident, and sliding another 150 feet on the street before coming to rest. Shorts, a T-shirt, and no helmet. I thought he was already dead as the paramedics scooped him up and rushed him to St. Francis Hospital. The new shape of his head earned him the nickname "Vegetable Soup." All of the responding officers on the scene felt that his skull was just a big container holding in his brain, which now had all the potential of a bowl of vegetable soup.

We would learn afterwards that Hancock was driving on a ticket and had an outstanding warrant for multiple burglaries. He had made a run for the city border in the mistaken belief he might escape arrest.

The driver of the vehicle who waved us down was still frantic. Because of Hancock's speed, she never even saw him coming. She kept asking if she had killed Mr. Hancock. She felt so responsible for this piece of garbage of a man. I related the whole story of what happened to the Major Accident guys and I accepted their suggestion to ticket Mr. Hancock for going through the red light even though it would be academic. Hancock was going to die anyway, if he weren't already dead.

As he limped up to the bench, I wondered whether he even knew why he was there. I stared at him to see whether he would recognize me as the one who looked into his dead eyes and assured him that an ambulance was on the way. I wondered whether he knew how much I wanted to curse him out for running from the police. I wondered whether he was aware of the nickname he earned on that hot July night. The only thing I was sure of was that since his run for the border in July, he had been unable to burglarize anyone's home or run from any other police.

Looking at the Face of Death...

By Jim

I am several years into retirement on this Tuesday in late November at 6:30 p.m. A cold mist is falling, driven by a light southwest wind. Leaving my home, I am eastbound on Morse Avenue, approaching the T-intersection and stop sign at Central. It can be a long time before traffic breaks enough to pull out, but tonight there are no cars approaching from either direction.

I make an easy left turn to head north, and instantly, the scene before me does not compute. I slow instinctively. Immediately to my right is a van at the curb, lights and hazard lights on, engine running, but no driver. A bundle of clothing lies in the curb lane about twenty-five yards ahead of the driverless van. In the center lane, just past the clothing, is a tennis shoe, and another twenty-five yards north, I see a beige late model mid-size sedan not moving, straddling the center line. In less than a second, my brain finishes the first process of the scene. The bundle of clothing is in fact a body. The cop still left in me kicks in. I pull my car to the curb lane and pull into a protective position about ten feet short of the crumpled mass and hit my four-ways.

The body is now fully illuminated by my headlights. The un-natural, grotesque position lacks human form and belies a death pose. I look into her face and there is no doubt. A ghostly pallor, empty, unfocused half-opened eyes, an expressionless face lying in a pool of blood that is no longer spreading. The heart has stopped pumping. That old feeling from years ago comes back...a slight quickening of the pulse and a small twist in my stomach. It's been a long time since I looked into the face of death on the street. There's nothing to be done for her.

I look further north and just ahead of the beige sedan is another body. A man lies on his side, and as I kneel next to him, he seems almost to be asleep. He's motionless except for shallow breathing. There is no sign of blood.

"Don't move him!" cries a voice from the west curb. "I'm a nurse; just leave him until help gets here."

I look over to the curb and see a thirtyish woman squatting next to two more dazed persons sitting on the curb. Driver and passenger from the sedan, I learn later.

"I'm a police officer," I lie. It's an easy lie because for the moment I am.

There's a man next to me, now talking to 911, telling them about this terrible scene in Niles. Wrong! There's always been jurisdictional confusion along this stretch of street that borders the suburbs of Skokie and Lincolnwood and the City of Chicago. At this point, the street centerline is the border between Chicago and Skokie, but from the skid marks starting on the east side of the street, the scene belongs to Skokie. It is more than two blocks to the Niles border.

I dial 911 on my cell and the signal hits a Chicago tower.

"Chicago Emergency, Roberts," is the immediate answer. Five years ago, I would have known Roberts personally, but tonight, he's just an anonymous call taker at the other end of the line.

"Connect me with Skokie Emergency!" The tone of my voice does not leave room for additional conversation, but if Chicago call taker Roberts is doing his job, he will monitor the conversation and dispatch Chicago first responders as backup. In just a few seconds, Skokie answers.

"Skokie Police, Sergeant Rosen." Mike Rosen and I are members of a law enforcement professional association and good friends. What is he doing answering 911 calls?

"Mike, this is Jim Padar. You've got a traffic accident with multiple injuries on Central just north of Morse!"

"Shit! Jim, are you sure it's the Skokie side? We're getting swamped with calls and we're on the way, but I was hoping it would be Chicago's."

"No such luck, Mike, and one more thing—it's a fatal."

"Double shit!"

I stand there for a moment, looking for the second vehicle involved in the surrounding death and destruction. Why weren't they wearing their seatbelts? Where is the other car? There are a growing number of spectators, but still no emergency vehicles on the scene.

"Officer!" shouts the nurse. "Could you check on my kids? They're in the van back by Morse Avenue."

I walk slowly back through the scene, around the car with front-end damage and caved windshield, and it starts to dawn on me. The windshield is caved inward toward the passenger compartment. This is a car versus pedestrian accident. I pass the solitary white gym shoe and see her again, brightly illuminated in my headlights. I stop for a moment, turn off my headlights, and leave the four-ways blinking. Standing on the curb, a man with a small white dog on a leash stares, as if transfixed by death. The dog is sniffing curiously at the edge of the pool of blood and seems to me about ready to take a taste.

"Hey!" I yell. The man is startled and looks across the body at me. "Your dog!" He looks down and quickly pulls the leash back.

Just behind my car is the driverless van, and inside are two children. A twelve-year-old girl in the front seat and a toddler in a

rear car seat. They are both crying hysterically. I tap on the window
and show her my star.

"Mom told me to keep the doors locked! She's helping the
people!" screams the older girl.

"That's right. You keep the door locked. But there's something
I need you to do." She stares at me for a moment. "I want you to
turn around and talk to your sister. Don't look out the front any
more. Your sister needs you to talk to her." She releases the seatbelt
and slowly turns, kneeling on the seat now facing to the rear, and
the little sister stops crying almost immediately.

Back at Morse is a traffic nightmare. Northbound lanes
have been stopped for some time, and other northbound traffic
starts pulling over into the southbound lanes to pass them, up
to Morse where they can't go any further. All four lanes are now
filled with northbound traffic at a standstill. A siren and a blast
horn sounds from much farther south. Most likely Chicago's Fire
Engine Company from Lehigh Avenue, but they're never going to
get through. I start to motion traffic westbound onto Morse. The
first few cars look at my blue flannel shirt and khaki cargo pants
and hesitate for a moment. Who the hell am I? A young man in a
Pontiac Grand Am rolls down his window.

"I want to go north to Touhy," he complains.

"There are bodies all over the road up there," I say, waving
toward the north. He pales before my eyes and turns west on Morse.
Hesitantly, the first few cars behind him turn west on Morse, and
the following cars turn without hesitation, flooding our quiet
confusing neighborhood of curving streets with hundreds of cars.
The Chicago Engine Company gets through, followed by Chicago
Police beat car 1621. Roberts, the Chicago call taker, has done his
job correctly. Other suburban emergency vehicles are arriving from
the north. Lincolnwood and Skokie most likely. I would estimate

response time to be about ten minutes, but in actuality, it was probably much shorter.

I walk back to the nurse, and as I pass the front of my car, I see Chicago firemen covering the fatal victim with a tarp. The nurse has been relieved by EMS personnel, and she's telling a Skokie police officer what she saw.

"I was driving right behind her. We were just driving along and they started to cross the street. They were shielding their faces from the rain. They never looked. They just walked into the street. It was wet; she tried to stop, but—" She looks helplessly at the carnage around her.

I interrupt her, "Your kids are okay, but I think they really need you as soon as you can break away from here."

"Thank you. Oh, thank you so much!"

I start to walk back to my car, contemplating how I'm going to extricate my vehicle from the mess at Morse when a young Skokie police officer starts addressing me, several decibels louder than he needs to. The look in his eyes tells me this gruesome scene has him rattled.

"What are you doing here? Get out of here! You have no business here!" Yellow crime scene tape has miraculously appeared from light pole to light pole, and I am definitely on the wrong side.

Simultaneously, I feel a hand on my shoulder and turn to see Sergeant Mike Rosen.

"Jim! Thanks for the call. We didn't know what we had." The Skokie patrolman glances at his sergeant and retreats back into the shadows.

"You're welcome, Mike. I just wanted to stay around long enough to make sure you guys didn't try to push the bodies to the Chicago side."

Mike laughs, a hearty laugh. "Don't think we haven't done that."

"I know, Mike!" More laughter. Cops' macabre humor. It's the same all over.

Back at Morse, the Skokie patrolman is all Mr. Manners now.

"Sorry, sir. I'll move my squad and help you get out of here."

"Thanks…and officer…" he looks back at me expectantly. "You don't need to apologize for doing your job."

I reach my shopping destination about twenty minutes late, nose into a parking place, and turn off the engine. How many people's lives have changed in the past half hour? Those children in the van will never forget this fateful evening. The man and woman pedestrians; husband and wife? She is deceased. Will he recover? The driver and passenger in the striking vehicle; they will relive this moment far too many times in the coming months. How quickly our lives can change. The headlights on my car turn themselves off, having grown impatient with me to exit the vehicle. I bow my head for a moment and pray for them all.

As a homicide detective, I had more than my share of handling and examining deceased persons. Long ago, I decided that whatever we are while alive stops being represented by our bodies at the moment of death. At death, what was our physical being is no longer relevant. From that instant forward, the human body ceases to embody our spirit, our essence, our soul. A French theologian named Pierre Teilhard de Chardin perhaps said it best:

"We are not human beings having a spiritual experience.

We are spiritual beings having a human experience."

It's All in a Name

By Jay

My partner and I were finishing up a typical noise disturbance call when we heard a couple of our fellow officers get called upon by dispatch.

"Twenty-four thirty-three, take the auto accident with injuries at Clark and Norwood. Fire's rolling."

We decided to tag along and be like one of the other hundred or so gawking motorists causing a gapers block. After about thirty seconds into our commute to the accident scene, we heard the other officers on the radio in that unmistakable voice that says, "Things don't look so good."

"Twenty-four thirty-three, emergency. We need a supervisor and a fire engine now. We got two trapped in a car and one looks fatal. Notify Major Accidents."

We hit the lights and sirens and almost immediately skidded to a halt in front of the wreck. SUV versus compact car—things didn't look so good. We jumped out of our squad and started our attempt at prying open the passenger side door. It took four of us, but we were able to get it open. When I looked inside to see what we were dealing with, his eyes caught mine. The driver was a white male in his forties. His eyes and mouth were wide open. His head was cocked sideways, almost as if he were trying to look directly at us. I couldn't stop staring into those eyes. I was trying to read what I have read in many eyes before. "Hurry up and help." "Get me outta this thing." "Thank God you're here."

I stared and stared into the driver's eyes as we tried to determine the passenger's condition; she was a bloody mess, curled up in a ball on the passenger side floor. After what seemed like days, but was actually only seconds, the fire department pulled up and sprang into action like the professionals they were. The firemen cranked up the old jaws of life and began working on getting the driver out as the paramedics began extricating the female passenger. The female began to scream as her crushed legs were pulled from beneath the dashboard. Those screams were exactly what I was hoping for. They let me know that she was still alive.

On the other side of the car, the firemen were finally able to pop off the door and pull out the driver. As they threw him on the stretcher and raced him into the ambulance, I took a final stare into those eyes. I was beginning to understand what those eyes were trying to tell me.

"You're too late."

At the end of our shift, I was tempted to take a look at the accident report. For some reason, I wanted to know the driver's name, or where he lived. I wanted to know which member of his family was notified of his death—whether it was his wife or a sibling.

I couldn't do it. I just needed to go home and get some sleep. The driver's anonymity would help me to forget what I had seen, what his eyes had told me. Hopefully, without a name or any type of identity, this memory would quickly fade like so many others.

The Dummy: Part I
The Investigation

By Jim

Supreme Court decision at
www.OnBeingACop.com/gallery/decision.pdf

Heater case: Police jargon for an incident likely to garner unusual media attention for any reason; notoriety of the victim or offender, location of the crime, or an infinite number of political considerations. Heater cases are always assigned to more experienced, seasoned investigator teams.

Chicago, Monday, July 26, 1971

It was a warm summer day in Chicago, and I was working out of Maxwell Street Homicide with Phil Ducar. I was the "senior" investigator on the team, having been assigned to Area Four Homicide for some eighteen months. Phil had been with the unit for almost three whole months, so between us we had less than two years' experience investigating murders. Although they called Maxwell Street Homicide "The Murder Factory"—averaging five or more murders a week—we were definitely the most junior team in the lineup that day.

After roll call, we reviewed the active aggravated battery cases we had been assigned as paper jobs and discovered we had a hospital interview to do in Park Ridge and a witness to talk to on the far northwest side of the city. Perfect! We would head out, take care of business, and stop at my house for an early lunch. I called my wife Karla to tell her to expect us. It would be a great start to a beautiful summer day. We had no idea that before it ended, we would inadvertently become the lead investigators on a "heater case" that would later become the subject of a book and a made-for-TV movie.

The hospital interview turned out to be more time-consuming than productive, and our witness interview was an elderly woman who was thrilled to have any visitors to her home, much less two real live homicide investigators. The morning's activities dragged on much longer than anticipated. As a result, it was nearly noon when we climbed the steps of my Chicago bungalow on the city's northwest side to grab a quick lunch.

My two sons, Christopher, age three-and-a-half, and Craig, age two, greeted us at the door but quickly lost interest as a roomful of toys drew them back to the living room. We sat down to a cup of coffee and a newspaper that proclaimed Mohammed Ali's victory over Jimmy Ellis, the Apollo 15 *Endeavour* launch, carrying lunar module *Falcon* for another manned lunar landing, and oh yes, folks were in an uproar that the price of gasoline had skyrocketed to just over forty cents a gallon.

I called the office to check in and tell them we would be down for lunch. Phil and Karla were discussing recipes for deviled eggs when I hung up.

"Sorry to interrupt, but we have a body, partner."

"We do? Where?" asked a very surprised Phil.

"The Viceroy Hotel, 1519 West Warren, Room 201, on the scene."

"Our job or are we the assist?"

"Nope, it's all ours."

We gulped our coffee and Karla put some toasted English muffins in a bag as we headed for the door. The boys, engrossed in play, never noticed us leave. We were farther away from the crime scene than we would normally be, and when I reached the main street, I hit the flashing headlights and siren on our unmarked car until we reached the expressway.

Once on the expressway, we killed the lights and siren—they would only confuse other drivers and wouldn't save us any time. We headed inbound on the Kennedy and made the bend to the outbound Eisenhower. Midday traffic was light. We exited at Ashland and arrived on scene in a very respectable time. We parked at the front of the hotel just as the mobile crime lab was arriving.

The Viceroy Hotel opened in 1930 as the Union Park Hotel, apparently named for Union Park, directly across the street. The building was an example of the modern art deco architectural style popular at that time. As ghetto hotels went, it was several cuts above the typical flophouses located within blocks. But it was what we called a "hot sheets" hotel where some of the rooms would be rented several times in a twenty-four-hour period.

District personnel had secured the room and were awaiting our arrival. As Phil and I entered 201, we noted a putrid odor that we immediately identified as human decomposition, but it wasn't as overwhelming as we had previously experienced in more extreme cases. The window on the far side of the room was open and the curtains waved lazily in the breeze. The closet in the room could only be opened by closing the door to the hallway. Closing that hallway door reduced the summer breeze, but opening the closet intensified the smell. The source was a black female in a somewhat grotesque upside-down position. She was clad only in a white girdle pulled up to her midriff. Atop her body were two blood-stained pillows.

Homicide investigators lump their cases into three major classifications: "smoking gun" where the offender is on the scene, "known but flown" where there are immediate eyewitness accounts identifying the offender, and "mystery" where very little is known at the outset.

The crime lab technicians photographed and then removed the body from the closet, revealing that the woman had apparently been beaten about the head. Her upside-down position facilitated the flow of blood to the closet floor where we found a small purse with no identification.

"Mys...ter...ry," Phil elongated the word as we stared at the body.

District wagon personnel removed the woman for transport to the hospital and, ultimately, to the morgue. We gave the single bed a closer look. It appeared clean and freshly made even after removing the bedspread and sheets. The mattress was moderately soiled, but when we turned the mattress over, we found the underside soaked with blood that had also contaminated the box spring. We left the lab personnel to gather and catalog pertinent evidence and headed down to the lobby to interview the couple who had discovered the body.

They could add little, reporting only that upon entering the room to enjoy some afternoon ardor, they noted a strange odor and opened the closet to discover the victim. We gathered their identifying information and sent them on their way. Since they were both married to other spouses, they would probably be unable to share their story with friends and family. We promised to be discreet if we found it necessary to re-contact them.

Mattie, the hotel manager, was a bit more helpful. She recalled renting the room to a black couple shortly after midnight Saturday night, Sunday morning. At about 2 a.m., the male left alone. Mattie called the room, and receiving no response, she dispatched the night maid to check the room and remake it if it were vacant. The maid reported that the room was vacant but the sheets and pillows were missing. Mattie instructed the maid to remake the room with fresh sheets and new pillows. In short order, the room was ready to rent again. In fact, Mattie recalled that the room had been rented at least twice more before the couple with keen noses checked in this morning. Unfortunately, the registration tickets for the weekend had been sent to the property manager's office down-town, as was the custom on Monday mornings.

Mattie had one other nugget of information—a golden nugget, in fact. When the black couple had checked in Saturday night/ Sunday morning, Rufus, a gentleman friend of hers, was keeping her company in the lobby. The man had waved at Rufus, and Rufus had smiled and waved back, and at that moment, Mattie sensed that the man was a deaf-mute. An hour or so later when the man left alone, he again waved at Rufus. Yes, she knew where Rufus worked—Wieboldt's department store downtown.

We called our office and gave a verbal rundown of what we had. The office assigned us an assist: Investigator Frank Bertucci, a six-year veteran in the unit. Frank, with years of homicide experi-ence, as opposed to our months of homicide experience, would bring an extra hand to the investigation. Phil and I would remain the lead investigators, but we welcomed Frank Bertucci's help. He knew the streets, and he was an indefatigable worker. None of us yet knew that we were working a "heater case."

Frank would expedite the fingerprinting of the victim at the morgue and then head downtown to interview Rufus. Phil and I would go directly downtown to the property manager's office to retrieve the weekend registration records for Room 201 at the Viceroy Hotel. We would all meet back at our Maxwell Street office to compare notes.

Phil and I arrived back at the office shortly after 5 p.m., our quitting time. The case was still officially a Death Investigation, but Phil and I knew that as soon as the autopsy reports came back, it would become a murder. Still, pending those results, and with little else to go on, it was difficult to justify overtime at this point. That changed very quickly.

Pat Angelo, our man detailed to the morgue, had managed to expedite the autopsy. Preliminary findings were blunt trauma to the head and strangulation. At the same time, the records section called with a hit on the victim's prints, a street prostitute well known on West Madison Street. We had a murder and the victim's name was Earline Brown, thirty-eight years old.

Almost simultaneously, Frank Bertucci came bounding up the long staircase with an enthusiastic announcement.

"The man you're looking for is Donald Lang—they call him 'The Dummy.' He's probably working right now, over on South Water Market for Strompolis Produce."

Phil Ducar and I were surprised. We knew Bertucci was good but....

Bertucci continued to explain to us that he learned the name from interviewing Rufus—who had known Donald for nearly fifteen years and confirmed that Donald was indeed a deaf-mute. In addition, Frank had just recently had conversation with an individual who worked the market, stating that Donald "was back"— back from a previous murder charge that he had somehow beaten in court. "Police persecution" was the opinion of fellow workers in the market area. It was our first hint that the case was heating up, but we didn't know it at the time.

Phil and I headed over to South Water Market and found Mario Pullano on the loading dock. Yes, he knew Donald. Yes, Donald was here now. When Mario heard we were there to arrest Donald Lang, he exploded. We were treated to a diatribe, alleging harassment and persecution of a harmless deaf-mute. Reluctantly, Mario brought Donald to us. Donald Lang was of slight but very muscular build. His eyes were intensely observant, and he was obviously somehow absorbing what was happening, but we took him into custody without resistance. Our case was near boiling now, but we had no clue. We were only six hours into a mystery murder investigation, and we were heading back to the office with an offender in custody! It was probably only seconds after we left the market that Mario made his calls to the newspapers.

On the second floor of the Maxwell Street Homicide office, we handcuffed Lang to a heavy iron ring on the wall. Somehow, we located a police officer who was fluent in sign language, having been raised by deaf parents. In a very short time, he was there and our first real attempt to interview Donald began. We started with the Miranda warnings, but he gave us no indication that he understood anything that was being said or signed to him. We wrote some words with paper and pen…nothing. In short order, our sign language expert had an opinion.

"He cannot read, he cannot write, he does not sign, and I doubt very much if he can read lips to any extent."

I looked at my watch. It was well after our 5 p.m. quitting time, but it was obvious we were not going to be going home. I called my wife and told her not to expect me until late—very late. I said goodnight to our two sons. Christopher seemed to grasp the conversation and I actually had a few words with him and he said goodnight. Craig just listened intently, smiling, and at the end of the conversation, responded with a single word. "Bye."

Ducar, Bertucci, and I returned to the interrogation room and went through the motions again.

CAN YOU READ OR WRITE? We wrote in block letters on a blank page.

DO YOU UNDERSTAND ENGLISH?

No cogent response. But Donald was an anomaly. I sensed that his eyes were intensely perceptive. If he were truly deaf and dumb and unable to communicate in a normal way, he must have learned to interpret what was happening by uncanny powers of observation.

Suddenly, Donald grabbed the pen from Bertucci and began to draw. A crude drawing by any standard, but he was communicating! He drew three stick figures, pointing to one and then to himself, apparently indicating that was him. Two more stick figures, one with a mass of lines at the top, apparently to indicate hair. He pointed to that figure and pantomimed breasts by cupping his hands to his chest. Then he drew a third figure, again with hair, and he wrote a number above each figure, 5, 8, and 3. Then he drew a long line from the stick figure with breasts and redrew the figure at the far left edge of the page. He stopped for a moment and looked at the three of us; then he held up three fingers, pointed at the leftmost stick figure, X'd her out with great emphasis, and threw the pen forcibly down onto the table. He almost appeared relaxed at that moment. He had told us his story! He looked at us with an aura of satisfaction.

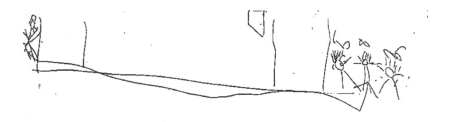

The three of us were astounded. Something very profound had just occurred, but what? We had no idea what the drawing meant. We each initialed the drawing, preparatory to inventorying it for evidence. I stood there for a moment just gazing at Donald. He stared back at me with that uncanny intensity. Intensity, not hostility. Then I motioned Ducar and Bertucci out of the room and closed the door. We walked several feet from the interrogation room into our office area.

"There's blood on his sock," I said quietly.

"What?" exclaimed Phil and Frank simultaneously.

"Reddish brown stains, probably dried blood on his one sock."

We returned to the interrogation room. Donald had rolled down both of his socks so the stains were no longer visible.

"The son-of-a-bitch can hear! I'm tellin' ya', he can hear!" shouted Frank.

"Frank! He couldn't have heard us—the door was closed, and we were all the way into the office," I replied.

"Then how does he do it?"

"I think he just watches everything that is going on around him. Maybe he caught my glance to his socks; I don't know…but I don't think he can hear."

We requisitioned a paper jumpsuit from the 12th District lockup and had Donald strip by pantomiming the motions. He was cooperative. We inventoried all of his clothing, including his socks.

"Padar!" It was the Third Watch sergeant shouting to me from the office. "It's City News Service on the PAX. They want to know what's up with Donald Lang?" The call on the restricted Police Auxiliary line confirmed it was an internal call, probably from the Press Office at Police Headquarters.

"Shit! How did they get a hold of this? Tell them we don't know—it's an ongoing investigation…. Tell 'em I'll call back." I knew it would only be a temporary ploy. No reporter worth his salt would believe that I would call back. They would call again for certain. But thanks to the sergeant, they now had my name.

Conference time. Ducar, Bertucci, the sergeant, and I sat down and reviewed what we had so far. We would need to tie up some loose ends, but we all agreed once the details were put down on paper, we would have enough to charge Donald Lang with murder. The sergeant called the State's Attorney's Office and requested a member of its Felony Review Unit respond to our office to review the case and approve charges.

Third Watch teams were dispatched to bring Mattie and Rufus in for formal written statements, which we knew the state's attorney would insist upon. Another team was asked to cajole some local denizens into participating in a lineup with Donald Lang. Rufus had known Lang for years, but Mattie did not have the same familiarity with him. A pair of positive identifications from a lineup would be the icing on the cake, and all it would cost us would be a few half pints of Richard's Wild Irish Rose fortified wine for the shill participants.

Things moved rapidly with the additional manpower that the Third Watch provided. By the time Felony Review arrived, we had tied up what we thought was a very neat package, but my heart sank when the state's attorney walked in. He was not one of my favorites, not at all what I would consider decisive. Other homicide investigators had a history of problematical rulings from him—but he was the man for the day, and we had no choice but to roll with it.

We sat down and began to review the case with him when he stopped us short.

"Donald Lang?" he asked. "The deaf-mute?"

"Yeah…I guess…if there's only one of him."

"Holy shit! I have to call my office."

"Sure thing," I replied. "You know where the phone is."

"No, no, no. I have to talk privately." And he promptly disappeared.

The sergeant shouted that the press was calling again….

Phil Ducar and I looked at one another.

"Who the hell is Donald Lang?"

We corralled Frank Bertucci.

"What's going on? What's with this Lang guy? What is it we don't know?"

Frank filled us in as best he could. Donald Lang had been arrested and charged with murder by our office several years previously in a very similar case. The case had languished in the court system because of Lang's inability to cooperate with counsel. The investigators on the previous case assumed that Lang had been dealt with appropriately, but suddenly, several weeks ago, Donald had reappeared in his old haunts and begun working in the market area again.

"He must have beat it somehow," Frank shrugged.

"Yeah, and now it looks like déjà vu all over again," I said.

The Felony Review attorney returned from his clandestine phone call. We sensed immediately that there was trouble with this case—big trouble. He went through the motions with us, the lineup, the written witness statements, the mysterious drawing, the bloodstained sock. He made a second phone call, very brief, covering his mouth and the mouthpiece with his hand.

"Photograph him and fingerprint him…"

Was there a glimmer of hope?

"and then release him!"

"Release him?" I almost shouted. "Who the hell is this guy?"

"Release him. Send his clothing to the lab and see if that's really blood. See if you can find some more witnesses who saw him with the victim…but send him home tonight."

I was incredulous. I was extremely upset and, most likely, it was in part because I had little respect for this particular state's attorney. But I also knew that it had not been a unilateral decision on his part. His office, his superiors perhaps, were no doubt supporting his decision.

We sent Lang back to the 12th District to be booked, printed, and photographed, along with signed release papers. Phil and I sat down at a typewriter to begin what would be an eight-page single-spaced murder format report.

"Padar! For Christ's sake, get this goddamn reporter off my back!" The sergeant called me away from the typewriter. I was nearing the end of my patience. I talked to Philip Wattley from the *Tribune*, and I am sure I was short with him, but I gave him the basics of the case, including the fact that Donald Lang had been released without being charged.

Almost simultaneously, a reporter from the *Chicago Daily News* showed up in our office. Barry Felcher was a pleasant, low-key guy, and I felt myself calm a bit as I reviewed the case for him. There was something about his physically showing up in the office that generated an element of respect.

Phil Ducar and I finished our report at 1 a.m, but we knew we had to be back in a little more than seven hours. There was a lot of work to be done on this case. It was 2 a.m. when I stumbled into my bed, and I was exhausted, but sleep was fitful as I reviewed every angle of the case over and over. Somehow, I would have to be ready for a very full day, starting first thing in the morning....

Tuesday, July 27, 1971

Morning came way too soon, but I was due at Second Watch Roll Call at 8:30 a.m. We briefly discussed the Earline Brown Homicide. Area Four Homicide Commander Charlie Azzarello and the Second Watch sergeant indicated that they had read our reports. Additional teams would be assigned to assist us in the follow-up on the loose ends. During roll call, the unit secretary took a phone call on the PAX line. It was Citywide Homicide Commander Frank Flanagan calling for Charlie. Charlie took the phone. It was mostly a one-way conversation, with Azzarello scribbling some notes. When he hung up, he stared at me for a moment. That was never good.

"Padar," he said, "report to the Chief of the Criminal Division at the State's Attorney's Office at 26th and Cal. Here's the room number."

"Me? Now?"

"Is your name Padar? Yes, now!" He swiveled his chair away from me, conversation over.

I shrugged and drew a set of car keys. No, this couldn't be good.

I was ushered into the office with very little wait. The chief of the criminal division had a very nice office, much nicer than the run-of-the-mill assistant state's attorney's. But the imposing surroundings made me ill at ease.

"Investigator Padar?"

"Yes."

"What's this about?" He tossed the morning edition of the *Chicago Tribune* across the desk to me with an article about the Lang case circled. "Read the underlined part."

The byline was Philip Wattley. The last two paragraphs were underlined:

[Padar] said the assistant state's attorney reviewed the evidence the police had gathered and ordered [Lang] released without explaining why.

Padar said the police would drop the case, and said it would be up to the state's attorney's office to pursue the matter or prosecute the man.

Well, I thought, that's not too cool. The Felony Review attorney had given us specific instructions on what additional investigative steps he wanted us to perform, but it was true he never explained why he was releasing Lang. Still, it was police responsibility to continue the investigation. My mind was racing. I had been tired and pissed when I talked to Wattley the night before, but had I actually said that? I had also talked to Barry Felcher from the *Chicago Daily News*, but that was a more relaxed in-person conversation in my office. I looked the large mahogany desk over—the *Chicago Daily News* was nowhere to be seen. Could I bluff? It would be a dangerous gambit for an inexperienced homicide investigator, but how much worse could it be for me?

"Boss, I never said that. I talked to the *Daily News* at the same time." (Well, almost the same time, I rationalized to myself.) "I'll bet they didn't print that." I thought I detected him soften a bit, so I decided to try to shift the tenor of the conversation. I leaned forward in my chair.

"Chief, who is Donald Lang? What's going on here? I must be missing something." My body language and tone of voice was student to teacher. It worked.

"Donald Lang was charged with another murder in your area over five years ago, very similar circumstances."

"I've heard about it in general terms, but I wasn't even a police officer when that one happened."

Gradually, the Chief of the Criminal Division, Cook County State's Attorney's Office, shifted modes and became a mentor, a tutor that morning in his office. Now he leaned forward in his seat.

"You know Lang was in custody on that other case and it kicked around here for the last five years. Then about six months ago, the Supreme Court of Illinois issued an opinion that ultimately re- sulted in Lang's release just a few months ago. And now you guys call us last night and you've got him again for pretty much the same thing. You understand why we're handling this with kid gloves?"

"Chief, honestly, my partner and I didn't know anything about that previous case when we—"

"I know, I know," he interrupted. "But that doesn't change the circumstances. This is going to be a high-profile case, and you guys will have to dot your i's and cross your t's before we approve charges.... You understand where we're coming from?"

"We're on it, boss, really. We're doing everything you asked last night." I was feeling a bit more emboldened. "But just do us one favor?"

"What's that?" he asked.

"When we finish everything you want and we call Felony Review again, send us a different guy."

He smiled as he stood, but he didn't answer.

"Have a good day, Jim," he said as he shook my hand. I took notice that he used my first name. "I'll have my office send you a copy of that Illinois Supreme Court Opinion. If we go to trial on this one, you should at least be aware of what's in it."

"Thanks. That would be great."

As I left his office, I dashed down the stairs to the newsstand on the second floor. I had one more item of business to tend to. I bought a copy of the *Chicago Daily News* and sat down on a nearby bench to scan the articles. There it was:

FREE DEAF MUTE IN SECOND KILLING
By Barry Felcher

Barry had written a much longer story than Wattley had in the *Tribune*, and while he quoted me extensively, there were no smartass comments about the police dropping the case. If the Chief of the Criminal Division took the trouble to read this story, I was home free.

I went back to the Maxwell Street Homicide office.

"Well?" asked the unit secretary.

"Well what?" I asked innocently. I knew that if the State's Attorney's Office had called the homicide commander downtown to complain about me, he was now calling back to tell him that everything was settled.

"What happened?" asked the sergeant.

"Oh yeah…26th and Cal…" I answered absentmindedly. "Yeah, we're cool. We talked about the case—he's sending me some legal background—keep an eye out for it."

They both looked at me quizzically as I left the office in search of my partner.

Phil and I spent the rest of the day looking for the couples who had rented Room 201 at the Viceroy Hotel after Lang had left but before Earline Brown's body was found. Apparently, some of them had used fictitious names…no surprise there. We called the Crime Lab for results on the blood tests. They told us that the blood on

Donald's sock was type B+. From previous medical records, we believed Donald was O+, so if that could be confirmed, we could prove that the blood on his sock was not his. But they were having trouble determining the victim's blood type.... Another day would pass.

Wednesday, July 28, 1971

The Earline Brown murder case dragged on for another day. We did a casual inquiry from some sources on South Water Market and determined that Donald Lang had returned to work there. If and when we got the green light from the State's Attorney's Office, it wouldn't be hard to find him.

There was some problem with the blood samples at the Crime Lab so we stopped in for some face time. The lab technician was pleasant, but the problem was typing Earline Brown's blood sample from the Coroner's Office. Because of decomposition, it was proving difficult, but the lab technician seemed certain that they would eventually be able to make a determination. Only about 10 percent of the population have B+ blood. If Earline's blood type turned out to be B+, it would be another factor to present in the case against Donald Lang. Of course, there was no DNA analysis available in 1971.

While we were at headquarters, we pulled the file on the previous murder for which Donald Lang had been arrested. A quick review showed marked similarities between the two cases.

We had no further luck locating the persons who might have rented Room 201 after Earline's body had been stashed.

Another day of dead ends.

Thursday, July 29, 1971

Thursday and Friday were our days off for the week. While we wanted to work the case to conclusion, we were doing nothing that made us indispensable and that could not be accomplished by other members of our unit. Indeed, many of them had already provided valuable witness accounts that placed Donald and Earline together on the night she disappeared, as well as other details that would become critical to the case.

Thus the arrest of Donald Lang became anticlimactic for Phil and me. The Crime Lab came through with a blood type for Earline: B+. Investigators from our office obtained a search warrant for taking a blood sample from Lang. They hand-carried it down to the Crime Lab. It was indeed O+. Other investigators from our office obtained an arrest warrant for Donald Lang, with the state's attorney's approval. Donald was arrested at the apartment of his father and stepmother at about 9 p.m. that evening.

While Phil and I were disappointed at not being present for the arrest, the case file indicated the total team effort that had taken place the previous four days. Phil and I were new guys, of course, and the assistance of our entire unit was testimony to the spirit that brought the investigation to a successful conclusion for us.

Now the ball would be in the state's attorney's court. This would become a history-making case.

The Dummy: Part II
The Trial & Epilogue
By Jim

If I thought this investigation itself was unusual, the trial of Donald Lang and the aftermath was truly a conundrum. As the weeks dragged into months, it became apparent to me that Donald Lang's notoriety was strictly due to the opinion by the Illinois Supreme Court that resulted in his release. That, and an unusually intense interest by the local media.

The Chief of the State's Attorney's Criminal Division, as promised, sent me a copy of the Illinois Supreme Court opinion regarding Lang's earlier murder case. I read the eight-page decision with great interest.

In a 1960 landmark case, *Dusky v. U.S.*, the United States Supreme Court established that a defendant must understand the charges against him and must have the ability to aid his attorney in his own defense. From what I knew about Donald Lang, that would be an impossibility. But when I read *Donald Lang v. Department of Mental Health* (September 29, 1970), the Illinois Supreme Court seemed to be saying, "Go ahead and try Lang anyway."

After Donald Lang had been arrested in November 1965, in a case remarkably similar to our present case, he was never brought to trial because he was unable to cooperate with counsel. His case kicked around for nearly five years while Lang was held at the Illinois Department of Mental Health. His attorney, Lowell Myers, moved that Donald be released from custody because he had never been given a trial and, therefore, had never been convicted of any crime. Furthermore, the Department of Mental Health had opined that Lang would "never acquire the necessary communication skills needed to participate and cooperate in his trial."

So the crux of Lowell Myers' argument was simply that Lang had been in custody for several years, never tried, never convicted, and there was no likelihood that he would ever go to trial. Under these circumstances, Lang was simply entitled to discharge, according to Myers.

The Illinois Supreme Court didn't quite see it that way, ruling instead that Donald Lang, "handicapped as he is and facing an indefinite commitment because of the pending indictment against him, should be given the opportunity to obtain trial to determine whether or not he is guilty as charged or should be released." While earlier acknowledging the principle mandated in *Dusky v. U.S.*, the Supreme Court gave no guidance on how that might be accomplished in the final portion of its ruling.

The first case went back to the Criminal Court at 26th and California. Upon review, the State's Attorney's Office found that two of its witnesses were dead, one was dying, and a fourth could not be located. In February 1971, the State dropped the case against Donald Lang and he was released from custody without trial. Less than six months later, Phil Ducar and I arrested Donald Lang for a second murder with eerie similarities.

The entire scenario seemed poised to repeat itself. Assistant State's Attorneys Joe DiNatale and Tony Corsentino were assigned to prosecute our case. They prepared to go to trial. When I asked about the inability of Lang to cooperate with his attorney, they cited the Illinois Supreme Court opinion mandating that Lang "be given the opportunity to obtain a trial...."

Donald Lang was going to be tried for the murder of Earline Brown, and apparently, questions regarding his competency, or lack thereof, would not be addressed. It seemed to me to be a formula for a legal disaster. But at that time, I was only a University of Illinois–Chicago junior, a student of criminal justice—what did I know? In retrospect, perhaps the Illinois Supreme Court was guilty of rolling the judicial dice. If Lang were tried and found not guilty, the problem would simply go away. But—and it was a big BUT— if Donald Lang were convicted, there would be inevitable appeals based upon *Dusky v. U.S.*, which would require the defendant to have the ability to cooperate with counsel.

DiNatale and Corsentino prepared with all the fervor associated with a major murder trial. They were relatively young but very experienced prosecutors. Over the next several months, they assembled the case based upon witness accounts and physical evidence, but no one had actually seen Donald Lang kill Earline Brown. It would be a circumstantial case, a strong one they felt, but still a circumstantial case.

Lowell Myers would once again represent Donald Lang. Lowell was an amazing man. He was born with impaired hearing, and by the time he was a teenager, he was essentially deaf, but those early years had provided enough hearing for him to learn to speak. As the years passed, however, his ability to articulate began to deteriorate. His lack of hearing resulted in his gradually losing the ability to form his words with clarity. He struggled continuously to maintain the capacity to speak. He became a CPA and went to law school part-time. He graduated number two in his class at John Marshall Law School. As he built a successful law practice, he dedicated himself to helping deaf clients.

Lowell Myers was a consummate gentleman. He would prove to be a tough opponent in the adversarial world of our criminal justice system. But there was never any personal rancor that so many times overshadows the world of the criminal trial courtroom. In short, I respected him and liked him as a person. When he passed away in November of 2006, I was out of town. I was saddened by both his passing and my inability to attend his services.

The trial of Donald Lang began on January 17, 1972, some six months after his arrest. He had spent the entire time in jail awaiting trial, much as he had in his previous case. Questions of his ability to understand the charges against him and cooperate with counsel were not addressed. The Illinois Supreme Court had mandated that he be tried on the first case; it never foresaw the possibility that he would be charged in a second murder. By its order, Lang would have to have his trial.

I was completing my second year as a homicide investigator, but this was my first major murder trial as lead investigator. In the early 1970s, the lead investigator sat at the counsel table with the prosecutors to assist with the details of the case. DiNatale and Corsentino didn't need much assistance, but nevertheless, it was a heady time for me. The trial would run six days, but in the month of January, I would spend nearly 100 hours at the Criminal Courts Building both in preparation and at the actual trial. They were simultaneously tense and mind-numbing hours.

My testimony came early in the trial, and I nearly derailed proceedings with a bonehead error born of inexperience. I had reviewed my written reports to the point of nearly memorizing them, and DiNatale and Corsentino had spent several hours preparing me for my testimony. But when I got on the stand, my mind raced with anticipation, a deadly enemy of courtroom witnesses. I had spent several hours on the stand and things had gone well. Corsentino had asked all the questions I had prepped for, and I sensed he was concluding as he turned toward the counsel table, but suddenly, he turned back to me with one final question, one very simple question, but a question we had not prepped for.

"By the way, did you make a determination as to the age of the defendant, Donald Lang?"

It was a fact that needed to be in the trial record to show that Donald was an adult at the time of the murder. But it was a question we had not prepped. Police officers spend classroom hours on courtroom testimony, appearance, demeanor, and other factors that impact credibility, but they also stress a cardinal rule: Only answer what was asked; never, never volunteer information beyond what was asked. A simple rule. And it was a simple question with a one word answer, "Yes." But the human brain is an amazing organ, and under stress, it can process thought patterns with amazing speed. My mind raced with anticipation—if Donald Lang were deaf and dumb and could not read, write, or use sign language, how did I determine his age? I, of course, knew exactly how I had determined his age, and I was happy to include that with my answer:

"Yes, sir, according to police records—"

Judge Strayhorn bolted upright and shouted.

"Strike that! The jury is instructed to disregard it. Wipe it completely out of your minds!"

Corsentino waited just a moment and then rephrased the question.

"What was age of the defendant, officer?"

"Twenty-five," I replied.

But Strayhorn wasn't done. He banged the gavel sharply several times. If the jury were not wide-awake and alert moments before, they certainly were now. Then he did a curious thing. With the jury and the entire courtroom's attention riveted on him, he repeated the offending phrase.

"The jury is instructed to disregard any statement that this officer made about 'according to police records.' I want you to wipe it completely out of your minds. We will have a short recess.... Take the jury out." If the jury missed the words the first time, they certainly did not the second time, and they were obviously aware that the phrase had enormous significance. They would never be able to wipe it completely out of their minds.

I think Strayhorn really believed that I had made the statement intentionally and maybe even that Corsentino had put me up to it, but neither was true. It was simply an error of an inexperienced investigator at his very first murder trial. Strayhorn vented on me for some time and would not allow Corsentino to come to my defense.

Meantime, the wheels were turning in the mind of the defense attorney, Lowell Myers. He immediately moved for a mistrial. My heart sank. After months of preparation, the thought of starting all over again was more than I could imagine. Apparently, Judge Strayhorn was sobered by the thought also. He denied the motion and Strayhorn, along with the attorneys, crafted a stipulation to be read to the jury. It was read to them when they returned to the courtroom:

"Donald Lang has never been convicted of any crime, either in the State of Illinois or anywhere else."

I could only believe that the reaction to my answer and the removal of the jury from the courtroom served more firmly to fix the offending phrase in their minds. They must have thought, "Where there's smoke, there's fire."

The trial proceeded.

Mattie, the Viceroy Hotel desk clerk, testified to seeing Donald Lang check in with Earline Brown and sometime later leave alone. Mattie's friend Rufus confirmed those facts with added credibility because he had known Donald Lang for many years.

Other witnesses from the seamy side of West Madison Street's bars, serving as dens of prostitution, painted a vivid, albeit sordid, picture of daily life on the street. The jury was being exposed to a side of ghetto life that I doubt many of them ever knew existed.

Personnel from the Crime Lab presented the blood evidence along with other trace evidence that strongly inferred that Donald and Earline had been together.

Donald Lang began the trial with a bored demeanor that over the days would gradually morph into impatience and restlessness.

I believe that as the trial wore on, his uncanny powers of intense observation brought him to the conclusion that not everybody in the courtroom was his friend. From early on, he scowled at Corsentino. In the courtroom, he seemed to interact mostly with Tony Corsentino and the net effect was negative. It was an inner boiling side of Lang that I had not seen before. Then one day before court had even convened, Donald began screeching and wailing in the bullpen cell behind the courtroom. It was disturbing to listen to and would have been disastrous if the jury were to witness such outbursts. Lowell Myers asked that Donald be excused from the courtroom. DiNatale and Corsentino objected, but Strayhorn wisely agreed with Myers. Donald was led from the courtroom, out of earshot of the jury. No reason for the defendant's absence was ever given to the jury.

As the case wound down, the state had presented an impressive case against Donald Lang. Impressive, but nevertheless circumstantial. With the exception of Lang, to the very best of our knowledge, there were no direct witnesses to the crime. And Donald couldn't tell us.

Lowell Myers offered some hypotheses as to other possible offenders, but while they might have been reasonable alternative explanations, he had no way of convincing the jury that they might be true.

After a six-day trial, final arguments were presented on Monday, January 24th, 1972. The trial and jury instructions concluded, the jury was sent out to supper in the late afternoon. Upon their return, they deliberated a scant two hours and returned a verdict of guilty. I think it was an outcome the courts, particularly the Illinois Supreme Court, had never anticipated. As a result of its decision in the earlier murder case and its mandate to provide Donald Lang a trial, the case resulted in the conviction of a person unable to understand the charges against him and unable to aid his attorney in his own defense. More than fertile grounds for appeal in this novice homicide investigator's opinion.

Judge Earl Strayhorn continued the sentencing hearing several times over the next five months while he wrestled with an appropriate sentence and an appropriate facility for Donald Lang. The latter was the most difficult—there was simply no facility that seemed to fit Lang's unique needs. In early May, Strayhorn pronounced sentence on Donald Lang. The transcript of that final hearing read in part:

It will be the sentence of this court that Donald Lang be taken from the bar of this court and turned over to officials of the Department of Corrections for eventual incarceration in the Joliet Reception and Diagnostic and Special Treatment Center. I want the record to show that he is not to be removed from that facility without prior approval of this court. I am sentencing him specifically to that facility with the understanding that he is not to be placed in the general prison population as long as he is suffering from his present physical disabilities, for a minimum period of fourteen years and a maximum period not to exceed twenty-five years.

It was a busy news day and the glow of the Donald Lang case had worn thin on the media at least for the moment. Some of the daily papers did not carry the story at all, while others buried it, grouped with other newsbytes of the day. But the saga of Donald Lang was far from over. Appeals would be filed by Lang's newly appointed legal team as the criminal justice system struggled with what to do with him.

Less than a year after his sentencing, I was told that a *Chicago Today* reporter, Dorothy Storck, would be researching a book about Donald Lang for Ernest Tidyman, author and screenplay writer noted for his recent films *Shaft* and *The French Connection*. I was told that if the book worked, a movie would follow. Cooperation with Dorothy Storck would be voluntary, but since she already had the department's blessing and seemingly unfettered access to case files and court transcripts, many of us agreed to talk with her. And talk to her we did—at length. The result of her research was a book authored by Tidyman titled *Dummy*, published in 1973. It turned out to be an exhaustive and authoritative account of both the murders with which Lang was charged as well as detailed background on Lang from childhood. Tidyman followed the book with a made-for-television movie by the same name. Starring Levar Burton as Lang, the movie covered only the first murder, and so many liberties were taken with the facts of the case and the police investigation that I was deeply disappointed. The book, however, is still part of my library.

In February of 1975, the seeds sown by the Illinois Supreme Court Opinion of September 1970 sprouted a literal minefield of legal weeds. The Illinois Appellate Court threw out Lang's conviction in the Earline Brown homicide. While it held that there was "ample evidence to show that Donald Lang strangled Earline Brown," it also stated that the trial itself was "constitutionally impermissible" because of Lang's disabilities. Because there were no trial procedures that could effectively compensate for the handicaps [of Donald Lang], his conviction was reversed. Once again, curious circular judicial reasoning caused the case to be remanded for retrial.

The front page headlines of the February 15, 1975, *Chicago Sun-Times* aptly described it as "THE CASE OF THE UNPROVABLE MURDER." The Appellate Court added, however, that if methods were not found to compensate for his disabilities, Lang should be committed to the Department of Mental Health and institutionalized—with his condition reviewed at "stated intervals"—for a period limited to the maximum sentence that could be imposed for the offense charged." Under the sentencing laws in effect in 1972, that meant that Lang might possibly spend the rest of his life in a mental institution…without the trial mandated by the Illinois Supreme Court in September of 1970.

The goal then was to train Donald to communicate so he would be able to cooperate with counsel and eventually stand trial. Although no one can argue that Lang was profoundly neglected by the social safety nets that might have helped him, it was also true that in every instance where training was attempted, it failed. It was unclear whether it was due to Donald's lack of cooperation or his inability to learn. His original attorney, Lowell Myers, suggested it was a combination of both. Lang would attempt to learn signing for example, would become frustrated at his inability to do so, and would simply shut out any further efforts. Lang was now twenty-nine years old, and his ability to communicate on any abstract level (e.g. What happened yesterday? Where are you going tomorrow?) was nil. It was against this background that the Appellate Court ordered the Illinois Department of Mental Health to develop a training program to teach Lang to communicate. It might as well have ordered the department to draw blood from a rock. Lang remained in Cook County Jail.

However, there was one difference this time around. Considering Lang's trial and conviction in the Earline Brown murder and documented violent outbursts while in custody over the years, part of the ruling read, "In light of the evidence of impulsive and explosive behavior which resulted in violent acts on the part of Lang, it is essential that he reside in a setting with sufficient security to insure the continuity of treatment and his appearance in court."

In January of 1976, the United States Supreme Court refused to review the Illinois Appellate Court decision that reversed Lang's conviction in the Brown homicide. There was clearly no magic bullet that could unravel the legal morass created by this case, and there were obviously gaps in Illinois law as to how to handle such cases, but in essence, the U.S. Supreme Court was telling Illinois to handle its own problems.

In March 1976, a Criminal Court judge formally pronounced Donald Lang not fit to stand trial, but he did not drop the still pending murder charges in the Brown homicide. This enabled the system to move Lang from the Cook County Jail to the Chicago-Read Mental Health Center. He was to return to the Criminal Court in six months for a reevaluation of his condition. But it didn't work that way. Another judge ruled that Donald did not meet the legal criteria for commitment and ordered him returned to jail. His bond on the pending murder charge was set at $50,000. Lang, who was destitute, needed 10 percent or $5,000 to be released from custody pending retrial. At this point, no one who knew the details of his background was willing to take a chance of having him released.

At some point, Lang was transferred to the Illinois State Psychiatric Institute and had reportedly "begun to learn to communicate." A Circuit Court judge ordered that Lang continue his training until he could be ruled fit to stand trial. The Department of Mental Health, however, appealed the judge's order because it claimed its department did not have the legal authority to treat persons who are not mentally retarded or in need of mental treatment. Its position was that Donald had a physical handicap, not a mental handicap. It sought to transfer Lang back to Cook County Jail. Three weeks later, the Circuit Court judge ordered the director of the Illinois Department of Mental Health to show cause why he should not be held in contempt for not developing a training program so Donald Lang could stand trial for the Brown murder.

It was beginning to appear that Lang was beyond the reach of the criminal law and perhaps beyond the reach of any meaningful training that might help him. He languished in a Never Never Land in our society, outside the purview of any social agency's existing programs. Given Lang's well-documented propensity for occasional violence, his unfettered return to life on the streets was not a logical option. What to do?

The Illinois Appellate Court stepped into the fray between the Circuit Court and the Department of Mental Health. The court ruled in favor of the Department of Mental Health. On October 4, 1977, Donald Lang was returned to the Cook County Jail.

Judge Earl Strayhorn summed it up as, "No one knows what the hell to do with him. The Department of Mental Health says it's not their job, the Department of Corrections says they don't know how to help him, and the courts just don't want him."

In an effort to chop its way out of the Donald Lang legal thicket, on September 24, 1979, the Illinois Supreme Court issued another ruling in the Donald Lang case. It ruled that Lang must be given still another hearing to determine whether he was fit to stand trial for the Brown murder charges. If he were found unfit and dangerous, he must be committed to the Department of Mental Health for treatment. The court was equating "unfit for trial" with "mental illness," which in Lang's instance was not correct.

Nevertheless, a hearing was held in June of 1980, and Donald Lang was found unfit to stand trial. Shortly after, I was called down to the Civic Center to testify at a civil commitment hearing with regard to any danger that Lang might pose. I was not asked for my opinion; rather, the assistant state's attorney guided me through the facts of the Earline Brown homicide and the subsequent trial. At the conclusion of my testimony, the ASA asked me two final questions.

"Detective Padar, did the jury reach a verdict in that trial?"

"Yes."

"And what was that verdict?"

"Guilty of murder."

There were no further questions. Donald Lang had been found unfit for trial and dangerous. In accordance with the order of the Illinois Appellate Court, he was to be committed to the Department of Mental Health. I would attend several re-commitment hearings in the next decade where I would repeat my testimony.

But the State of Illinois did not want to be on the hook for training Lang for what it considered a physical disability, not a mental disability. It appealed to the U.S. Supreme Court to over-rule the Illinois Appellate Court. On January 21, 1980, almost exactly nine years after Lang's conviction, the U.S. Supreme Court refused to hear the case. It looked like the Department of Mental Health would become Donald's home for the indefinite future. He was transferred to the high security Manteno facility of the Department of Mental Health. Almost two years later, in November of 1981, Lang was transferred to the less restrictive facility at Chicago-Read Mental Health Center where it was thought he could get better training.

On Thursday, March 4, 1982, at about 8 p.m., Donald Lang "escaped" from the Chicago-Read Mental Health Center on Chicago's far northwest side. After nearly eleven years in custody and unable to speak, hear, read, or write, he somehow made his way to the far South Side on public transportation and telephoned his sister with the help of a bystander. He used money he earned in the center's workshop to board a CTA Rapid Transit train to the South Side. He was carrying a note with his sister's name, address, and phone number. His sister returned him to Chicago-Read less than twelve hours later. No, Donald Lang was most definitely not retarded.

Over the years, the Department of Mental Health has documented several violent outbursts by Lang. His handicap frustrates him and causes him to lash out at times. In addition, he has problems relating to women in social settings at the mental health facilities. These incidents, along with his documented history of two murder arrests and one conviction serve to place him in the "dangerous" category, thus insuring his continued incarceration.

As of this writing, Donald Lang remains in custody at the Chicago-Read Mental Health Center. He is legally blind in one eye and his sight is failing in the other. For a person whose survival literally depended upon his sight and keen powers of observation, this situation must indeed be devastating.

Lang turned sixty-seven in 2013. I would hope and assume that he enjoys supervised family visits in his later years if his sister and brothers are still alive. I respected Donald Lang. He was street smart and learned to hone his remaining senses to insure his own survival. He was a bright young man in spite of his disability. I have a great deal of empathy for Donald Lang. Our system truly failed him every step of the way in spite of the best efforts of his parents to seek help for him. Given the proper training at an early age, he might have avoided this entire scenario.

But being so closely involved in the investigation and prosecution of the Earline Brown homicide, I feel that he was correctly convicted of her murder. And after reviewing the circumstances of the Ernestine Williams murder five years previously, there seems little doubt that Lang was also responsible. Despite an abundance of societal failings with regard to Donald, I cannot translate that into justification for their murders. They deserved better than to die by Donald's hand.

CTA Sniper!

By Jim

Few occupations allow a person to get some idea of how his workday will go by merely listening to the news on the way to work, but homicide detective is definitely one of them.

It was an end-of-season summer day in the late '70s, and as I drove to work that morning, the local all-news radio station was reporting breaking news. A female passenger on an eastbound Lake Street elevated train (the "L") had apparently been shot as the train proceeded past a public housing project en route to the famed Chicago Loop. A reporter was on the way to the hospital to determine her condition; police were unable to confirm that the shot came from a sniper. Details to follow....

Hmmm, I thought to myself. On a heater scale of one to ten, that's definitely a ten.

A "heater case" is police jargon for an incident likely to garner unusual media attention for any number of reasons—a sniper shooting at passing trains would definitely qualify.

Once I was in the office, the sergeant didn't waste any time with preliminaries.

"Padar, Shull...take a supposed gunshot victim from the L at Pres/St. Luke's Hospital."

Just the two of us? No multiple teams fanning out?

"You'd better get over there right away. She wants to get on to work and they're fixin' to release her."

Okay, okay, maybe not a ten.

"You got a name, Sarge?" I asked. "Ya know it's on the radio?" I continued, trying to maybe work it back up to a ten. Or at least a nine.

"Here's what we have," he said as he handed us some notes, "and the media doesn't know any more than we do—probably less."

Mike and I read the one-and-a-half pages of handwritten notes on the case. Gertrude Engstrom, thirty-three, of Oak Park was sitting in the window seat of a Lake Street elevated train when a gunshot struck the window next to her, striking her in the right upper arm. She was to be released after treatment in the Emergency Room of Presbyterian/St. Luke's Hospital. Passengers pulled the emergency stop at the Ashland Avenue platform and notified the conductor; an ambulance was called and the train was evacuated and removed from service. The train was deadheading to the Forest Park terminal where it would be met by Chicago Police Crime Lab personnel.

"Shull, you and Padar head to the hospital first before she gets away from us," said our sergeant. "Then go straight to the terminal and interview the crew. I'll call the Crime Lab guys and see if they can hold the crew until you get there."

• • • •

At the hospital, Mrs. Gertrude Engstrom's "gunshot wound" was several notches below minor. Her upper left arm bore the tell-tale signs of an orange Betadine scrub that had highlighted perhaps a half-dozen very superficial abrasions. A precautionary x-ray was negative for any foreign matter, according to the preliminary read by the ER resident. She would be released when a radiologist confirmed the findings. I had a feeling this nine or ten heater case was rapidly cooling.

Gertrude presented a mixture of embarrassment and anxiety—embarrassed at all the attention she was receiving and anxious about proceeding on her way to work. She worked at a downtown publishing firm and we offered to call her office for her. No need; she had already called from the hospital and left a message, giving a brief description of what had happened to her.

"Can you tell us what happened?" we asked.

She took a deep breath—she had already told her tale many times this morning.

"I was sitting on the Lake Street elevated. We were on an 'A' train, so we went right past the Damen platform, and before we got to the Ashland stop, I heard a loud snapping sound and a bullet came through the window and hit me in the right shoulder.... At least, I thought I got hit by a bullet...." She gestured to her upper right arm. "But now they tell me I just got hit by some glass."

"But you heard the shot?" asked Mike.

"No, not a shot...more like a loud snapping sound when a stone hits your car windshield on the highway...and I felt the pain right away, and I saw the bullet hole at the same time."

"And then what happened?"

"I screamed, and some other passengers had heard and seen what happened, and everybody started to get excited. When we pulled into the Ashland station, someone pulled the emergency handle over the door and told the conductor what had happened. I was holding my arm and crying. They made everyone get off the train and then the ambulance came. That's all I really know."

"Can you estimate where the train was when you got shot?"

"Oh, God, no!" she laughed. "I was just riding in kind of a trance—you know how you do...especially in the morning on the way to work. All I can tell you is we were past Damen and coming into Ashland."

"Mrs. Engstrom," interrupted a nurse, "your office is on the phone. Do you feel well enough to take the call out at the nurses' station?"

We couldn't help but overhear the one-sided conversation.

"Yes! That was me!"

"No, no, I'm coming to work."

"I'm fine.... No, I'm not going home."

"Oh, my goodness!" she giggled. "Well, okay." She hung up the phone.

"They're sending a car for me," she giggled again.

"If you play your cards right, they'll probably buy you lunch," I said.

She laughed and then suddenly she burst into tears.

"I thought I had been shot...I really did...and now I'm joking about it."

The emotional roller coaster.... She composed herself once again.

"I'm all right. I'm really all right," she said, as though trying to convince herself.

The nurse reappeared.

"Mrs. Engstrom," she said, "the radiologist said there is nothing there—you can go now."

• • • •

Out at the Forest Park terminal, we learned that the train crew had been sent home, but we connected with our Crime Lab personnel. They were scouring the elevated car for the bullet.

"There's no question it was a gunshot," said the lab man. "Looks to be a small-caliber, maybe a .32. It penetrated the window, but we can't find the damned bullet!" They had apparently been at it for some time.

"Well, it's not in the victim," I said. "All she has is a few scratches from the glass."

"Screw it," said his partner. "It's not here. Maybe someone picked it up…or maybe it got caught up in someone's clothing."

"If it came from the projects, those windows are at least thirty to forty yards from the tracks. Ya think a .32 would have pretty much expended its energy by the time it penetrated the window?" I asked.

"To tell you the truth, I'm surprised a .32 even went through the window from that distance," said the lab guy.

"Maybe it didn't," said his partner. "That's reinforced safety glass. Maybe it almost made it through and then fell back to the street. You say all she had was scratches from glass particles?"

The four of us peered closely at the window. There was no way to tell whether the bullet had actually entered the L car or not, but the hole in the glass was just about where a passenger's upper arm would be; however, apparently the bullet never touched her.

"Chalk it up to one of the mysteries of life."

"Yeah, that's it…a mystery of life. You're never going to find the offender anyhow."

• • • •

Mike and I called our office and brought it up to date. We headed back to Lake Street to canvas for any possible witnesses.

We walked Lake Street, under the elevated tracks, heading east from Damen on the south side of the street, adjacent to the Henry Horner Housing projects. There were literally hundreds of windows, but the horizontal distance from the windows to the tracks was about forty yards. Quite a distance for a .32 caliber bullet to be effective on safety glass. Every time a train passed, the noise was intense, intense enough certainly to drown out the sound of any gunshot. It was early afternoon now, so we decided to return to our office and bring the sergeant up to date.

• • • •

In the office, we grabbed some coffee and sat down to review our notes. The media had not called all morning, probably due to the minor nature of Gertrude's injury. The #10 Heater Case had rapidly dissolved to a routine aggravated battery, to be vigorously investigated by our office, of course, but not worthy of intense media attention...or so we thought.

"Padar! Shull! One of you guys pick up the PAX." The PAX was the restricted Police Auxiliary Line, an internal phone system for the department. We picked up simultaneously.

"You guys handling that L shooting from this morning?" asked a 12th District patrol officer.

"That's us," we replied.

"Listen, I would have called you guys sooner, but I didn't know about your case. I think maybe I got your shooter."

"Who is he? Where is he?" we asked at the same time.

"He's in the lockup here at 12. He had a beef with his girlfriend early this morning, so he took a shot at her and missed—then he took off, and ran to his momma's down the hall. We arrested him with an old .32 caliber Colt Police Positive loaded with .32 caliber shorts. It's a pissant gun with pissant ammo, so I don't know if it fits with what you're looking for—"

"It sounds like exactly what we're looking for!" we interrupted. "Put a hold on him; don't let him bond out. We need to know exactly where this happened. We'll want to talk with the girl and look over the apartment to see if it could fit what we think the trajectory is."

"Oh, the apartment fits all right. We looked for the bullet hole, but the girl told us she thought it went out the window...right toward the elevated tracks. She never mentioned a passing train, but she was pretty shaken up...and he's not going anywhere; the gun is stolen and he's on parole. He'll be held over for court."

"Thanks, officer—great pinch and thanks for calling us!" We were grinning ear-to-ear when we hung up.

"Padar! Shull! Pick up the PAX!" came the shout-out from our sergeant.

"Sarge, we've got something going on this L sniper. Can you give it to someone else?"

"It's the homicide commander; he asked for you specifically—pick it up!"

"Hey, boss, what's up?" we asked. Both of us were on very good terms with the commander.

"Listen, guys; I want you to meet a reporter and camera crew at Ashland and Lake, eastbound platform, and give 'em an interview on this L shooting from this morning." He mentioned the reporter and I recognized her name. She was relatively new in town, an attractive blonde. Maybe the commander was as big a sucker for blondes as I was.

We briefed him in detail on what we had going.

"Well, talk to her first and then go over and talk to the girl in the projects—but don't tell her about this lead. It might not pan out. Give me a call when you finish the interview."

• • • •

We met the major network new gal reporter and camera crew on schedule. They set the scene so the camera was facing westbound, toward any oncoming trains, and the cameraman stood at the very edge of the platform so he could get a shot of Mike and me and the new gal, with the eastbound tracks as a backdrop. I didn't realize it at the time, but they apparently timed the start of the interview to coincide with an approaching elevated train.

New Gal asked some very general questions about the shooting and we answered likewise, giving her some indication that we were working on some leads. Then she took a strange tangent and asked a series of question of both Mike and me as to how often these incidents happened. Well, never before to our knowledge. She pressed the issue; a train was approaching; I glanced at the cameraman as

I heard the train. He was standing, I thought, dangerously close to the edge of the platform. New Gal couldn't seem to believe that this was an isolated incident. I kept glancing at the cameraman, expecting him to be momentarily sucked onto the tracks by the on-coming train. The train came and went and I heaved a sigh of relief.

• • • •

At the Henry Horner apartment, we interviewed the girlfriend and scoped out the apartment. Physically, everything fit. The apartment was on level with the elevated track outside, but the rails did appear to be at least fifty yards away.

Without ballistics, we would have a weak case, but with added charges, bad guy would be more inclined to negotiate a plea with some of the charges being dropped in exchange for a guilty plea. The case of the L sniper would be cleared by arrest before the end of the day. I called home and alerted my wife to set the VCR to record the afternoon news. Mike and I were going to be on TV!

• • • •

I arrived home late, after the conclusion of the early evening newscasts, and my wife reported that our story had not been aired. But the station was hyping the story repeatedly in promos, billing the incident as some sort of battle between the police and CTA motormen. Stay tuned—details at ten! Had my roller-coaster heater case regained another life?

At ten o'clock, I sat on the edge of my seat. New Gal appeared with Mike and me on the Ashland L platform. As she spoke with us, I kept glancing at the cameraman, expecting him to disappear at any moment. I was, without a doubt, the most shifty-eyed cop ever to appear on the ten o'clock news. New Gal harped on how unusual we thought the incident—"Never occurred before" according to our experience. Cut to an interview in the office of the president of the CTA motorman's union where he regaled New Gal with how dangerous the job of a motorman was....

"My men get shot at every day," was his closing line.

It was not true, of course, but Mike and I had been set up in a trumped-up story for the sake of creating a headline.

I called the homicide commander at home. He was laughing.

"Well, she snookered us," he said lightheartedly.

"What 'us' boss?" I replied. "I didn't notice your name mentioned in this story."

He laughed again.

"We'll check our facts with our records, but I'm sure we'll be able to have News Affairs issue a statement in the morning to correct the situation. But the station won't cover it, so we lose this one."

He was taking it much more lightly than I, for certain.

New Gal remained in Chicago for the rest of her broadcasting career, but I never spoke to her again. She would never get one scintilla of information from me ever again. And given my prestigious position in the department...I'm sure she never noticed.

Shoot! Shoot Now!

By Jim

photo at www.OnBeingACop.com/gallery/station.jpg

For the most part, I can remember circumstances surrounding an incident with reasonable clarity. There is one event, however, indelibly etched in my mind, that has no beginning—and really no end when I stop to think about it. The pundits will say that a good story has a beginning, a middle, and an end. So quite possibly, this is not a good story—maybe you should stop reading now—but I need to tell it because the middle is so crystal clear even these many years later.

It is a bright and crisply cold day. I am inside a Chicago Transit Authority station on the Eisenhower Expressway. I stare down the long ramp that goes down to the platform on the expressway level. That platform runs for about a block and then becomes another long ramp that climbs to street level at the far end. The entire stop—consisting of a station at each end, the ramps, and the plat-form—runs for two city blocks.

I am extremely familiar with these surroundings, having worked as a part-time ticket agent for the CTA during my college years. Many a long hour was spent in the ticket booths that nest inside each station. But today, I am a cop on assignment at this location. I am outside the ticket booth, and my back is to the street where the occasional bus stops to pick up and discharge passengers to and from the rapid transit trains that run in the center of the expressway. I watch down the ramp as a young man approaches, climbing steadily upwards toward me.

He looks to be in his early twenties, and although he is Caucasian, he sports afro-style light brown hair. Coupled with his white skin, he presents a non sequitur image of an African American. The overall look is no doubt intentional, but it just doesn't work. He vaguely reminds me of a guy I went to school with—I never liked that guy. He's wearing a heavy three-quarters-length tan corduroy jacket, similar to what I saw in a mail order catalog just a few weeks ago. He walks with determination, staring at me as he approaches. The sun catches a bright reflection off of an object he is carrying in his right hand.

My alert level rises several points as I strain to identify the object. As he gets closer, I can make it out to be a hunting knife, identical to the size and style my cousin Howard and I used to carry when we were tramping the north woods of Wisconsin as teenagers. We used the knives to cut underbrush and saplings. Somehow, here at this transit station in the city, I do not believe that is his intention. I reach under my coat and clumsily draw my little five-shot snubnose. It takes too long. He is rapidly closing the distance between us. My "Surviving Edged Weapons Attacks" training vaguely flashes before me—wasn't there something about a "twenty-one foot rule?" No time to think about that now—he's definitely closer than twenty-one feet.

I call to him to stop, and I gain a few feet by stepping rapidly backwards, but he is a man on a mission. It is astounding how quickly your brain can process information under extreme stress; I do a quick assessment of the consequences of shooting. Directly behind him is the ramp sloping downwards toward the platform. If I miss, or if the shot is through and through, the bullet will hit the corrugated metal roof of the ramp. The decision is made in a fraction of a second. Shoot! Shoot now!

At this distance, it's an easy shot. He's too close, but a well-placed shot or two will most likely take him down before he can do much harm, but...

...but my trigger finger will not work. It's like my finger has fallen asleep. Whose finger falls asleep? Even with every ounce of effort, I cannot pull the trigger. I step even further back, stumble into the turnstile, and fall on my back between the walls of the turnstile. I cannot roll. My trigger finger is paralyzed. He is on me now; he raises the knife and strikes, the blade just a few inches from my chest.

I awake with a start. My heart is racing. My head is wet on the pillow. My wife sleeps quietly at my side. It's "the dream." In my case, it's a recurring dream, and it is nearly identical each time it happens. Thankfully, it only happens two or three times a year.

Most law enforcement officers have experienced "the dream" in some fashion or another, but some won't discuss the details. For many, the situation may vary from dream to dream, or the hanging point may be different. Several have told me they pull the trigger, the gun fires, but the bullet falls out of the barrel, harmlessly to the ground. For cops, such dreams are not unusual and their meaning can be debated ad infinitum.

In my case, I am certain that it was the manifestation of a subconscious doubt as to whether I would be able to shoot another human being. The power to take a life without protracted legal procedure is one of the most awesome powers possessed by every police officer. Much of our training addresses the laws that cover the use of deadly force. We talk about the fact that state law details the precise circumstances under which deadly force is permissible. Then department policies will usually prescribe additional limitations, and finally, most law enforcement officers personally limit themselves even further. Is it any wonder why we might dream about deadly force? My subconscious doubt was erased on a cold February night in 1974 at thirteen minutes past midnight when my partner and I exchanged gunfire with armed robbers. My revolver worked just fine, as did my trigger finger. From that day forward, I never had that dream again. That was "Shootout at the High Rollers Pool Hall," which you can read elsewhere in this book.

The Dream

By Jay

It is a common recurring dream among police officers. The details vary a bit, but the outcome is always the same. You find yourself in a scenario where you must draw your gun and shoot the bad guy. You pull your weapon, line up on the target, and here is where it varies. Some officers say they don't have the strength to pull the trigger. Others pull the trigger and the bullet lodges in the barrel. Some say they have bad rounds and others say they just can't hit the target. My rounds fire from the barrel, but either drop to the ground before they make it to the bad guy, or they just bounce off him. The dream doesn't come as often as it used to—maybe once every couple of months now.

"Seventeen-twenty-two."

"Twenty-two. Go ahead, squad."

"And seventeen-twenty-four."

"Two four, go ahead."

"Seventeen-twenty-two, seventeen-twenty-four, units on city-wide, we have a battery in progress, domestic-related, at 4776 N. Kedvale on the two. Husband is beating the wife and just burned the child with an electrical cord.... Okay, the ticket is being upgraded to shots fired. The call taker is still on the line and hears loud reports and screaming. All units use caution; possible shots fired."

"Seventeen-twenty, send me that job."

"Seventeen-thirteen's going."

"Seventeen-eleven's going."

"Seventeen-twenty-two, give a slow down squad. I'm on scene, offender's gone, and no one's shot."

A husband and wife had fought two days ago and the husband had stormed out. The wife was asleep this morning with her two kids and her sister sleeping in the adjacent rooms. As the family slept, the husband quietly entered the apartment and proceeded to the kitchen. He took a fan and cut the cord from it. The ends were split with a knife and the wires were exposed. He slowly crept into his wife's bedroom, plugged in the cord, and held his sleeping wife hard against the bed by her neck. As she woke up in a panic, he repeatedly plunged the cord into her chest, leaving numerous burn marks. In between shocking her, he delivered multiple punches to her face. The rest of the family woke up to her screams and her sister called 911.

As all of us were responding, the husband ran out the back of the apartment and disappeared. We spent the rest of our tour looking for him, but we were unsuccessful. The child was never burned, and there were no shots fired. There was a lot of confusion and screaming during the call. The heavy accent didn't help things either. As I went in for check off at the end of my shift, I sent one more flash message over the air so all the Second Watch officers just starting their tour would keep an eye out for this guy. I locked my equipment in my locker and fought through the morning rush hour to get home. I climbed into bed and hit the sleep timer on the TV. I slowly drifted off to sleep, and here came the dream….

He's got his wife by the neck with his right arm, and he's pointing a gun at me with his left. He's screaming at me to drop my gun or he'll kill her. She's screaming. The two kids in the apartment are screaming. My gun is pointed at his head. I take a deep breath and slowly squeeze the trigger. There's a loud bang and a flash. The bullet fires faster than ever and strikes its target. Dead center head shot. The gun drops from his hand and he drops to the floor. The wife runs frantically screaming out of the apartment. The two kids run to me, crying and grabbing me by each leg.

"Why'd you kill our daddy? Why'd you kill him?"

I kneel down, hug them back, and start to cry.

I sit up in bed and search for my watch on the nightstand. I hold it close to my face and squint at it. I still have a couple of hours left to sleep. I roll over, take a deep breath, and drift back off.

After seven years of having the same dream, I'm not exactly sure why my gun worked this time. Maybe I just really wanted him dead. Maybe the husband angered me more than I thought. Maybe a shrink will read this someday and explain to me why my bullet found its target and did its job this time. I guess I really don't care why. Perhaps the dreams may stop altogether, or they may just go back to the way they've always been. Only time will tell. Whatever happens, I'll be looking forward to those nights between the dream.

Janitors in a Drum:
Part I—The Crime Scene
By Jim

photo at www.OnBeingACop.com/gallery/drums.jpg

Friday, July 5, 1974

Tony Russo sank into his bed, bone-tired. His wife was asleep instantly, but Tony stared at the ceiling.

This sandwich shop was draining him physically and emotionally. It was one of those things that seemed like a good idea at the time. When the owner, Sam Rantis, disappeared the previous December, Sam's wife tried to continue the business on her own, but when Sam's body was found in February with his throat cut in the trunk of an auto parked at O'Hare Field, the Widow Rantis found everything too much. She implored Tony and his wife to take over the operation of the shop just to keep the business running.

It wasn't bad initially, but now, in early summer, business had picked up and the hours became longer. Between Tony and his wife, they spent almost every waking moment in the kitchen and behind the counter.

And now there was that damned smell. Not strong, but lingering, and neither Tony nor his wife thought it was food-related. Of course, they cleaned the kitchen and the walk-in refrigerator. They even moved every piece of equipment and cleaned again. The faint but putrid smell persisted. Tonight, after a long day, Tony and his wife got into an argument.

"Tony!" she shouted. "You've got to do something. Maybe I'm more sensitive to it, but that kitchen stinks!"

Tony had to admit, silently, that although faint, the odor seemed to be slowly getting worse.

As he tossed and turned, his mind drifted back to his days as a corpsman in the Navy. On several occasions, he had dealt with decomposed bodies, but over the years, he had successfully blocked them from his mind.

It was nearly midnight when Tony Russo sat straight up in bed. That was it! This was the same smell as a decomposing body.

He eased himself out of bed and dressed quietly; then he drove the short distance back to the shop. He kept most of the shop lights out—he didn't want people to think the store was open for business. Tony didn't waste his time searching all the places he and his wife had already covered, but he stood in the kitchen, scanning the overall area. His eyes came to rest on a door to an unused storage area under a stairwell in the kitchen's very back corner. They had looked in there earlier, but they hadn't moved anything. He opened the door slowly in the dimly lit kitchen.

Empty plastic bread racks from their previous vendor were stacked almost to the ceiling, filling the cramped little room. Was it his imagination or was the smell just slightly stronger in this unused closet? He began slowly to remove the layers of bread racks, revealing two tightly sealed 55-gallon drums, lids securely clamped with bolt rings. About twelve inches of heavy plastic sheeting hung over the drums' edges. Was it his imagination, or was the smell definitely stronger in here?

Tony searched the junk drawer in the kitchen and found a small crescent wrench. He dearly wanted to turn on some lights, but he also knew he didn't want any visitors. He stepped into the dark, cramped area and began gingerly to loosen the bolt ring on the closest drum. Someone slammed a car door in the alley and he jumped a foot. He could hear his own heart beating and realized he was perspiring profusely. He paused and took a deep breath, and then he slowly broke the seal on the lid and raised it very slowly. When he peered inside, the hair crawled up the back of his neck. He retreated from the kitchen and called the police. The odor, now strong and pungent, filled the little sandwich shop.

Saturday, July 6, 1974

It was a warm summer evening when Mike Shull and I reported a bit early for the 12:30 a.m. First Watch roll call. Roll call would be informal—there were only four of us working tonight; a Friday night/Saturday morning summertime shift. With only two teams working, the odds were that at least one would draw a fresh homicide before we finished our tour of duty. The phone rang and the sergeant answered and started taking a notification. When he hung up, he looked at the four of us.

"The 12th District has a body in a garbage can." He looked at us expectantly, waiting for the four of us to determine who was going to take the night's first assignment.

"We'll take it," said Mike. I looked at him quizzically. But moments later, we were en route to the Korner Sandwich Shop at 1015 South Western.

"And tell me again, just why we're taking this job?" I asked facetiously as we drove the nearly deserted streets.

"Because…" he feigned the part of a patient teacher speaking slowly, "it's summertime and it's not going to be a body. It's going to be a dead dog…or rotten meat…or something like that. And that will be our job, and the next one…the real murder…will go to the other team."

It was nearly 1:00 a.m. when we pulled up to the corner of Taylor and Western, and it was immediately apparent that we had something more than rotten meat. There were two beat cars and a field sergeant, along with a wagon, all clustered at the corner. Mike was quiet as we climbed from our car. The one beat car was covering the front door to secure the crime scene. The second beat officers and the sergeant were inside, talking to Tony Russo. All the lights were on now, and when we entered, we immediately recognized the all too familiar stench.

The field sergeant nodded toward the kitchen and walked back to the tiny closet with us. The beat officers had fully removed the lids of both drums. The contents of one drum appeared to be nothing more than clothing, winter clothing. The other drum revealed two feet sticking up, covered with winter galoshes.

"I told the wagon guys to wait for you guys before emptying the drums," said the sergeant.

"Empty the drums?" I asked incredulously.

"Yeah, we really don't know what we have, and we have to empty them to transport whatever it is. We don't know whether we have two bodies, or half a body in each drum, or just one body and some clothing. How will we know until we empty them?"

"In my kitchen?" asked Tony from the front counter. "Please! No!"

"Officer, get that man outside!" shouted the sergeant.

"Sarge, he's right," said Mike. "First off, the Crime Lab should empty the drums, and secondly, I don't think they should be emptied here in this kitchen."

"Well, the last time I looked, I was a sergeant," he said looking down at his sleeve, "and you're a detective, so I think I win."

It was one of those moments of marvelous providence....

"Jimmy, Mike, what you guys got?" came a voice from the front counter.

We looked out to see William Keating, the Chief of Organized Crime, walking into the kitchen. Keating was the acting street deputy for the night and, as such, was the ranking department member on the street. More than that, he had been the citywide homicide commander for the past several years, having just recently been promoted to chief. Mike and I knew him well and he knew us well. Now it was my personal protocol always to address command members by rank whenever in the presence of other officers, no matter how well I knew them, but I felt this moment called for an exception.

"Hey, Bill!" I said. "We were just talking about that. We're not sure what we have, but I was thinking to have the Crime Lab shoot some pictures and then take the drums over to the morgue."

"You can't take anything to the morgue that hasn't been pronounced dead," said the obviously irritated sergeant. "And we don't know what we have!"

"Good point," said Keating. "Have the wagon transport the drums to the morgue intact. On the way, they can stop at the back door of County and have each drum pronounced dead."

"No doctor's going to do that without knowin' what's in the drums," said the sergeant, growing even more agitated.

"You know what?" answered Keating, showing a bit of his own irritation. "I think my guys can handle it." He nodded toward Mike and me.

The field sergeant glared at us.

Keating walked to the closet entrance, peered in, and then looked up. The room's back wall was actually the backside of a stairwell, and the ceiling was unusually high—twelve feet or more. There were very high shelves on the back wall.

"Check all those shelves," said Keating. "There might be the murder weapon or who knows what up there. And go to the hospital and the morgue with the drums. I don't want these drums out of your sight, and I want you to be there when the drums are emptied. Then give me a call with what you've got. I'll be on the street all night."

Mike and I looked up at the shelves, wondering how we were going to get high enough to search them.

The Crime Lab arrived and started shooting pictures, while Mike and I looked for a ladder. Tony Russo located a ladder for us, and we examined the empty shelves and had the lab shoot pictures. The lab groused.

"What are we doing this for?" the technicians complained as they teetered on the ladder.

"Because the chief wants us to," we replied.

As we prepared to leave, we double-checked the closet's very upper areas again just to be certain we hadn't missed anything. It was almost 4:00 a.m. when we sealed the premises and slowly followed the wagon over to the Cook County Hospital. We still didn't know exactly what was in the drums.

At the back door of the hospital, the wagon pulled up on the driveway close to the entrance while Mike and I parked several car lengths ahead. We walked back to the wagon.

"Why don't you guys wait here?" we said. "We might have to finesse this a bit."

"Hell," they answered, "just have 'em pronounce each drum DOA. Ya know…whatever is in this drum is dead and whatever is in that drum is dead."

"Yeah, I know," I said laughing. "But there's the paperwork thing—they do like to know who or what they're pronouncing."

Inside the Emergency Room, we grabbed the first nurse we could.

"Hey, we got a stinker in the wagon out back—I don't think you want us to bring him in. Who can pronounce him for us?"

"That would be Markie," she said, fluttering her eyes toward a very handsome, very young looking resident on the other side of the room. The blond, blue-eyed doctor appeared to be so much younger than his actual years. I made a note in my notebook, "Pronounced DOA by Dr. Markie."

"Markie!" she called across the room. "These gentlemen have a stinker for you...out on the driveway." She fluttered her eyes again, but the resident was obviously not interested or amused. As he approached us, he took his stethoscope from the front pocket of his scrubs and put it around his neck.

"I don't think you're going to need that, doc," I said.

Mike nudged me and tapped his finger on his left chest and nodded at the resident. I read his nametag: Mark Wolf, ER Resident. I crossed off "Markie" and wrote "Wolf" and we explained to Dr. Wolf what we had out in the wagon.

"Well...this is highly unusual," said the resident, trying to salvage some dignity by using his most officious tone. "You know we have to fill out some paperwork, and we need to know exactly what you have out there."

"Well...I suppose..." I said, speaking very slowly, "I suppose... we could just bring the drums inside and empty them here rather than the morgue."

Mark Wolf stiffened a bit and pursed his lips while fingering his stethoscope.

"Well...let me take a look before you do that," he said with all the authority he could muster.

Outside on the driveway, we swung open the wagon door, and all the pent up odiferous fumes spilled out into the warm summer air. Doctor Wolf had no choice but to climb into the cramped unvented wagon to take at least a cursory look. He took a hurried look into each drum and then, pale as a ghost, he literally staggered out of the wagon to the curb, squatted, and threw up. And then he threw up again, and again, until there was nothing left but retching. He steadied himself with one hand on the curb and looked up at Mike and me, vomitus spittle dripping off his chin and onto his scrubs, narrowly missing his shiny stethoscope. Mike and I truly felt sorry for him.

"Well, what say, doc? Should we bring the drums in?"

He shook his head feebly and gave a single wave at the wagon. "No…go," he said weakly.

"Should we make the time 4:40 a.m.?" asked Mike.

The resident nodded his head and gave an "I don't care" wave.

"We'll call you in a bit and tell you what we find. You can hold the paper until then," said Mike.

Mark Wolf had crawled up the side of the wagon to a standing position. He was a mess and looked like an underage 4:00 a.m. Rush Street drunk as he walked slowly back toward the door to the ER. Mike and I took no pleasure in his condition—we knew our turn might be coming soon as we really emptied the drums.

The Crime Lab team was waiting for us when we got to the morgue with the two 55-gallon drums, but before we started, we had the same argument with Freddie, the midnight attendant.

"What do you have? How many toe tags? How do I register this?"

"Freddie, just give us a few minutes! We'll come up and let you know as soon as we know."

In the basement, we laid two body trays on the floor and positioned a drum at the end of each tray. With the help of the wagon men, the Crime Lab team slowly tipped the contents of each drum onto the trays.

Drum #1 was a medium build male Caucasian fully dressed in heavy winter clothing, but we were surprised to find both legs were missing as we gingerly untangled the clothing. The drums were double-checked, the clothing carefully examined, but there were no legs.

Drum #2 was a heavyset male Caucasian fully dressed in heavy winter clothing, wearing the rubber galoshes we had observed earlier at the sandwich shop.

We stood for a moment and pondered the situation. Strangely, the smell did not seem to be overpowering. We were in a large room with excellent ventilation and maybe, just maybe, we were getting used to the disgusting odor. More photos were in order. I won a coin toss and elected to go upstairs, leave the street deputy a message, notify our office, and get two toe tags from Freddie. The missing legs were a problem, so our sergeant elected to send a Second Watch team back to the sandwich shop to do a leg search. Almost as an afterthought, I called County Hospital to notify Dr. Mark Wolf of our findings so he could complete his paperwork.

"Is Doctor Wolf available? This is the homicide detective with some information for him." I sensed I was talking to the inappropriate flirty nurse. She muffled the phone, but I could hear her shout across the room.

"Where's Markie? Showering? With who?" she giggled when she came back to the phone and put on her professional voice: "I'm sorry; Doctor Wolf is not available." I left a message and felt even sorrier for the hapless resident. The nurse was sorely in need of some supervisory correction, but that was not my battle.

Back in the morgue basement, the crime lab crew was trying to lift at least partial fingerprints from the badly decomposed bodies. In the far corner, Mike and I spotted a mop bucket and a wringer. Next to the bucket was some "Janitor in a Drum" cleaning solution packaged in a green container shaped exactly like a 55-gallon drum. From that moment on, Mike and I dubbed the case "Janitors in a Drum."

Neither body bore any jewelry or identification. In the shirt pocket of body #2, we found three checks payable to "Sam Marcello" and signed by Sam Rantis, the deceased owner of the sandwich shop. Once we were able to get them dried out and copied, these checks would be a good starting point for our follow-up investigation.

Back at our office, we spent several minutes in the men's room, scrubbing as best we could. Afterward, we felt good enough to grab a cup of coffee as we set ourselves up in a side room to begin our report. The Second Watch personnel were already out on the street, and one of the teams had broken the coroner's seal at the sandwich shop and was beginning its search for body #1's missing legs.

We started our report, which would wind up as nine typewritten pages, but we made good progress with minimal interruptions—the other detectives claimed we stunk and they wouldn't come near us. One unwelcome interruption was a call from the "leg search team." It had found the missing appendages to body #1 in a large Baby Ruth candy bar box in a corner of the floor in the same closet where the drums were found. Mike and I were surprised and embarrassed. There was no excuse for an oversight like that, except that we perhaps concentrated too much on searching the upper shelves.

About an hour later, Chief Keating stopped by our office on his way home and stuck his head in our room for a quick briefing on what we had working. He already knew about the legs, and I knew I had to at least mention it; perhaps I could turn it back on him, jokingly, of course.

"And," I concluded my briefing of our Janitors in a Drum case, "We sure did miss those legs, didn't we, boss?" He stared at me for just a split second and my heart sank—maybe he didn't see any humor in my wisecrack, but then he laughed out loud.

"Yes, we did—*we* certainly did," said the chief with a broad smile.

We finished our report about 1:00 p.m.—a thirteen-hour shift—and we typed our final line at the bottom of page nine:

"Investigation continues...."

I called my wife:

"Honey, take my robe and slippers and hang them in the garage. Make sure the washer is empty—I've got clothes that need to be washed...the rest dry-cleaned."

"What happened?"

"Ya don't wanna know."

Less than an hour later, I walked in the back door of our home in my bathrobe, carrying my clothes under my arm.

"Where are your shoes?" she asked.

"In the garbage…."

"What happened?"

"I really don't think you want to know, honey…at least not right now."

Janitors in a Drum:
Part II—The Investigation
By Jim

Saturday, July 6, 1974

Finally home after a thirteen-hour shift, I was bone-tired, but I lingered in the shower in a futile attempt to wash the smell from my body and nostrils. Your skin does well with a good deodorant soap, but the odor in the hairs of your nose just seems to hang on forever. I knew from experience that when I woke up, the smell would be gone. Until then, there was nothing to do but attempt to ignore it as a temporary annoyance. In six short hours, I would need to leave for work; my next shift would begin at 12:30 a.m.. My poor wife's task would be to try to keep our three young children quiet enough for me to get some semblance of sleep. It was a Saturday—maybe she would take them to her sister's house for the rest of the day.

Most folks think that homicide detectives spend a large part of their time with bodies, but nothing could be further from the truth. Most cases, of course, start out with a body and a crime scene, but the real work, the fun part of the job, is always the investigation, and as my head hit the pillow, that's where my mind was going. I knew teams from our office were following up at this very moment, and that was frustrating. My part for now would be to get some sleep and be fresh for my next tour of duty in a few hours, and that meant, for the time being, I wouldn't be part of the fun. Mike and I had spent about four hours with the victims in this case—an unusually long period of time, but the bizarre circumstances demanded it. Now, with that behind us and as our teams from Area Four Homicide embarked on the investigative journey, I don't think any of us realized that the trip would take some two months. No less than fourteen investigators would work crucial portions of the case in an effort that exemplified the team spirit of our unit. During the course of the investigation, we would be aided by other units within our department, suburban departments, and the FBI, not to mention witnesses (some reluctant) and confidential informants.

The pieces of a case like this never develop in a chronological order, and our first clue that we would be dealing with a long-term timespan was, of course, the fact that our bodies were dressed for winter and we discovered them in July. Identification of the victims is always of prime importance, and in this case, there was a bit of a delay due to the bodies' conditions. Our crime lab personnel came up with partial prints from each victim, and by the end of the first day, we identified the person in drum #2 as Sam Marcello, reputed to be a juice loan collector for the mob. Marcello had been reported missing to the Rosemont Police back in February. Rosemont had information that indicated a Joseph Grisafe had been reported missing that same day in another jurisdiction. Late in the first day of investigation, an anonymous informant called our office and told us that our victim #1 was in fact Grisafe. The following day the lab would confirm Grisafe's identity from a partial print lifted from the body, and the pathologist confirmed that both had died as a result of gunshot wounds to the head. We had the solid information we needed to start the grunt work that makes up every murder investigation. In addition, we were fortunate to have a "date marker" that would help people remember when certain incidents had occurred; both men had disappeared on the Saturday after Thanksgiving, November 24th, 1973, over seven months prior to the bodies' discovery.

Reconstructing Saturday, November 24, 1973
The Little Old Lady in the Window

"Knock on one more door…" was the homicide supervisors' mantra. They would preach to us at roll call:

"There's always a little old lady in the window who saw what we need to know."

Sophia Conti lived in the 900 block of South Claremont, scarcely a block from the Korner Sandwich Shop at Taylor and Western. We didn't find her by knocking on doors, but rather from a radio dispatch card. During the course of the investigation, we learned that Grisafe's car had been ticketed and ultimately towed for parking at a hydrant at 930 South Claremont. On a hunch, we searched through the November 1973 dispatch cards stored at the 12th District, and there it was: November 24, Parked at a hydrant, 930 S. Claremont, complainant Sophia Conti. We knocked on her door.

Sophia was old-school Italian and a one-woman neighborhood watch. She was well into her eighties and walked with a stoop, but she spoke with a strong voice and Italian accent.

"Did you call the police for a car parked at the hydrant November of last year?" we asked.

She looked at us quizzically. How could we possibly expect her to remember something like that?

"It was the Saturday after Thanksgiving."

Her face lit up.

"Yes! Yes, I called. Hoodlums! Mafiosi! They park like they own the street!" She flicked her fingers under her chin in a gesture of disdain. "And I called the next day and the next until they towed the car."

"Do you remember what time you saw them?" I asked.

"I don't know…it was dark."

"Maybe around seven?" I asked, looking at the dispatch card; 1856 hours (6:56 p.m.).

"Could be, maybe," Sophia shrugged. "They do something bad? Those hoodlums?"

"No ma'am, not anymore—they're dead."

Her demeanor changed visibly—she had spoken ill of the dead—she made the sign of the cross as she showed us to the door.

About 8 p.m. that same evening, Don Borman, a neighborhood regular at the Korner Sandwich Shop, stopped by to grab a cup of coffee and visit with the owner, Sam Rantis. The lights were on, but the front door was locked. It was unusual for the shop to close this early. Borman knocked insistently. He saw Sam peer around from the back room and disappear. Borman knocked again. Eventually, Sam came to the front door.

"I was wondering if he was in some kind of trouble, and I just kept knocking until he answered the door," Borman said. "He only cracked it a bit, and he looked nervous and he was perspiring. He told me he was closed, and then he locked the door and went back to the rear of the store."

"Did you think that was unusual?" we asked.

"Absolutely. Since we were friends, he would have talked to me instead of closing the door and just walking away. I thought that was rude, considering we were friends. At our next meeting, he made no mention of it and I didn't ask him."

Which came first? The bodies or the drums?

Sam Rantis had a problem—well, really two problems. He had two bodies in the walk-in freezer of his sandwich shop. Teenage part-time employees recalled seeing a couple of drums at some point around the Thanksgiving holiday, but they didn't think anything of it, and they couldn't recall whether it was before or after Thanksgiving. Sam reached out to a couple of friends, James Erwin and Wayne (Billy) Cascone, and asked for their help in disposing of the bodies. Just what help they provided is open to speculation, but somehow Grisafe's legs were chopped off and Grisafe and Marcello were stuffed and sealed into 55-gallon drums. It is unlikely that Rantis could have accomplished this physical feat by himself; both victims were big men. The major problem was that Erwin and Cascone talked about helping Rantis…and they talked where others could overhear them.

The best laid plans…

No one knows exactly what Rantis's plan was, or if he even had one. Was he making it up as he went along? Or was his plan merely unraveling before his eyes? Whatever the case, at some point, the sealed drums and Grisafe's legs were moved to the unused storeroom at the sandwich shop's rear and concealed behind the bread racks. Rather hastily, one could assume, because the legs were merely wrapped in heavy plastic and set atop an empty Baby Ruth candy bar box. In fact, in the aftermath, it was most likely the legs that people smelled and not the drums, as the drums had been very tightly sealed.

On Wednesday, December 5, 1973, attorneys for the families of Grisafe and Marcello served a writ of habeas corpus on the FBI, seeking the immediate release of Joseph Grisafe and Sam Marcello, who were assumed by the family to be in federal custody. They, of course, had been murdered eleven days earlier and lay moldering in drums at the rear of Sam Rantis's sandwich shop. Apparently, the mob grapevine had not yet reached the families with that information, but the hierarchy most certainly was aware that Marcello and

Grisafe had gone missing, and further, that their last business call had been to Rantis.

Retribution can be a terrible thing...

Two days later on Friday, December 7, Sam Rantis disappeared. His frozen and partially decomposed body was found two-and-a-half months later in the trunk of an auto parked at O'Hare Field. His throat had been cut.

On February 26, the body of Wayne (Billy) Cascone was found in the rear seat of his car. He had been shot in the head.

The mob was closing the ring around all those involved with the deaths and disposal of their two trusted couriers.

Have a sense of decency...

The only one still alive was James Erwin, but he didn't seem worried. At his friend Billy Cascone's wake, he stood with friends, singing the chorus of the "Beer Barrel Polka": "Roll out the barrel, we'll have a barrel of fun.../Now's the time to roll the barrel, for the gang's all here."

Some laughed and some chastised Erwin for his lack of sensitivity, but at that point in time, March 1974, the drums containing the bodies of Marcello and Grisafe had not yet been discovered, so perhaps some did not understand the significance of his little joke. Nevertheless, it was an important break for our yet to be discovered case. Erwin's tasteless gag rankled certain people and encouraged them to come forward and give us statements as our case got underway some three months later.

Our Area Four Homicide teams continued to chase down the numerous minutiae that makes up a complex case. Each statement we took, each interview we did, continued to draw us closer to the conclusion that Marcello and Grisafe had been murdered by

Sam Rantis on the Saturday after Thanksgiving, 1973. It seemed unlikely to us that Rantis had any accomplices at the time of the actual shooting; rather it appeared to be a simple crime of opportunity. Rantis knew they were coming, and he got the drop on them.

In late August, 1974, Mike and I spent a whole day reviewing the entire file, along with the homicide files of Rantis and Cascone. On the wall in our office hung a handwritten chart of all of the recent homicides. At the far right of the page were two columns: "Not Cleared" and "Cleared." The Not Cleared column bore X's optimistically drawn in pencil. The X's in the Cleared column were in ink. Every homicide detective in the city understood that his or her job was to "move the X." The Marcello/Grisafe case was especially significant; there were two X's.

Our review of the total body of evidence convinced Mike and me that if Sam Rantis were alive, we would have a strong enough case to arrest him and charge him with the double homicide. Rantis was himself a murder victim, of course, so he was not amenable to prosecution. There was another way to clear murders, however—Exceptional Clear Up. We would present our detailed evidence to a coroner's jury, seeking a finding of "Murder, by Sam Rantis, now deceased."

We typed a summary report that ran five typewritten pages. Perhaps too complex, we thought, so we prepared a single secondary page enumerating the major points. Then, just to cover our bases a day in advance, we visited the deputy coroner who would be hearing the case. Tony Scafini was one of the more talented deputies in a sea of deputies where, all too often, innate intelligence was not a consideration. Tony reviewed the case with us in detail.

"You're good to go," he announced. "See you tomorrow."

The next morning, the coroner's inquest into the deaths of Marcello and Grisafe was duly convened at 9:00 a.m. Tony guided me through the preliminaries and then threw the testimony open to me. As I methodically presented the facts, I glanced over and suddenly realized there was one crucial area over which I had no control—the actual members of the jury. The coroner's jury was made up of six very elderly men, most likely friends or relatives of staff of the coroner's office. As I proceeded, I noticed that at least two of them were sound asleep. The others looked, at best, glazed over by the complex case. The court reporter dutifully clicked away as I talked, but I honestly felt that she was the only one paying any attention to what I was saying.

At the conclusion, Scafini dutifully inquired whether there were any more witnesses. There were none. He then charged the jury with the case, and they woke up and slowly shuffled out to deliberate in the hallway outside the hearing room. They always took five to ten minutes. I think that most of them took this as an opportunity for a bathroom break. After the semi-obligatory ten minutes, they shuffled back into the hearing room.

"Gentlemen of the jury, have you reached a verdict?" intoned Scafini.

"We have," responded the most alert of the six.

"And what say you?"

"We find this case to be murder, by person or persons unknown."

My heart sank—there went our clear up—but Scafini leapt out of his chair.

"No! No! No!" he shouted as the jury suddenly awakened at his outburst. "You've got it all wrong. Go back out in the hallway, and I'll come out to help you."

Tony Scafini waited until they had oh, so slowly shuffled out of the room, and then he rapidly followed. He returned in a few minutes, and once again, we waited several minutes until the men laboriously hobbled back in.

"Gentlemen of the jury, have you reached a verdict?" intoned Scafini as though he were saying it for the very first time.

"We have," responded their leader.

"And what say you?"

"We find this case to be murder, by Sam Rantis, now deceased."

I heaved a sigh of relief as I gathered my papers.

"Thanks, Tony," I said.

"My pleasure," he responded.

Back at the office, Mike and I reviewed our summary report. No less than seven homicide teams, comprised of fourteen men, had participated in this intense two month-investigation. Together, we had brought a most bizarre case to a successful conclusion.

Two years later, the Cook County Coroner's Office was replaced by the Office of the Medical Examiner, thus doing away with inquests and coroner's juries.

James Erwin was the only participant in this case to survive... for a time. In May of 1976, he was killed in a hail of gunfire, hit thirteen times as he stepped from his car at 1873 North Halsted Street. I wondered whether anyone sang "the gang's all here..." at his wake?

Author's Note: This story is dedicated to my longtime homicide partner, Detective Michael Shull. Upon his passing several years ago, I "inherited" his personal files and case notes—without those, this story would not have been possible.

Why Now? Why Here?

By Jay

November 18, 1999

Standing there, taking a deep breath, I saw one of the most amazing sights I had ever seen. It was a meteor shower emitting the most incredible colors I could ever imagine. It had to be a mile long with every shade of blue, red, and yellow. This was the view I had often hoped for while lying out at a campsite in Wisconsin or the Upper Peninsula of Michigan. It would be the perfect scene while relaxing next to the glowing embers of our dwindling campfire. It would be the icing on the cake after a long day of appreciating the beauty around me. A blink of the eye and it was gone. I realized that I wasn't camping in Wisconsin or Michigan. I realized that this wonderful sight was viewed from a place I could have never imagined seeing it from.

My legs grew weak again after remembering that I had just climbed twelve stories in search of an offender. Last night, he had a gun. Tonight, he came back with the same threats but no weapon was seen. I found myself perched along the balcony at 660 W. Division, the heart of the Cabrini-Green housing projects. I looked down over a hundred feet at my squad car parked on the front lawn, parked over broken glass, broken crack pipes, and broken dreams. I was praying that no one would bust out the windows or tag my car with spray paint. It would be too much paperwork if that happened.

A quick glance back up at the horizon and I realized that the meteor was gone. The rainbow of lights over the city skyline had vanished. I could hear another officer enduring the pains of the hysterical victim from behind me. He had to take the report and listen to her life story. I had to walk back down twelve flights of stairs, hoping to avoid cockroaches and rats.

I wonder whether I would have appreciated this sight more if I were camping in Wisconsin or Michigan. Maybe it was just a little image of beauty in such an ugly place. Maybe it was a reminder always to look for good when surrounded by bad. Maybe it was just a way to make me smile when I was certain that I wouldn't smile until my shift was over.

I might forget where I saw the meteor shower from that night. I might forget the whores and hoodlums whom I ran across that night. But I will never forget that most magnificent sight that, for an instant, swept me away from the squalor and desperation that surrounded me.

Thusly, a Scuffle Ensued...

By Jim

Mae Beth Jefferson eased her late-model sedan slowly down the dark country road. She had driven west from Chicago for over an hour, avoiding the expressways—she couldn't risk being stopped by the police.

Miles of farmland were on each side of the road, crops plowed under for the winter. It was bitter cold and her headlights picked up occasional flakes of glistening white snow. She had no idea where she was.

The man slumped awkwardly in the front seat beside her moaned softly and it startled her. She knew he was there, of course—she had shot him an hour earlier as they sat parked at the edge of Chicago's Douglas Park. This would be the end of his journey.

Mae pulled the car onto the frozen shoulder, walked around, and opened the passenger door. The man was quiet now as she tugged on his arm. He didn't budge. Leaving the door open, she returned to the driver's side and pushed; still there was very little movement. She glanced nervously up and down the deserted road; her white nurse's uniform contrasting with the surrounding night. No one was in sight.

She seated herself in the driver's seat, braced her back against the door and her feet against the body, and pushed with all her strength. He tumbled silently out the door onto the solid cold ground. She went back around the car to close the passenger door, but the body was blocking it so she pulled the car ahead a few feet and finally got the door closed. For a final time, she returned to the driver's seat and proceeded slowly down the road.

Mae Beth was an intelligent and educated woman—a licensed registered nurse no less. Where others might have struggled with the curriculum, things came easy to her. With little effort, she had graduated, passed the state license exam, and taken a job at a local hospital on Chicago's West Side.

Her supervisors would tell you that she was a pleasant woman and an eager worker, but she needed close supervision. She was just shy of being the complete package, and the element that was missing was common sense, a flaw that would stalk her relentlessly over the next forty-eight hours.

Twenty-four hours later, Mike and I were cruising the West Side when we were paged to call our office. We found an outdoor public phone and I stood shivering in the cold as I spoke to our sergeant.

"Padar, Shull…you guys have a homicide, one in custody, now at the Kane County Sheriff's office."

"Kane County? For Christ's sake, how can that be ours?"

"It's ours and now it's yours."

"Where's the body?" I asked.

"Kane County Coroner's Office."

"Wait!" I yelled into the frozen phone. "There's a homicide in Kane County, and a victim, and an offender, all in Kane County, and it's ours?"

"That's right," replied the sergeant. "Call me when you get out there." He hung up the phone.

Mike was incredulous.

"How in the hell can that be ours?"

"I don't have the faintest idea," I said. "But do you want to call the sergeant back and argue?"

Silence...both Mike and I knew that would be a lose-lose scenario.

We stopped at the 12th District and called Kane County for detailed directions on how to get there. Less than an hour later, we walked into the sheriff's office.

The Chief Deputy ran it down for us:

Early that morning, a local farmer found a partially frozen body along a county highway. Examination showed the man had died from a single gunshot wound to the abdomen. A wallet on the body tentatively ID'd him as Deshawn Carter. They were waiting fingerprint confirmation, but a name check showed that he had a record in Chicago for battery and burglary as well as several arrests for disorderly conduct.

"So you had a mystery," Mike interjected.

"Yep, a stone cold whodunit with no leads, but that changed fairly quickly. The little lady in there..." he nodded toward an interrogation room, "started calling local hospitals out here inquiring about a Deshawn Carter. One of the nurses recognized the name as the homicide DOA from this morning, so she had the lady on the phone call our office."

"And she did?" I asked in amazement. "Who is she?"

"She claims to be Deshawn's girlfriend. Her name is Mae Beth Jefferson, and she's an R.N. at one of your local hospitals. But she was evasive when we asked why she was calling out here...so we sent a couple of our guys into the city to talk to her. They sweet-talked her into coming back here to ID the body."

"And so now, you not only had a lead, you had a hot suspect," I said smiling. I always liked it when a mystery began to unravel.

"Sure did, and when she saw the body, she broke down and admitted to shooting him during an altercation, and driving him out here and dumping the body, although she claims he was alive when she dumped him at the side of the road."

"So let me get this straight," Mike said as pleasantly as possible. "You've got the body, you've got the offender, and you've got a confession, and you want to turn it all over to us?"

"Well…he was shot in Chicago…."

"Yeah, but he was transported to Kane County…. Hell, he might have even died in Kane County, but regardless, the venue for prosecution lies anywhere along the path of the body."

"But the real crime scene is the car, and that's back in Chicago," said the Kane County Chief Deputy. "And there's one other thing—our assistant state's attorney talked to your assistant state's attorney, and they agreed that you should take it just from a logistical point of view."

That was the trump card—I knew this would be our case.

"Just one more thing," I said. "She's in custody in Kane County. We'll have to bring her before a judge to get an order permitting us to take her back to Cook County."

"Ah, but she's not in custody," said the chief deputy. "We haven't charged her. There's a possible element of self-defense and the investigation is ongoing. She's free to go, but *we* brought her out here, and I'll bet she'd really appreciate a ride back to the city." He was smiling broadly now.

"Let us call our assistant state's attorney," Mike said.

A quick call to our Felony Review assistant state's attorney confirmed he was up to date on the case.

"Look," he said. "Tell her she's free to go—make sure the chief deputy and your partner are in the room when you tell her. Then offer her a ride back to the city. She'll go for it—they tell me she's as dumb as a box of rocks. Then suggest she come back to the homicide office to talk to me and clarify a few things."

"And if she insists on going home?" I asked.

"Then take her home. We'll pick her up tomorrow morning...
but if that happens, and I don't think it will, we'll have to post a car
on her vehicle until the mobile crime lab can process it."

And so it came to pass that Mae Beth, Mike, and I found ourselves in an unmarked squad, heading back into Chicago. She chat-
ted amiably—she was indeed intelligent and educated.

She jumped at the chance to accompany us to our office to tell
the felony review ASA her story. She really wanted to straighten the
whole mess out.

At the Maxwell Street Homicide office, Mae was Mirandized in
writing in the presence of the ASA. She told her story willingly and
without hesitation, but when the ASA asked whether she would
give a formal written statement to a court reporter, she was thrown
for a moment.

"That would make me very nervous," she said. "Can't I just
write it out for you in my own words?"

The ASA, Mike, and I stared at one another for a moment.
Neither Mike nor I had ever taken a handwritten statement.

"That'll work," said the ASA after a brief pause. "Let's get you
some paper."

Pads of lined paper were not to be had in our office, but the
ASA managed to dig one out of the bottom of his briefcase.

Mae Beth Jefferson began to write in earnest as we watched
from a distance in the squad room.

"Let's see what she comes up with," said the ASA. "We can
always go back to a formal court reporter statement if we need to."

Mae wrote for nearly an hour, and the results were nothing less
than eloquent...and incriminating.

She wrote of a relationship that was *"steeped in passion but
punctuated with tumultuous tirades."* On the day of the incident,
Deshawn had called her at work and asked to see her. She took a
break from her duties and met him in the park near her car. They
sat in her car and the conversation became *"...intense and irratio-*

nal and thusly, a scuffle ensued." Mae had a .25 caliber automatic in the side pocket of the driver's door. She shot Deshawn once in the stomach. She returned to work briefly and asked to be excused for the rest of her shift. Then she went back to her car and drove Deshawn to a *"dark and desolate road"* where she *"pushed him out of the car into the stygian night and hoped he would get help in time."*

Mae had written an elegant essay on murder, and she appeared pleased with her composition, but would it stand on its own as a confession for court? It was detailed, but if it had been a Q & A court reporter statement, there were items that would have been clarified:

- What was the exact nature of the "scuffle?"
- Why didn't she seek help at the hospital less than 100 yards away?
- How did she expect him to get help on the dark and desolate road in the "stygian" night?

A copy of the handwritten statement was faxed to the Chief of the Felony Review Unit. It was now well past midnight, and while he was not thrilled with being awakened, he studied the document carefully. Ultimately, it was decided that the raw power of a coherently handwritten statement would carry more weight in court than a sterile typewritten page transcribed by a court reporter. Mae Beth Jefferson was charged with murder and sent to the women's lockup.

Epilogue I

The bond court judge initially set a very high bond in spite of the fact that Mae had no previous record. Later, her attorney petitioned for a reduction in bond, which was granted, but she was still unable to make bail.

Months later, as a trial date was being discussed, a negotiated plea was suggested. The defense attorney felt he would be unable to surmount the fact that Mae had driven Deshawn over fifty miles and dumped his body on a deserted road, believing he was still alive.

Mae ultimately pled guilty to a reduced charge of voluntary manslaughter in return for an indeterminate sentence at the bottom of the sliding scale. She would do penitentiary time, but as a relatively young woman, she would be out with time to rebuild her life.

Epilogue II

Over the next several years, Mike and I would often lift a phrase from Mae's handwritten statement. When writing a case narrative recounting an altercation, we would begin the paragraph with...

"Thusly, a scuffle ensued."

"You Saved My Baby!"

By Jim

audio at www.OnBeingACop.com/soundtracks/risk.mp3

Chicago's West Side, 1975. The radio call was a man stabbed.

Mike and I trotted in between the buildings of the Henry Horner Homes, but we instinctively slowed, approaching the play lot. There was a crowd as one would expect on this warm summer evening, especially at the scene of a stabbing—but the people were strangely quiet—there was clearly something else going on here. Just a few months earlier, a Chicago police officer had been shot and killed by a sniper from these buildings. It was not a nice place to be, and tonight, we were the first officers on the scene.

We slowed and unsnapped our holsters, keeping our hands on our snub-nosed revolvers as we continued more cautiously toward the group. Our uniform was "summer homicide," short sleeve dress shirts, ties, and slacks. Our sports coats hung on the rear seat hooks in our unmarked sedan, now parked at the curb on the south edge of the housing project. Our lifeline, our radio, was firmly affixed to the car dashboard; the Detective Division would be the last in the department to be upgraded to the new handheld personal radios.

As we got closer, the crowd took note and created a path for us. In the center of the group lay a muscular teenager, staring wide-eyed at the sky. No one was within twenty feet of him, and we stopped in our tracks when we saw why. The shirtless young black male had been stabbed in the neck—the right carotid artery to be exact—and with each contraction of his heart, a stream of blood shot ten to fifteen feet from his body. He writhed about from time to time, and the direction of the blood would shift slightly with each movement. The crowd would murmur and shift even further away. We snapped our holster straps closed.

"Oh shit!" Mike and I exclaimed simultaneously. No matter how many first aid movies you may have seen, nothing can prepare you for this sight in real life.

"I'll get a compress," said Mike as he headed back to the car.

"And call for an ambulance!" I yelled after him as I approached the young man.

In our police careers, both Mike and I had witnessed people bleed out from massive head wounds or other horrendous trauma that simply could not be staunched with the 4" gauze compresses we carried in our case. But this was different. The point of bleeding was immediately identifiable. If I could just get my fingers on that point and apply pressure until Mike returned, the young man might have a chance. I wasn't quite sure how we would apply a compress with enough pressure and avoid strangling the young man at the same time, but that was not the present problem.

Somehow, I got close enough to his body without getting a direct hit. I knelt next to him and placed the fingers of my right hand directly on the wound. I could feel the carotid pulsing, but miraculously, the bleeding stopped. With that accomplished, I had time to contemplate our next move, but I didn't have the faintest idea what that would be. I looked at his face, still wide-eyed but conscious. Primal fear was the only way to describe his expression. The crowd stared silently. In the background, I could hear the wail of responding sirens. What seemed like several minutes was in reality probably only seconds.

Mike, 12th District uniformed personnel, and two paramedics, burst through the crowd at the same time…and they stopped in their tracks.

"Oh, shit," said the paramedics as they looked at the streams of blood spatter that had streaked across the concrete.

"No shit," I muttered to myself.

They showed a light on the man's neck and my hand.

"Don't move your hand!" they said as they opened their case of magic.

"Flatten your palm against his neck, but don't move your fingers. Pressure! Maintain pressure!"

Okay, I'm doing that, I thought to myself.

Imagine my surprise when their magic appeared to be yards and yards of Ace bandages wrapped around my hand and the victim's neck.

"And your plan is?" I asked.

"You're coming with us," they said. "And don't move your fingers!"

One of the paramedics retreated to the ambulance and returned with the stretcher. It wasn't easy, but somehow, they maneuvered the patient, now totally unconscious, onto the stretcher, raised it to about waist high, and all of us began to glide slowly toward the street. Once at the ambulance, it was apparent that I was on the wrong side for conventional transport.

"You'll have to kneel next to him."

I looked at the corrugated steel floor. "Not without a pillow."

"Give the pussy a pillow," said one of the paramedics with a glint in his eye.

"Don't fuck with me or I'll move my fingers."

"Okay, okay!"

Once inside the ambulance, it was all business. The one paramedic started oxygen and was attempting to start an IV line while the other was radioing vital signs to the hospital. It was the first time I recall hearing the term "hypovolemic shock" among other medical terms, and the hospital responded in a terse exchange with the paramedic on the radio.

The silent crowd had come alive, surrounded our vehicle, and begun pounding on the sides.

"What choo doin?"

"Ain't you goin a take 'em?"

"Go! Go! Go!" They began to chant, all the while pounding on the sides of the ambulance.

The paramedic was still struggling with the IV.

A blue-and-white-checkered hat appeared at the sliding window on the rear door.

"Hey, guys, ya gotta move. There's too many of them here."

"Goddammit!" cursed the paramedic on the radio.

"Standby, we have to move!" he shouted into the radio.

He climbed into the driver's seat and we sped a few blocks to a parking lot on the far side of the Chicago Stadium.

"If we don't get an IV started, we're going to lose him," he said as he climbed back with us.

"Negative on the IV," ordered the hospital. "Transport stat!"

"Give me five more seconds," said the paramedic next to me.

And then miraculously, "Got it!"

"Let's move!"

I had never ridden in anything other than an old fashioned Cadillac ambulance, and I was astounded to observe that the newer ambulances were built on a truck chassis. Every block of our ride reminded me of that fact.

At the back door of County, we once again had to gyrate and contort to get the two of us out of the ambulance, my right hand and his neck remaining securely fastened together. That accomplished, we snaked our way through the Emergency Room corridor—which strangely was not our destination. We rolled out into the hallway where an elevator took us to the second floor trauma unit, known simply as Ward 32. I had been there dozens of times, investigating various shooting and stabbings. The Cook County trauma unit was probably one of the most competent in the world, but this visit would be quite different for me.

If I thought the patient and I were to be immediately released from one another, I was mistaken. The paramedics described the incredulous scene to the doctors, and they turned to me questioningly.

"That's right," I said. "He was pumping ten to fifteen foot streams."

"And that's where your fingers are now?"

I nodded.

"Don't move your hand."

And they started to work their medical magic. The victim was smoothly transferred from the fire department stretcher to the trauma unit gurney. His blood pressure was perilously low, called out with a single number rather than the pair of figures we are used to hearing. "Sixty!" And a few moments later, "Fifty-five!" Pulse was rapid. There were no breath sounds in his right lung. A urinary catheter was inserted—that always caused me to shudder no matter how many times I had seen the procedure. They couldn't start their own IV and the one started in the parking lot of the Chicago Stadium was now being used to push a unit of blood while they started a cut-down in his groin to provide for a more rapid infusion of blood.

At any given moment, four or more persons were working on him. The medical terms being thrown about by doctors and nurses alike sounded like a foreign language to me. I understood enough to know that they suspected that internal bleeding might have drained into his pleural cavity, causing the right lung to collapse. They called for a chest tube to be inserted immediately next to where my right elbow was positioned. I shifted away a few inches, but I couldn't move any further. The incision and insertion without anesthetic resulted in a low moan and some movement on the patient's part, and I took that as an encouraging sign. But when the tube was finally inserted, bright red blood flowed out, confirming internal bleeding.

"Clamp it! Clamp it!" someone shouted. "We need to get more blood into him."

Every step was a balancing act, but slowly, I began to get the general impression that the plan was to prepare him for transport to the operating room. A vascular surgery team had been assembled and was in place. How far would I go? I wondered silently.

Suddenly, they were concentrating on the ace bandages around my hand and his neck.

"Don't move your hand until we tell you! Maintain pressure!"

They started to unwrap several feet of blood-soaked elastic bandages.

"Okay…when we tell you…remove your hand and step away."

I checked the path behind me and nodded my head.

"Now!" shouted the doctor.

I pulled my hand away and stepped into the pathway behind me without looking back at the patient. We had been joined together for well over an hour. As I flexed my hand and elbow, he and his gurney were disappearing out the door on the way to the OR. I found a wash station at the back of the trauma unit and scrubbed with a hexachlorophene-impregnated sponge for several minutes. While I was drying, Mike appeared at my side.

"Where's that 4" compress I sent you for?" I asked with mock indignation.

"Go fuck yourself," he responded. "Can we leave now, doctor?"

We laughed and the medical people still in the trauma unit shot us a look.

I had blood on my shirt, and I was sure there had to be some on my trousers. We only had about ninety minutes left on our shift.

"Let's go in to the office. I'm going to ask to be excused so I can go home and clean up. Do we have any idea who this guy is?"

"I know who he is," said Mike facetiously. "Wiggins. Larry Wiggins. He's nineteen, and he lives in the Henry Horner Homes."

"Well, I'm glad you were doing something useful while I was… tied up." We both laughed again.

Back at our Maxwell Street office, Mike started typing a Serafini Report, an unofficial note detailing what we knew, in the event Wiggins expired before we returned to work the next afternoon.

I headed home to shower and throw in a load of laundry.

• • • •

For the next two days, we immediately checked on Larry Wiggins' condition when we arrived for work. The first day post-op, he was listed as "critical." The second day, he got a half-notch upgrade to "critical but stable," a meager improvement.

We attempted some interviews at the Henry Horner Homes, but the attitude toward the police was several steps beyond hostile. The offender was nicknamed "Pookie," and we got a general physical description, but nobody would identify him beyond that. We enlisted the help of a robbery detective from our adjoining office. He was an encyclopedia of ghetto nicknames. Problem was, he told us, there were about a dozen Pookies on the West Side. But with Larry Wiggins very slowly improving, he began to drop lower on our priority list. Homicide was the game, and our Maxwell Street unit had earned the nickname "The Murder Factory" the hard way. Wiggins was alive and improving—time enough to interview him in person in a week or so.

The third day when we arrived for work, there was no need to call the hospital. The sergeant handed us a report from our morgue man reclassifying the Wiggins Aggravated Battery to Homicide/Murder. Larry Wiggins had expired suddenly during the early morning hours. The autopsy listed his cause of death as "Cerebral

Thrombosis secondary to Traumatic Laceration of the Right Carotid Artery" (stab wound). In short, Larry had suffered a stroke from a blood clot that had probably originated from the site of the knife wound. That put Larry back at the top of our priority list for the evening.

After roll call, we trekked over to the Henry Horner Homes once again, but this time we went directly to the apartment where Larry had lived with his mother and sisters. As we entered, the mood was quiet and somber. A girl I would later learn was Larry's younger sister turned to her mother.

"Mama, this is the detective I told you about," she said, nodding toward me.

"Oh, sweet Jesus!" she shouted as she took about three steps and put me in a bear hug. "You saved my baby! You saved my baby!" She sobbed as she held tightly to me.

Didn't she know? Hadn't they told her? Her son had been dead now for well over twelve hours. I held her tightly, not knowing what her reaction was going to be, but she had to know the truth.

"Ma'am! Ma'am!" I put my mouth close to her ear. "Larry passed away early this morning."

She released me and put her hands on each of my arms just above the elbow.

"Don't you understand?" she said. "You gave him a chance; oh Lord, you gave him a chance!"

I stared dumbly at her as she regained her composure.

"Jesus put you there so we could see him and tell him we loved him…and say goodbye. You did that for us."

"Yes, ma'am," was all I could say.

"We're looking for Pookie," I added lamely after a short pause.

She stood straighter and stronger, taking on the persona of the tough, resilient black matriarchs whom I had seen so often in the ghetto.

"We know Pookie," she said. "We'll bring him in to you."

"Mrs. Wiggins, that's our job. We don't want anything happening to you…or to Pookie."

She smiled, indulgently, I thought.

"His mama and I—we bring him in to you—ain't nothin' goin' to happen to him. We be doin' the right thing." Her tone left no room for argument.

Two hours later, an entourage arrived at the Maxwell Street Homicide office with Pookie in tow. He was a big young man, but with his mama at his side, he looked meek and bedraggled. The whole entourage stayed at the office while we took statements from Pookie and several witnesses. The assistant state's attorney from the Felony Review Unit arrived, reviewed the case, and approved murder charges.

It was well after midnight when we called for Pookie to be transported to the lockup. The two mamas, Larry's sisters, and two witnesses left together. Everybody's lives had changed the past few days, but the mamas walked out arm in arm, solid and straight. In a very real sense, they had each lost a son to ghetto violence, but no pair of mothers ever appeared more resolute in adversity.

I should have felt good—investigation, arrest, a cleared homicide—but in one way it was a hollow accomplishment: I really hadn't "saved" anybody.

Back on Home Turf
By Jim & Jay

*Another story from Jay. All of us in law enforcement have those inci-
dents where we have felt our finger tighten on the trigger. Often, time
is compressed or expanded while your mind whirls...do I pull one more
ounce, or do I wait? I'm convinced, from experience, that most times, in
this city, the police wait and someone lives to see another day. But when
the situation resolves, it's no less traumatic on us as police officers. We
came within an ounce of taking someone's life. Just part of the job....*

December 9, 1999
Back on home turf—The 24ᵗʰ District (Rogers Park)

After a couple of long weeks on temporary assignment in
Cabrini-Green, my partner and I finally returned to the 24th
District. It was a slow night. Not a soul on the streets or a gang-
banger in sight. We searched for drug dealers and any vehicle that
deserved to be stopped. We stopped for the young black male who
was yelling, "Officer!"

We were on Juneway Terrace and Marshfield. It's an area the
locals call "The Jungle." He was probably around twenty years old

and was being chased down the block by a larger and older black male. The younger of the two kept yelling at us, "He's gonna cut me! He's gonna cut me!"

I curbed the squad car and jumped out of the vehicle. The larger of the two held a meat hook in his hand, swinging it violently from left to right. He was right up against the passenger side door so my partner was unable to exit the vehicle. The only thing that stood between me and the meat hook was the 1996 Chevy Caprice that I complain about every day for its terrible pickup and lousy handling.

"Drop it, drop it, drop it!" The meat hook never dropped to the ground. I could feel the butt of my handgun in the palm of my right hand. My finger tightened a bit on the trigger. It took precious seconds of concentration, but I looked up and saw the street sign. I called in our location and asked for another unit to back us up. Before I got a response from dispatch, I saw another squad car pulling in right behind us. Our offender's weapon finally hit the ground. He was placed in the back of our squad car and the weapon was recovered.

The victim was the stepson; the offender was the stepfather. It turned out to be a simple domestic dispute. The stepfather had drank about a fifth of whiskey and got upset when the stepson started laying the sofa cushions on the floor to make his bed up for the night.

I can't even tell you what their names were because I couldn't stand being near them when my partner took their information and ran their names. I just paced back and forth a couple of yards from the car.

I could've shot the stepfather and been justified. I could've missed and struck the innocent person two blocks down. I could've just ignored the calls for help and let the beat car handle the outcome. I can't solve their problems or give them hope. I can just help them to live another day and hope that they solve their differences tomorrow.

Good to be back on home turf? My home turf isn't the 24th District, it's a small two-bedroom condo up in Edison Park. It's the place where I can watch a little TV, go to sleep, and dream about the good things in life. It's the place where I wake up and thank God for the day ahead of me. It's the place I return to at night and pray to God, thanking Him for once again getting me home safely.

The Wrong Guy

By Jim

Just after midnight, the black limo with heavily tinted windows pulled to the curb in front of White's Shrimp House on Chicago's West Side. Before the chauffeur could exit, Leon Woods opened the door, stepped out to the sidewalk, and turned to help Theresa Dodson from the car. While she slid across the seat to grab his hand, Woods turned suddenly and exchanged words with a young man. A shot punctuated the Saturday night noises, and for a moment, everyone was quiet. Woods crumpled to the ground, curled into a fetal position, and moaned softly. The young man fled east toward Kedzie Avenue.

"Woody! Woody!" screamed Theresa as she stumbled from the car and knelt next to her boyfriend.

The chauffeur ran around the front of the car and started east after the gunman, but he had disappeared, so he ran into White's to call the police.

I was working days with another new homicide detective. Even though we were both experienced street cops, between the two of us, Jason Moore and I had less than eighteen months' homicide experience, but we perceived ourselves to be sharp and we worked well together.

At the Sunday 8:30 a.m. roll call, the sergeant called our names.

"Padar, Moore, you guys have a fresh one from last night. We just got the call that he died on the table at Cook County. See the midnight crew; they can bring you up to speed." The midnight detectives were just finishing a lengthy Aggravated Battery Supplemental Report when they got the word that Woods had expired.

"You guys are fresh," they told Jason and me. "Why don't you retype this and reclassify to a Homicide/Murder Supplemental?"

Jason and I looked at on another…. We were new, but not dumb, and the last thing we wanted to do was spend the next several hours retyping someone else's report.

"Why don't you guys just retype the first page reclassifying? The rest of the pages will be the same. We'll cover the new information in our report at the end of the day," said Jason.

They looked at us as if we were trying to trick them somehow.

"That'll work," said the older detective after a moment's reflection.

Jason and I headed out the door to re-interview Theresa Dodson.

"Hey! You guys!" shouted the midnight crew. "They found this under his body…. Don't know what it means, but we're going to inventory it as possible evidence."

We stopped and looked at an extension cord that had been wrapped in black electrical tape.

"Looks like a homemade blackjack. Are we sure it was his?"

"We don't know, but it was under his body, so most likely it belonged to him."

After some difficulty, we found Theresa at her sister's apartment where she had gone after leaving the hospital while Woods was still in surgery. Thankfully, she had been notified of Woods' death before we arrived. Although distraught, she agreed to talk with us about the shooting. She seemed sincere and anxious, but she couldn't tell us much.

It had been the one-year anniversary of their first date, so her boyfriend had wanted to make it a special night. He hired a limousine and driver and they were to spend the night hopping from club to club. Around midnight, they were hungry and stopped at White's Shrimp House for a late-night snack. Her dear Woody was shot as he exited the limo.

She had the impression that Woods had exchanged words with the shooter, but she didn't hear the conversation. After the shooting, she went to Woods' side and did not pay any attention to the gunman. She thought he appeared young and was wearing jeans and a tan T-shirt. Woods lay moaning softly until the ambulance arrived—he did not speak. The homemade blackjack belonged to Woody—he carried it for protection. To the best of her knowledge, he did not own any firearms.

Leon Woods worked with his father in a wholesale import business on Pulaski Road. It was family owned, and he spent five to six days a week at the warehouse. He had no enemies to her knowledge.

As we were concluding Theresa's interview, we received word that Woods' autopsy was about to begin, and since our "morgue man" had the day off, our office sent us to observe.

As we arrived, Woods had just been moved from a morgue tray to an examination table. There was evidence of the large, closed surgical incision, but as the diener (the pathologist's assistant) opened the abdominal cavity, it was filled with free blood. A single bullet hole was located about four inches above the navel. After clearing the blood, examination of the liver showed evidence of a lacerating bullet wound and attempted surgical repair.

"They should have had a successful outcome; it's unusual for County to drop the ball on a case like this," said the pathologist as he gave us a running narrative.

He gently removed the liver and handed it off to the diener.

"Ah, but they were doomed along with Mister Woods," said the doctor as he suctioned residual blood.

"Look here," he exclaimed. "The bullet transversed the liver and lodged at the edge of the anterior spine, but look, look right here."

He took the handle of the scalpel and gently probed the aorta, exposing a small ¼" laceration.

"The bullet nicked the aorta. The surgeons were dealing with a blood-filled abdominal cavity and a lacerated liver. But hidden deep behind the liver was a second more serious hemorrhage source, the aorta. I doubt anyone could have saved him."

After photographs, he gently removed what appeared to be a .25 caliber bullet. We would be looking for a .25 caliber semi-automatic pistol as the murder weapon, but if it were a semi-auto, where was the shell casing?

We checked back with the office where the midnight crew had finished its report. No casing was mentioned—in fact, the scene had not been processed as a homicide. At the time of the initial investigation, Leon Woods was a shooting victim, not a murder victim.

Jason and I headed back to the sidewalk in front of White's Shrimp House. With the aid of bright sunlight, we found a shiny .25 caliber shell casing nestled in a sidewalk crack. The mobile crime lab responded, took pictures, and recovered the casing.

We looked to the east. Witnesses had reported that the shooter had fled in that direction and quickly disappeared. Several doors down was a shoeshine parlor. It was a large establishment with about a dozen shine stations along one wall and chairs for waiting customers along the other. Manned mostly by teenagers from the neighborhood, it was a thriving business. The owner did not tolerate drug or alcohol use on the premises, and the boys worked hard and probably made a good buck. It was favored by cop and civilian alike, some coming from great distances. In my estimation, it was by far the best shoeshine in the city.

Jason and I decided we both needed a shine, and as we walked in, we were immediately descended upon by the boys.

"Shine, officer?" they shouted over one another. They recognized detectives and uniformed officers with equal accuracy. They knew that the owner would not charge the police, and most officers tipped generously, double the cost of the shine. We were desirable customers.

We settled into our chairs and casually inquired whether our polishers had been working last night. We dared not ask anything more with the other boys all ears. We finished and tipped the boys and approached the owner at the counter. He waved us out, indicating that the shines were on the house, but we stopped and asked him whether he was there last night at the time of the shooting.

Yes, he had been there. No, no one had seen the shooting from inside the shop. Yes, he would call if he learned anything. Fat chance. We left business cards.

Jason and I had inherited the case from the midnight crew. It was technically their case, but it would be difficult for them to do any in-depth investigation during midnight hours. We tackled the assignment with great enthusiasm.

Witnesses were re-interviewed and then interviewed again. The best of the lot was the limo driver who described the shooter as 5'10", dark complexion, wearing a tan T-shirt and blue jeans. He had run east on Madison and disappeared quickly.

After a week, the investigation languished. We felt the key to the case was in the shoeshine parlor. It was a community gathering place, and while the gunman might not be one of the boys, we felt that they knew who it was, and in fact, we strongly suspected that the shooter may have fled through the store to the alley to make good his escape. But no one was talking.

Eventually, our nearly constant pressure in the 3200 block of West Madison made enough people so nervous that bits and pieces of anonymous tips and clues began to filter in to us. It was all second- or third-hand information, none of which could be attributed to any individual:

- The shooter was not from the neighborhood
- The shooter was not one of the boys at the shoeshine parlor
- The shooter did run through the store to the alley behind
- Nearly all of the workers at the shoeshine parlor knew who he was

Most of the information came from emissaries of business people in the area. In short, they didn't want us hanging around constantly—it was bad for business. We couldn't have cared less, of course; we would continue to stop in every day until we got something substantial enough to clear the case. We needed to step up the pressure somehow.

Jason and I came up with a plan. We would find the shoeshine worker who most closely matched the description of the offender and bring him in for questioning. It was certainly a legitimate thing to do—question someone on the basis of a physical description. Hopefully, skilled questioning would yield information that would help us identify the real killer. It all seemed so simple, but in reality, it would lead us down the path of multiple errors in judgment, born in part of our inexperience. Would we blow the case entirely?

The hapless lad was Larry Wilson, age seventeen. He was 5' 10", dark complexion, and on the day we snatched him from the shoeshine parlor, he was wearing a tan T-shirt and blue jeans. We put the word out on the street that Larry was our man and he would be charged with murder. Nothing could be further from the truth, of course—we had no case against him other than his physical description.

Back at the homicide office, we cajoled Larry with the promise that if he were the wrong guy, giving us information leading to the right guy would earn his immediate release. Larry was a pleasant young man, but he told us nothing. Time to increase the pressure—thus began our series of mistakes.

We could have held a faux lineup and told Larry he was identified as the offender. But we contacted our best witness, the chauffeur, and held a real lineup, and much to our surprise, the chauffeur positively identified Larry Wilson as the shooter. Because Jason and I were inexperienced, our supervisors were doing their job and watching us closely. Of course, we had not advised them of our masterful scheme, and they were convinced we had cleared the case by the arrest of Wilson. Department regulations required us to notify the State's Attorney's Office in any case where a lineup identification was made. Jason and I were convinced that the chauffeur was basing his identification solely on the clothing Larry Wilson was wearing, but the assistant state's attorney wasn't buying it. He advised us to book Larry and charge him with murder.

Our pleas for release, or at least delay, fell on deaf ears. Both our supervisors and the ASA felt we had done a fine job wrapping up the case and making an arrest. Larry Wilson had remained silent, offering neither a denial nor an alibi. He was transported to Central Detention to await a bond hearing.

For the next several days at morning roll call when the sergeant asked each team what homicide it was working, we would respond, "Woods."

"Woods is cleared. Pick another case."

"But we got the wrong guy!"

"You can't work a cleared case; pick another one."

We would reluctantly give him another name, but when we hit the street, we worked the Woods homicide.

Back at the shoeshine parlor on West Madison, if we were greeted coolly before, we definitely were persona non grata now. Our shoes had been shined about a half-dozen times in the preceding days, but when we walked in now, none of the boys pleaded for our business.

"Look," we told the owner. "We don't think Larry did this either, but if you want to help him, you'll have to help us find the right guy."

A week went by and Larry Wilson was assigned an initial court date well into the following month. It was a Friday just after noon when we popped into the shine parlor once again. The owner nodded to us, the first recognition he had afforded us since Larry's arrest. Then he looked to the far end of the counter and nodded to an older gentleman who had watched us walk in. We approached him and he held out his hand as if to shake ours. I felt a slip of paper in my palm, but I kept my fist closed.

"What's this?" I asked in a low voice.

"It's the right guy," he answered as he turned and walked away. We needed to know who the old man was, so we headed back to the owner.

"Who is that?" we asked.

"Larry's grandfather. Don't worry, man; he's solid to the bone, but he won't talk to you. Ya jus gotta take what comes to ya."

We drove several blocks away before we stopped and opened the crumpled piece of paper. Scribbled in pencil was: Herman Wilson, Goldmine, Apt 510.

Both Jason and I had worked the Cabrini projects and we recognized "Goldmine" as being the ghetto designation for the building at 714 West Division Street. We stopped by the 18th District, cornered a friendly youth officer, and ran an alpha name check on Herman Wilson. He had a juvenile record for burglary and a couple of curfews, and he lived at 714 West Division in Apartment 510. He was now seventeen, which under Illinois law made him an adult.

It was past lunch and we had skipped breakfast. If this case broke this afternoon, we might not get to eat at all, and besides, we needed a plan.

We headed back to West Madison Street again, to a cop favorite, the Palace Grill, a tiny diner with good food. The lunch crowd had cleared out, and Jason and I took a seat at the counter's far end. Hungarian goulash was the special, and ours arrived when Uncle Mike slid the plates to us from the counter's other end. They miraculously skidded to a halt in front of each of us, a bit of the rich red/brown gravy sloshing over the plates' edges onto the counter.

"Presentation is everything," I grinned.

"Yeah, but it's the best goulash in town, so don't knock it."

We ate slowly, each silently wondering how to handle what appeared to be a major break in the case.

"What do we do now?" I asked.

"We pick him up, of course," said Jason.

"And then what?"

"He must suspect that we know something," said Jason. "If he's the right guy, he might even be expecting us—you know, the homicide mystique."

I laughed.

"Yeah, we're so mysterious we arrested the wrong guy."

"Let's just come on strong and confident; let him think it's all over except the paperwork, and see where that takes us."

"Oh, I love these crystal-clear plans," I said. "What could go wrong?"

"That doesn't sound 'strong and confident,' Jim. Do you have a better plan?"

"You mean a better plan than no plan?" I answered sarcastically.

"Okay, I'm listening…" said Jason. Silence.

"All right, let's do it, but I just don't want to dig ourselves a bigger hole," I answered, not exactly strongly or confidently.

We had a Task Force unit meet us at the 714 building, and on the fifth floor, we pounded on the door to apartment 510. A heavyset black woman answered.

"Herman Wilson," we said without further explanation. She held the door open and we cautiously stepped in.

"Herman!" she called. "You all come here, boy.... They're here for you."

Jason and I glanced at one another with raised eyebrows. Mama didn't seem surprised. We searched Herman thoroughly and then cuffed him behind his back, looping the handcuff chain through his belt.

"Herman," I said, "you're under arrest for murder. You have the right to remain silent. You have the right...." I ran through the Miranda warnings, mostly for effect—we normally did that back at the station in the interview room.

"How'd you find him?" asked Mama.

"We're detectives, ma'am; it's what we do," I answered curtly. This "strong and confident" thing was growing on me.

Once out in the squad, Herman tried to speak...

"You probably—"

"We don't want to hear it," I cut him off. "It's all over, Herman."

We pulled out onto Division Street and headed west. We caught the red light at Halsted and Herman tried again.

"You probably won't believe me, but..."

Jason was driving, but he turned in his seat.

"Believe what, Herman?"

"I threw the gun off the bridge right up here."

We stopped just short of the single lane bridge over the Chicago River.

"Where?"

"I'll show you...right up here."

We exited the car and the Task Force unit pulled up behind us.

"He's showing us where he threw the gun," we explained.

"What kinda gun was it?" I asked.

"A little one, a .25 automatic. On the way home, I got scared and threw it in the river."

Bingo! He knew what kind of weapon was used.

"What happened that night?" asked my partner in a kinder, gentler tone.

"I was coming out of the Shrimp House when this gangster pulls up in a black limo with tinted windows. He looked at me and reached under his coat and started to pull out something black.... I got scared and shot him."

"How many times?" I asked.

"Just once. He went right down and I ran."

"What was he pulling on you?"

"I don't know, but he dropped it when I shot."

"Where did you run?"

"Toward Kedzie Avenue, but I cut through the shine parlor. Those kids in there didn't have anything to do with this, I swear.... I just ran through there to the alley and then walked home. I threw the gun in the river when I crossed the bridge."

Ten minutes later, we were marching Herman Wilson into the Area Four Homicide office on West Maxwell Street.

"Who's this?" asked the sergeant.

"The right guy...the Woods homicide...and his story is corroborated by what actually happened."

It was mid-afternoon on a Friday when I found myself and a state's attorney along with Larry Wilson standing in front of a bewildered judge, explaining why we wanted Larry released immediately.

"Well..." said the judge as he pondered the facts, "this case is not on my docket, but I understand that Judge Murphy has left for the day. I won't interfere in his case, but I'll release Larry Wilson to your custody, Detective. You have him back in Murphy's court first thing Monday morning, do you understand?"

I nodded, but I didn't understand. Released to my custody? What the hell did that mean? Was I supposed to bring this kid home with me for the weekend?

Back at our Maxwell Street office, I walked in with Larry in tow, and as we passed the interview room where Herman was manacled to the wall, they caught each other's eye and almost imperceptibly nodded to one another.

In the office, out of earshot, I asked Larry Wilson whether he knew Herman Wilson.

"He's my cousin," answered Larry.

"Did you know he did this?" I asked.

Larry hung his head and nodded.

"And you were going to take a murder rap for him?"

"Well, when we was kids, we burglarized a factory. He got caught and I got away; he never told on me, so I wasn't going to tell on him."

"Larry," I said patiently, "do you understand the difference between a juvenile burglary and an adult murder?"

Larry looked at me, totally mystified.

I dropped Larry off at his home near Central and Lake Streets... with the warning that I would hunt him down and kill him if he were not waiting for me Monday morning.

"Larry, do you know that if you go back to court with me Monday, this will all be over...but if you don't, you'll either be dead or back in jail, depending on who finds you first. Understand?"

Larry nodded silently. He met me at the appointed time Monday and his case was dismissed. I bought him lunch and drove him back home.

Herman Wilson went to trial for murder about two-and-a-half years after his arrest. He spent the whole time in custody. At a bench trial, the judge found him guilty of voluntary manslaughter, based upon the "black object" that victim Leon Woods was pulling from under his coat. Herman was sentenced to five years in prison, but the remaining portion of his sentence was suspended.

And the two rookie homicide detectives, Jason and I, considered the whole case a learning experience. Jason left the department a few years later in a major career change. I stayed on, of course, vowing not to repeat the same mistakes.

7:00 a.m.?

By Jay

Senators, Naked Gays, Schizophrenic Homeless, and a Polish Sausage. How do you tie that together in a short story? It's easy...for a cop.

Where will you be tomorrow at 7 a.m.? In the car on the way to work? Getting your kids ready for school? Maybe you'll be lucky enough still to be sleeping in your bed. I don't know where I'll be tomorrow at 7 a.m., but I can tell you where I've been the last few days.

Three days ago at 7 a.m., I was standing on a street corner, drinking a soda, and discussing the political ramifications of the current situation in Israel. I was having this discussion with an Illinois State Senator. He had stopped by the house we were guarding. The house belonged to a rabbi who was the target of a drive-by shooting incident earlier in the shift. The conversation was pleasant and the break from the previous night's activities was greatly appreciated.

Two days ago at 7 a.m., I was officiating a homosexual domestic violence call. Despite my begging and pleading, the offender, Junior, refused to put on any clothes until my partner and I listened to his side of the story. This was a less than ideal sight after a big breakfast of gyros and eggs. We complied with the victim's wishes and escorted Junior out of the building. He later returned and severely beat the victim for calling the police.

At 7 a.m. yesterday, we were enjoying the sunrise at the lakefront and having another stimulating conversation. This time, we were talking with Crazy Mary. She was explaining to us how agents from Social Security are following her around and forcing her to take invisible liquid medication that causes her legs to swell. "You know, that same stuff you have in the bathrooms at the police station," she further explained. According to Mary, at the same moment we were talking to her, these Social Security agents, possibly FBI agents, were circling her like "Indians circling a wagon train." We tried our best, but we were unable to apprehend any of these invisible drug-toting scoundrels.

And finally, today at 7 a.m. my partner and I were trying to decipher gang graffiti as we enjoyed a Polish sausage at a twenty-four-hour hotdog joint on Maxwell Street. It was a small perk for having to take fingerprint cards down to headquarters. These fingerprints were from our hospitalized, aggravated, battery victim/criminal damage to vehicle offender. Quick hint: If you're going to break out someone's windshield, you'd better be able to run faster than he can.

So I ask you again, where will you be tomorrow at 7 a.m.? I can't tell you where I'll be. I wouldn't even be able to give you an educated guess. I figure I'll find out tomorrow, say somewhere around 7 a.m.

Lights, Sirens, and Angels

By Jim

Chicago, 1967

Roy Pedersen found himself alone for the first time the entire weekend. Alone alone. His parents had driven him in from central Iowa early Saturday morning. When they arrived at the Moody Bible Institute, there were back-to-back activities—a welcome luncheon, an afternoon family prayer meeting, and an icebreaker reception with all the other new students and their parents. A late afternoon, somewhat tearful farewell to family was followed by an upbeat evening meal with songs of prayer and rejoicing. By the time he fell into bed, he was exhausted, both physically and emotionally. Early Sunday morning, breakfast and church services were followed by detailed tours of the facilities and more fellowship activities for the new students.

Evening found him sitting alone on the edge of his bed. He was more than a successful farm boy from an even more successful farming family. But his great-grandfather had been a country preacher, and Roy felt a calling, a calling that led him to this place. However, this day, his eighteen-year-old bones began to feel the first twinge of doubt.

• • • •

Roy entered the county fair auction pit with mixed emotions and his blue-ribbon sow. The auctioneer spoke a few sentences in plain English:

"This is Roy's last year with the 4H—he's goin' off to that Bible school in Chicago—let's do right by him—give him a good send -off. He's from the Pederson Farm, east a town."

Roy heard it all, but he kept his head down, face expressionless, concentrating on guiding his nearly 300-pound hog away from a collision course with one of the three ringmen. It was a bittersweet moment; it would indeed be his last appearance in this place. He almost wished the auctioneer hadn't emphasized that, but deep down, he knew the man was just trying to garner him top dollar, which might even cover his first-semester tuition.

"Okay, folks, this is a 295-pound blue-ribbon winner here. Do I hear...?" The auctioneer began his rapid chant.

The bidding opened with a rapid staccato of competition. The ringmen called the bids at a pace that surprised even Roy. The community was clearly voting its approval of Roy, his prize-winning animal, and perhaps even his chosen vocation.

"Going once, going twice, sold!"

Suddenly, it was over; the winning bid was a record for the day, far above any reasonable market value. Roy allowed just a hint of a grin to cross his face. He liked this moment and everything that had led up to it. He enjoyed the science and challenge of raising high-quality livestock. He loved the unique combination of physical labor and brainpower required to be a success. Still...there was this other voice deep inside his soul.

• • • •

Roy stood up slowly from his bed. He needed to get outside to clear his head. "Lord, will I ever get used to spending this much time indoors?" he thought to himself. It was nearly dusk when he hit the Chicago streets on a cool late summer evening.

He walked north on LaSalle and looked curiously at the neighborhood around him. A mixed bag, he thought. Not real good, but not real bad. But when he crossed Division Street, he found an oasis of white upscale buildings. He cut east through the area and noticed a sign, "Sandburg Terrace." He was on Clark Street now, heading south, deep in a mental inventory—home, school, his calling....

He didn't notice the deteriorating neighborhood, and when he crossed Chicago Avenue, deep in his own thoughts, he was definitely in an area that just didn't register with anything in his prior experience. Drunks lay in the curb, littered with wine bottles, the wind blew trash about, and he noticed for the first time it was dark out. A man approached him with a determined look in his eye, walking on a collision path. Roy made a tactical error and sidestepped toward the building side of the walk. The man grabbed Roy's jacket and pushed him into a doorway. His face was just inches away from Roy's, and Roy smelled his putrid breath of stale wine and cigarettes. They were face-to-face, chest-to-chest now in the doorway as the man wrapped his arms around Roy, pinning his arms at his side, reaching for Roy's back pockets in search of his wallet.

• • • •

The police chaplain once said, "Sometimes angels come with lights and sirens." Now, my tactical partner John Klodnicki and I considered ourselves good cops; however, I doubt we ever would have used the term "angels." But the Lord works in mysterious ways, and I always liked that phrase about lights, sirens, and angels.

Early evening found us in the second-floor tactical office of the 18th District on Chicago Avenue between LaSalle and Clark. We were working soft clothes, and our unmarked sedan was parked at the front curb. Completing the office duties of the moment, we bounded down the front stairs of the station to hit the street. I drove the fifty yards east and then headed south on Clark for no particular reason. We had traveled less than a block when John called out to me.

"Jim! Doorway!"

I glanced to the sidewalk to see two figures, one pushing the other into the doorway, obviously in some kind of struggle. I nosed the squad into the curb, hit the doorway with our spotlight, and activated our bright lights, which began the trademark alternate flashing. John was out of the car before it stopped moving. As I opened my door, from across the street came a short burst of a siren and a blue Mars light began to flash as a northbound squadrol crossed oncoming traffic and nosed into the curb next to us for an instant assist.

Bad guy took one look, threw his hands up in exasperation, turned to the wall, and assumed the search position.

"He was trying to get my wallet!" exclaimed Roy.

"We got him; we got him," I said as I covered John while he searched one pissed off offender. We cuffed him and marched toward the squadrol, but the wagon men had a momentary look of uncertainty.

"You guys got the paper on this, right?" asked one of them.

"Yeah, yeah, we got the paper. But you'll have to write the Honorable Mention." They laughed.

"Meet ya in the tac office."

Up in our second-floor office, things moved rapidly. Roy agreed to sign complaints, but he expressed reservations about how he would do in court. Not to worry, we told him. We would tell him what to say.

We called the Robbery Unit, which told us to charge him with misdemeanor strong-arm robbery and book him for local court, Branch 29, right here in our building.

"But I won't know what to say," complained Roy from a chair in the room's far corner.

Bad guy shot him a look.

"Wait 'til we get yo-yo to the lockup," we said. "We'll tell you what to do in court."

Once we got the arrest report completed along with the signed complaint, we were able to get the prisoner out of the room and down to a cell. We briefed Roy on the court procedure, and he promised us he would appear. We drove him safely back to his dorm. A thirty-second robbery had taken almost three hours to process, and we felt we had done a very respectable job.

• • • •

With the "normal" delaying tactics on the part of the defendant, it was over four months before the defense answered that it was ready for trial. Roy was present at each hearing, and it became readily apparent to the public defender that he wasn't going to go away.

The trial was quick and certain. The prosecution presented only two witnesses, Roy and me. The verdict was guilty of a reduced charge of attempted strong-arm robbery. The judge indicated that Mr. Robber was about to be sentenced to four months in the House of Correction. Since the defendant had been in custody the entire time, awaiting trial, that meant he would walk out of court today, time considered served. But apparently, he wasn't listening or he couldn't do the math.

"Is there anything you would like to tell the court?" the judge asked him.

"Yes, sir, your honor, there is. That officer there," he said pointing to me, "told him how to testify so I would be convicted," now pointing at Roy.

That got the judge's undivided attention.

"Young man," said the judge, addressing Roy. "Step back up here and let me remind you, you are still under oath. Did this officer tell you how to testify?"

"Yes, sir, he did," answered Roy in his most sincere Midwestern Bible student voice.

My mind raced, my pulse quickened. What the hell had I told him? For the life of me, I couldn't remember. I recalled that Roy was anxious about his testimony, but what had I told him? It was all Roy's show now, and I knew for certain this Moody Bible Institute student would take his oath most seriously, and rightly so...still.... The courtroom was dead silent; all eyes were on Roy.

"And just what did he tell you, son?" asked the judge, now peering over his glasses and directly at the young man.

"He told me..." Roy turned and looked directly at me now. "He told me to just tell the truth. Don't add anything and don't leave anything out."

"That'll be all, son," said the judge as he turned to the defendant. "Make that six months in the House of Correction. Mister Bailiff, take him away."

Out in the hallway, Roy looked me in the eye and shook my hand with a firm grip, his left hand just as firmly grasping my shoulder as he thanked me profusely. He was just eighteen and had only a few months under his belt at Moody, but I almost got the sense that he was ministering to this urban cop ten years his senior. He had the gift.

"You guys just swooped down out of nowhere. It was like you were...you were...." He was at a momentary loss for words.

Like we were angels? I couldn't bring myself to say the words, but I knew I felt good about my job and the work we did each day. I smiled broadly.

"Lights and sirens," I said aloud.

"Pardon?"

"Lights and sirens, Roy. We come with lights and sirens."

My New Partner...
If only for a Moment

By Jim & Jay

The last day Jay worked his district assignment prior to his promotion to sergeant, his tactical partner told him, "Jay, ya know...this is the last night in your police career that you'll ever work with a partner."

It was a profound statement of fact. Sergeants, lieutenants, and captains ride the streets alone.

In police work, your partner is a big part of the job. You are ecstatic when you have a good partner. You are unbelievably unsettled when you have a not-so-good partner. You're apprehensive each time you work with an officer new to you. A good partner becomes a sibling. It sounds overly dramatic, but you share life and death each tour of duty. But that becomes taken for granted very quickly. On a day-to-day basis, you share much more. Personal problems, family scenarios, philosophies, idiosyncrasies...the list is infinite.

In over fourteen years on the job as a patrolman and detective, I worked countless tours of duty with other officers. I count but three of those officers as "partners." When I left the last one, I was leaving Homicide for an assignment that would lead to a sergeant's promotion. It makes me sad that I did not realize nor did I mark the last day in my police career that I worked with a partner. I considered all of them brothers. All of this is the backdrop for Jay's story of his first night as a sergeant on the streets of the 11ᵗʰ District.

Every new recruit gets the benefit of being teamed up with an experienced field training officer, or at least another officer with some time on the job. The recruit gets to sit back for the first couple of days and just take things in while his trainer drives the car, operates the radio, and does all the talking. He listens intently as his partner points out old crime scenes, gives up a few tricks of the trade, and chimes in with his own opinion after every radio call is dispatched.

Every new sergeant gets a supervisor's log, a radio, and if he's lucky, maybe even a map of this new district he will be patrolling. My watch commander was nice enough to show me where the radio room and locker room were located. He couldn't find a map of the district, so he rattled off the boundaries, handed me the evening's roster, and told me to handle roll call. After roll call, I wandered out to my squad car, started it up, and tried to remember the district boundaries. I looked up the station's address so I would know how to make it back at the end of the shift.

As I rolled out of the lot, another sergeant walked up to the car and handed me a district map. "You might need this," he said, "… and welcome to Eleven."

I studied the map for a moment, put an "X" where the station was, and proceeded to drive along the borders. After one circle, I found a nice little park where I could sit and get my thoughts together. A moment later, a call of "a robbery just occurred" was broadcast.

"Eleven-eleven, take the robbery just occurred at Lake and Homan. The complainant was just robbed at gunpoint by two black males. Number one was wearing a camouflage jacket and had the gun. Number two was wearing all dark clothing. Last seen heading south from Lake Street."

Well, here was my chance to log a couple of cars and respond to a felony call, just like any good sergeant should do. From the park, I could see blue lights racing down the street. They disappeared before I could get in behind them and follow. I pulled out my trusty map, but before I could even find where I was, the radio crackled.

"Slow down at Lake and Homan, squad. No one's out here. We'll tour the area and see if we can find anything."

All right, now I found where I was and found Lake and Homan. On my ride over there, I saw an older black male waving me down. As I pulled up to him, he was yelling that he was just robbed.

"Eleven-ten, I just found the victim at Homan and..." Typical West Side intersection—only one street sign. "Stand by squad."

"Get in," I said to the victim. I cleared off the passenger seat and opened the door. He was to be my new partner, if only for a moment.

"Okay, where are we at?"

"This is Washington, Sarge. Go right. I just saw them run this way."

"Eleven-ten, squad, the victim said he just saw them running.... What direction is this?"

"That's east, Sarge."

"All right. They're running east on Washington from Homan. I think I see them now halfway down the block."

"That's them, Sarge, right there on the right."

"All right, squad, they just cut through a gangway at 3319 heading south. They're gonna pop out at about 3320.... What's the next street over?"

"It's Warren, Sarge, Warren."

"All right, they're gonna pop out around 3320 Warren. Get some cars over here."

Again I saw blue lights flashing and heard engines racing on the next block.

"Eleven-eleven, slow down on Warren. We got two on the hood at 3320. See if the Sarge can bring the victim over here."

"Eleven-ten, on the way."

As we pulled up, I put the spotlight on the two.

"That's them," yelled the victim.

"Eleven-ten, we got a positive I.D. on these two over here."

"All right, sir. These officers will take it from here."

"Thanks, Sarge," he said as he got out of the car.

"Take care, partner," I replied.

As I parked the car to fill out my log, the radio crackled again.

"Eleven-eleven, the weapon's recovered, proceeds recovered. We're taking the victim into Eleven, and eleven-seventy-one is taking the two offenders. Thanks for all the help."

"Well, that went fairly well," I thought to myself. I smiled as I thought about what had just happened. I parked the squad and waited for the next call, and looked over at the empty seat, wishing my new partner could have finished the tour with me.

End Notes

By Jim

As I sat at my desk and put the final touches on the stories in this book, I was humbled. One seldom sees snippets of his entire life gathered in one place. When Jay and I decided to assemble these stories into a book, a major goal was to humanize the police. We've attempted to do that with stories of a variety of experiences on the streets of Chicago. Stories written from the heart, stories with soul, crafted to lift the curtain and give others a glimpse of what cops call "the job."

We shared a story of family tragedy because police officers experience family tragedies like anyone else. Adversity is part of everyone's life, and no one knows that better than police officers because so much of what they do is deal with other people's misfortunes. Noted author and psychotherapist Virginia Satir said, "Life is not the way it's supposed to be. It's the way it is. The way you cope with it is what makes the difference." That perhaps best sums up why some survive better than others. Jay and I are blessed with a family structure that has provided and continues to provide limitless love and support on a daily basis. Many of the stories here attempted to reflect that.

Some wondered why I stayed with the police department after my first wife's death left me the sole support of three very young children. "It's so dangerous," they would say. I stayed because I knew I could give a voice to homicide victims. I could come to the aid of those in danger who had no one else to call. I stayed to carry on the fine work of the hundreds of officers whose lives were taken from them while doing this job. There are currently 567 fallen Chicago Police officers, and unfortunately, but inevitably, that number will continue to grow.

A police career has many hazards, but some exist where you might not expect. Both Jay and I have experienced the gut-wrenching psychological toll of police suicides. Together, we have lost a partner, a teammate, and a best friend to police suicide as was chronicled here in several stories. We make no effort to explain these losses because in the words of an unknown poet, "'tis hard to understand."

Police come to experience more than their share of criticism simply because what they do makes the news. The media covers stories that are unusual and extraordinary, and if you accept that, then tens of thousands of police stories each day are never reported because they are simply ordinary and routine.

Perhaps Theodore Roosevelt said it best when he was Police Commissioner of New York City:

It is not the critic who counts, nor the man who points out where the strong man stumbled, or where a doer of deeds could have done them better. The credit belongs to the man in the arena whose face is marred by dust and sweat and blood, who strives valiantly, who errs, and who comes up short again and again, who knows the great enthusiasms, the great devotions, and spends himself in a worthy cause. The man who at best knows the triumph of high achievement, and who at worst, if he fails, fails while daring greatly, so that his place will never be with those cold timid souls who never knew victory or defeat.

Jay and I are proud to be men "in the arena."

About the Authors

Jim Padar is a married father of four and a grandfather of six. He holds a degree in Electronic Design and Technology from what is now DeVry University and a degree in Criminal Justice from the University of Illinois–Chicago. He is also a graduate of the 139th Session of the FBI National Academy. He joined the Chicago Police Department in 1966 where he worked as a patrol officer, tactical officer, homicide detective, sergeant, and lieutenant. In 1995, he accepted a position as Operations Manager for the City of Chicago's 911 system. He retired in the year 2000. In retirement, he spends his time writing and participating in Live Lit events in the Chicago area.

Jay Padar is a married father of two. He holds a Bachelor's degree in Law Enforcement Administration from Western Illinois University and a Master's degree in Criminal Justice from Lewis University. He joined the Chicago Police Department in 1998 and has worked as a patrol officer, tactical officer, and currently holds the rank of sergeant. Jay is also a member of the Public Safety Writer's Association.

On Being a Cop was born when Jay first hit the streets of Chicago as a rookie cop. Like most new cops, he would arrive home after a midnight tour of duty, his residual adrenaline not conducive to sleep, so he started writing emails to his dad, chronicling the night's experiences. Dad read and smiled with pride and admiration—his son was capturing in writing the wonder of being a new cop, but more than that, Jay wrote with soul and a sensitivity seldom seen in police stories. "Keep writing, son," he emailed back. "For every story you write, I'll write one."

Thus began an exchange of several years. Point and counterpoint, laughter and tears, triumphs and tragedies, rookie and old man. And when they paused and put all the stories together, they thought it was good. More importantly, others told them it was much more than good, and so a book was born.

* * * *

Join us at www.OnBeingACop.com to view new stories posted on a regular basis, interact with other readers and connect with the authors.

Jim and Jay are available as speakers for your next event. Contact them at info@OnBeingACop.com